# INSIDE THE
# CARTEL

**DEY**ST.
*An Imprint of* WILLIAM MORROW

# MARTIN SUAREZ
with IAN FRISCH

# INSIDE THE CARTEL

### HOW AN UNDERCOVER FBI AGENT

### SMUGGLED COCAINE, LAUNDERED CASH, AND DISMANTLED A COLOMBIAN NARCO-EMPIRE

**DEY**ST.

Without limiting the exclusive rights of any author, contributor or the publisher of this publication, any unauthorized use of this publication to train generative artificial intelligence (AI) technologies is expressly prohibited. HarperCollins also exercise their rights under Article 4(3) of the Digital Single Market Directive 2019/790 and expressly reserve this publication from the text and data mining exception.

In accordance with my obligations as a former FBI employee pursuant to my FBI employment agreement, this book has undergone a prepublication review for the purpose of identifying prohibited disclosures, but has not been reviewed for editorial content or accuracy. The FBI does not endorse or validate any information that I have described in this book. The opinions expressed in this book are mine and not those of the FBI or any other government agency.

INSIDE THE CARTEL. Copyright © 2025 by Martin Suarez. All rights reserved. Printed in the United States of America. No part of this book may be used or reproduced in any manner whatsoever without written permission except in the case of brief quotations embodied in critical articles and reviews. For information, address HarperCollins Publishers, 195 Broadway, New York, NY 10007. In Europe, HarperCollins Publishers, Macken House, 39/40 Mayor Street Upper, Dublin 1, D01 C9W8, Ireland.

HarperCollins books may be purchased for educational, business, or sales promotional use. For information, please email the Special Markets Department at SPsales@harpercollins.com.

hc.com

FIRST EDITION

*Designed by Patrick Barry*

*Title page photograph courtesy of the FBI*

Library of Congress Cataloging-in-Publication Data has been applied for.

ISBN 978-0-06-335401-2

25 26 27 28 29  LBC  5 4 3 2 1

*For Maria, my two sons,
my daughters-in-law, and
my grandchildren*

\*

**Life isn't about finding yourself.
Life is about creating yourself.**
—GEORGE BERNARD SHAW

# AUTHOR'S NOTE

**THIS IS A WORK OF NONFICTION. I HAVE, HOWEVER, ELECTED** to use pseudonyms for specific individuals. These are dangerous people, many of whom are fugitives or out of prison.

I am taking a serious risk in publishing this book. The cartel never forgets.

# CONTENTS

| | Prologue | xi |
|---|---|---|
| 1: | *A Smuggler's Paradise* | 1 |
| 2: | *Mi Amor* | 23 |
| 3: | *¡Están Tirando Coca!* | 42 |
| 4: | *I Know Not to Say a Damn Thing* | 62 |
| 5: | *Going Home* | 79 |
| 6: | *Wearing the White Hat* | 99 |
| 7: | *I Can Smell a Cop from a Mile Away* | 111 |
| 8: | *The Wire* | 123 |
| 9: | *De Noche, Todos los Gatos Son Negros* | 137 |
| 10: | *The Black Market Peso Exchange* | 153 |
| 11: | *Carnage* | 166 |
| 12: | *Two Wagons* | 181 |
| 13: | *Vamos a Matarte* | 193 |
| 14: | *I Am Not Afraid of Death* | 205 |
| 15: | *Salud* | 220 |
| 16: | *Sicario* | 238 |
| 17: | *Indictments* | 253 |
| 18: | *Never Enough Time* | 271 |
| | Epilogue | 283 |
| | Acknowledgments | 289 |

# PROLOGUE

**THE ASSASSIN POINTED HIS GUN AT THE BACK OF MY HEAD.**
It was just after eight in the morning on a blazing hot day in August 1994. My wife, Maria, had already taken our two young sons to school, where she also worked as a teacher. I had decided to go for a long run through our neighborhood, a gated community an hour west of San Juan, Puerto Rico. It was a gorgeous place to live. The small but comfortable home was wedged between an expansive golf course on one side and the Caribbean on the other. My running route took me on a loop down to the beach and back. I wore short-shorts typical of the mid-nineties, pulled my socks high up my calves, and laced my Nike sneakers tight around my feet. I pushed my legs to keep up a fast pace. My lungs burned. The tropical sun beat down on my neck. I arrived at the beach, turned around, and made my way back home.

I opened the front gate and walked over to a chair on my patio. I plopped down, dropped my head, tried to catch my breath, and closed my eyes, my mind lost in the recovery of a tough run. Then, the hitman emerged from the bushes. I never saw him coming.

"*Tsst, tsst, tsst,*" he hissed.

# PROLOGUE

I turned around and he pointed his pistol at my face, its six-inch, stainless-steel barrel gleaming in the morning sunlight. I cursed myself for being caught off guard, for letting my one personal indulgence become my greatest vulnerability. I stood up and raised my hands above my head, my back slick with sweat, my heart pounding.

"Turn the fuck around," he said. I complied. I could feel his gun's cold metal snout inches away from my skull. "Walk, motherfucker," he said. "Let's go."

I knew that *El Toro Negro* hired this hitman—this sicario—to kill me. Toro was the money boss of the North Coast Cartel, one of the largest, most powerful, and deadliest criminal organizations in Colombia. But how did Toro figure me out? I had been a deep-undercover FBI agent for the past six years. I smuggled $1 billion worth of cocaine through the Caribbean's choppy waters and into Miami for the Medellín and Cali cartels. After moving to Puerto Rico, I worked for Toro and North Coast as a high-echelon money launderer. Almost every day for the last two years, I picked up millions of dollars in cash from drug lords and washed the dirty money. And I almost always wore a wire—the most dangerous part of the job.

Although I'd had many close calls, I never slipped up. Not once. But here I was, death staring at me. The hitman led me up the steps to the front door of my home. I knew he wanted to shoot me inside the house, so my wife would come home and find my bullet-ridden corpse lying in a pool of blood. The cruelty was the point—the hallmark of any cartel worth their salt. Being an undercover FBI agent, especially back then, during the heyday of the craft—where many of the policies and procedures of becoming someone else to catch criminals were being written on the fly—required more courage than most

## PROLOGUE

men possessed, especially with a gun pointed at the base of your skull.

I couldn't let myself die like a dog, shot in the back of the head, my wife's worst fears made real. I couldn't let my two young sons grow up without a father. I couldn't let my own father down, the reason I became an FBI agent in the first place. It was for Maria and my two boys that I would make sure to live, not for the bureau. The FBI had me when I was "Manny," my undercover alter ego, a dirty smuggler and money launderer. But here, in my own home, I was Martin, and the only duty I cared about was to my family.

I gathered up everything that filled my heart: the pride I had in my job, the deep love I held for my family, the sense of duty instilled in me by my father, all the strength that I could muster. Courage. Maybe even bravado. I spun around and pushed the hitman down the steps. If he wanted to kill me, he was going to have to fight me first.

And then his gun went off—and all I saw was blood.

# CHAPTER 1

# A SMUGGLER'S PARADISE

**I KNEW THE CARTEL SENT HER. THE WOMAN STRODE INTO** my office wearing blood-red stilettos and a matching dress cinched at the waist by a white belt. She had her luscious brown hair pulled back in a tight ponytail, gold hoops hung from her ears, a Cartier watch wrapped around her wrist, and her red nails were sharpened like daggers. Two more women, dressed in crisp pantsuits, their heels clicking in unison on the hardwood floor, sauntered in behind her. It was a procession of glitzy excess, women who knew power and wealth intimately. Each of them carried a large box wrapped in ribbon, gifts of which I was the sole recipient.

It's common knowledge in the world of drug smuggling that women from Medellín are Colombia's most beautiful. Their accents, gentle lilts that jump from sugar-soaked tongues, have turned many men into puppy dogs. This is especially true when the women represent a faction of the Medellín Cartel, Pablo Escobar's powerful drug empire that, during the

1980s, controlled much of the transcontinental cocaine trade and smuggled nearly two million pounds of the drug into the United States each year. It was at the behest of Escobar's closest associates that these three women visited my office in Miami, Florida, on a seasonally warm day in December 1989. In the eyes of the cartel, I was one of the most prolific drug smugglers in South Florida. I had marine and aviation skills, a reliable crew, and the guts to get their dope across the border. But the truth was even more cinematic: I was a deep-undercover FBI agent tasked with infiltrating Colombia's most menacing narco-empires.

I was in my personal office, down the hall from the main entrance of the building, and didn't see the women come in. My secretary, Carla, a cartel associate who had agreed to cooperate with the FBI and work undercover with me, knocked on my door and poked her head in.

"There are some ladies here," Carla said, "and they have gifts."

"Yeah?" I responded. "Bring them in."

The three women came into my office and, without a word, placed the boxes on my desk. They spun on their heels, went back out to their two matching luxury Land Cruisers, and brought in another stack of boxes. And then they left again for a final round. Nine boxes sat atop my desk, over four feet tall. I stood up from my chair so I could see over the tower. I met eyes with the woman in the red dress.

"We know you were expecting this," she said, the words dripping off her tongue as if a siren's song, a mischievous smile spread across her face.

I knew what the boxes contained, didn't even have to open them to check: bundles of cash stacked from base to brim. I tried to hide my excitement at this turn of events. These couriers coming to my doorstep signaled we had truly infiltrated the Medellín Cartel. We had been working for months to garner their trust; our patience and precision had paid off. Now, I was convinced that our credibility was locked.

"Thank you, ladies," I said. "I hope you enjoy your weekend." They nodded, turned out, and left. The clacking of their heels reverberated throughout my office even after they closed the door behind them.

\* \* \*

I HAD BECOME A smuggler less than a year prior. I was the first FBI agent in history to be thrown into a long-term, deep-undercover operation that targeted Colombia's most ruthless drug cartels. Ever since Pablo Escobar catapulted the Medellín Cartel to international infamy in the early 1980s—and helped replace coffee with cocaine as Colombia's leading export—the FBI had his organization in their sites. What's more, Escobar had utilized one place as his main point of entry: Miami. My home city became the nucleus of the international drug trade. As the War on Drugs grew in scale and importance, even conducting thousand-pound busts wasn't going to cut it anymore. The cartels were making so much money that they chalked up the losses to merely an overhead cost. The FBI needed to infiltrate the cartels—not only to better understand their methodologies and internal structures, but to thwart the flow of drugs from the source. That's where I came in.

After the FBI created an airtight alter ego—what we call a "legend"—I was no longer Martin Suarez. I became "Manny," a guy who had no qualms helping Colombian cartels transport hundreds of millions of dollars' worth of cocaine into the United States, all of which would eventually be seized. The

## INSIDE THE CARTEL

FBI gave me the funding to secure an undercover office in Miami, where I posed as an import-export businessman. Stationed in a warehouse on the city's industrial southside, where all the smugglers lived and worked, my "company" actually did some legitimate business, moving oranges and other produce into the United States. It was a convincing enough public front that even our neighbors were fooled. The glass-paneled office, however, became my drug fiefdom—the center of an underground operation in a city that had, during the 1980s, become a smuggler's paradise.

I quickly began trafficking cocaine into Florida for Colombia's most premier drug cartels. I had help with getting started. First was Carla, who posed as my secretary. Second was Diego, her husband, who posed as one of my employees. Diego was a former pilot for José Gacha, who ran the Medellín Cartel alongside the Ochoa brothers and Pablo Escobar. Diego and Carla were plugged into the highest levels of the most powerful drug empire in the world and had recently become cooperating witnesses for the FBI. They were tasked with helping convince drug barons that I was a legitimate doper. They lent me credibility and introduced me to high-ranking members of the Medellín Cartel. It worked. I installed long-range radios and obtained numerous satellite phones, so I could communicate with Escobar's traffickers. The FBI's technical agents installed hidden cameras and microphones throughout the space so every conversation I conducted was recorded for future prosecutions. As the months went on, a snowball effect occurred. The momentum of my connections and the services I offered culminated in a rock-solid reputation, and I continued to worm my way deeper into the underground world of high-end drug trafficking. But what was I supposed to do with these boxes wrapped in ribbon, delivered to me by a trio of gorgeous women, and filled to the brim with cash?

The money came from a subgroup of the Medellín Cartel led by Tigre Valencia. Everyone called him *El Viejo*. The Old Man. He was one of Colombia's largest manufacturers and exporters of cocaine, and one of Escobar's right-hand men. He held complete control over the rural jungles in southern Colombia near the Peruvian border, where he established massive cocaine-processing laboratories and secured an alliance with the Marxist-Leninist guerilla group the Revolutionary Armed Forces of Colombia (FARC). By the late 1980s, with his wagon firmly hitched to Escobar, he had emerged as one of South America's richest drug kingpins. By some estimates, he owned over a hundred homes. His success was due in large part to his affinity for smuggling via aircraft. He established ironclad routes through the Caribbean Corridor—for which my team and I had now become an integral part.

My initial negotiations with El Viejo's organization lasted for months and required a great deal of perseverance. To start, I was a newcomer to their organization, and they weren't going to bend over backward to instantly slot me into their rotation of smugglers, no matter my bona fides. They did, however, want to diversify their roster of traffickers and soon put me through their vetting process, which included tours of my office in Miami—where I showed them my telecommunication devices; I even let one of their more senior smugglers use them a few times as a favor—and my personal boats at the marina. I knew from speaking with Diego that a legitimate trafficker would always hold back showing their smuggling boats, as a security precaution and to not appear overeager. I did the same, knowing that if I came across as too trusting of the cartel, it would backfire. Similarly, I refused to divulge where

## INSIDE THE CARTEL

I stashed the loads once I smuggled them into Miami. On top of these tours given to El Viejo's Miami-based counterparts, El Viejo directed that I travel to Panama, Puerto Rico, Guatemala, Houston, Boston, Honduras, New York City, the Bahamas, and Rhode Island to meet with the cartel's other associates, so they could form an opinion of me for a group vote. I didn't mind the grunt work; it gave the FBI valuable intelligence on how their operation worked. In all, I met with over seventy-five members of the Medellín Cartel over an eight-month period.

This type of hoop jumping was how they weeded out cops and informants: only law enforcement worked on deadlines imposed by overzealous management figures; were held on a short leash with international travel; and had to be mindful of strict budgets. Luckily, the FBI was extremely patient. We were willing to commit ourselves to an expensive operation for a long period of time in order to infiltrate a high-level core group of criminals. To us, time was not an adversary but an asset.

I primarily dealt with El Viejo's deputy Pedro, who also lived in Miami. Pedro was highly intelligent, brilliant with logistics, well-dressed, a smooth talker, and from a very wealthy Colombian family who owned vast rice and coffee fields. A few of his family members were also in the drug trade, and they got their start rum-running and smuggling cigarettes into Colombia. During the cocaine boom, however, they aligned themselves with El Viejo. Pedro enjoyed the fine things in life—bespoke clothes, expensive art, fancy cars, keeping up with world events—but he was also ugly: a square head, ruddy face, and a worn-leather complexion, all exacerbated by his love of whiskey and late-night parties. And yet, he had an endearing quality to him, which I exploited with an air of friendly nonchalance, as if we were old buddies. I knew, however, that deep down, he couldn't be trusted. I needed to stay on my toes. Nevertheless, I enjoyed his company. He was a fun guy to hang out with.

As the weeks went on and our conversations continued, Pedro confirmed that he wanted me to smuggle a load for them. Back then, there were a few ways I could be paid as a transporter, all of which Pedro offered. First: I would be paid a higher cash fee in a lump sum once the drugs were sold in the United States (which didn't help me because the FBI would seize the drugs before they hit the streets). Second: an even higher cash fee if I smuggled the drugs, kept possession of them in Miami, and let his dealers sell them piecemeal over time (which also didn't help us because, in order to conduct a seizure, they had to be in someone else's possession). And lastly: a lower cash fee, with a portion paid up front and the rest upon delivery to his men in the States. I always picked this option. I explained to Pedro that, sure, I made less money, but I was able to avoid potential violence, risk from law enforcement, waiting to get paid, and the headache that came with babysitting hundreds of millions of dollars in cocaine. (This, too, was the sweet spot for the FBI: We could seize the up-front payment *and* the drugs, and I could theoretically still force the cartel to pay me the rest of my smuggling fee after our seizure, since I held up my end of the deal. We'd get to have our cake and eat it, too.) My thought process made sense to Pedro, and he agreed to my payment structure. He said the deposit money would show up on my doorstep soon.

Neither I nor my case agents knew the money was going to show up that day—or from such enticingly beautiful couriers. A vibration shook my office after the women left, a subtle confirmation of our collective talents and how deep this undercover operation could go. I was elated. And yet, I didn't have time to fully prepare for what I would do if they actually brought the money to my office and expected me to immediately put together a plan to get their dope from Colombia to Miami. I needed to buy some time before I presented Pedro with a concrete plan or committed to anything he might propose.

I brought Ricky Mansilla, my partner and fellow undercover FBI agent, into my office. A Cuban who spoke fluent Spanish, Ricky had recently transferred to Miami from the Los Angeles field office and was my right-hand man for this operation. A savant with numbers, he was an accountant for Eastern Airlines before joining the bureau, and held a psychology degree from the University of Miami. Ricky also had a photographic memory. He could take one glance at a phone number, cross-reference it with a host of other data in his head, and come up with a firm conclusion as to how it folded into the larger criminal conspiracy at hand. Ricky was the brains to my brawn; while I was building relationships with smugglers, he was securing covert bank accounts, warehouses, apartments, cars, boats, planes, and other crucial assets to help deepen our cover. We were ideal partners.

I opened one of the boxes. The money was dirty, rank, and covered in a slick film. It reeked of cocaine, a pungent mixture of gasoline and cleaning fluids. I knew that the cash had likely just come off the street.

"How much?" he asked.

"If I had to guess, close to a million," I said.

"We have to figure this shit out, and quick. We have no idea who knows that we have this *billullu*. We could get robbed, or worse."

"I know," I said. "We need to establish chain of custody, too."

"Well, I guess I'll call the brass."

Our superiors instructed us to bring the cash to the FBI's covert warehouse at the airport, where we stashed our smuggling planes. We had to be as inconspicuous as possible every time we met. There was no way I could just waltz into the Miami field office with a trunkful of drug money; I never knew who was watching me. Ricky and I quickly loaded the cash into the back of my black Ford Bronco. I hit the road, with Ricky following me in another car. We had to make sure that the cartel, or a rival faction, wasn't following us; we took a circuitous route so we could see if we had a tail. We were clean. We pulled into the airport parking lot where our case agent waited for us. He threw open the hangar's overhead door. Ricky and I zoomed inside, quickly unloaded the cash, and rushed back to our undercover office. Our boss, Pete Paris, was going to call us. I was now responsible for a million dollars of the cartel's money, but I also had to deal with the added pressure of hoping that Pete would let us go through with the rest of the mission. The phone rang. I picked it up.

"Pedro had the money delivered?" Pete asked.

"Yes, sir," I said. "I had no idea it was coming today, but Ricky and I got it down to the warehouse. It's being logged now."

"Were you followed?"

"No," I said. "We made sure of it."

"Good. But it's really bad timing for us to launch a big operation. Christmas is right around the corner, and everyone is taking time off. We just don't have the manpower to do this right now."

"I think I can buy us some time," I said. "Pedro and El Viejo are really eager to work with us, now that I've been vetted by the cartel. I'll make them understand."

"What are you going to tell them?"

"Well, I can't use Christmas as an excuse. The cartels actually move a lot of their dope between now and New Year's, so if I blame the holidays, it will tip them off that we might be law enforcement. I'll tell them that we already have a few loads going for other clients, and we can't take on any more work until February. That will give us plenty of time to prepare both the pickup and the seizure. If we make it seem like we are too busy for them right now, they will be that much more eager to work with us."

I heard Pete breathing on the other end of the line, mulling over my proposal. "Well," he said, "if you can convince them to wait, we'll make sure you have the assets that you need when the time comes."

Coincidentally, I had already laid some groundwork with Pedro in this department. A few weeks ago, Pedro told Abassi, another member of the Medellín Cartel, that I was a top-notch trafficker who was going to start smuggling loads for him and El Viejo. In turn, Abassi randomly dropped off some money at my undercover office—basically a gift so I would move his dope. He was a priest for the Santeria religion—a *babalawo*—and routinely blessed loads when they left Colombia so they would avoid law enforcement detection. He also fancied himself a witch doctor. He always wore an all-white outfit that beamed off his ink-black skin, comically long pointed shoes, awful-smelling cologne, and a stack of the seven powers necklaces common in his religion. Abassi really wanted to work with me. I told him that, although I very much appreciated the money and that I was also eager to work with him, the timing was off, and I didn't want to take any unnecessary risks with his product. Abassi grumbled, frustrated that he had wasted his time arranging the cash, and took the money back. Afterward, he complained to Pedro that I had denied him access to my smuggling operation. This raised my status with Pedro. In his mind, he had access to someone other people didn't. When I called Pedro a few days after the women dropped off the money and explained I needed some time to arrange transport, he wasn't fazed. He was willing to wait however long it took to have me move his drugs.

After my call with Pete, I sent Carla home, locked up the office, and went to my undercover apartment. Ricky and I shared a three-bedroom unit in Miami Lakes, where all the real-deal smugglers lived. I resided there more or less full-time, save for a few weekends here and there when I was able to go home and see my family. I tried to relax in that place, but often in the silence of the night, after shuttling stacks of cash or a truck full of drugs, the pressure of working undercover weighed heavily. I never knew if the windfall I'd just received was being tracked by a rival faction, who would kick down my door and start a firefight. I always felt most confident in the moment, shooting the shit with drug lords and cartel bosses, playing the game off my wits. But it was here, having just driven to a covert FBI warehouse with one million dollars in my trunk, that my nerves began to get the best of me. The FBI, however, trained me well: my gun was always loaded.

To make matters worse, I hadn't seen my family in almost two weeks. I wanted to spend as much time with them as possible for the holidays. I was scheduled to go back that night to see my wife, Maria, and our two sons, both of whom had just started elementary school. I had only been working undercover for a year, but it was putting a strain on all of us. I always had to be available for the cartel, day or night, which meant I always had to be Manny. I lived in an undercover apartment, drove an undercover Porsche, and had an undercover license.

I always dressed the part, too: Italian silk shirts, gold jewelry, and fancy shoes. When I was able to transform back into Martin Suarez, I would drive into an underground parking garage where my real-life identity waited for me. I'd change clothes, swap cars, and emerge back into the world as the real me. I always counted down the days until I was able to see my family again, but sometimes, out of the blue, a trio of gorgeous Colombian women would drop by my office with boxes full of cash and plans had to change.

I called Maria. My gut knotted up. I knew what I had to do. This became the first of many plans broken during this all-consuming operation.

"Hello?" she said.

"Hey sweetie," I said. "It's me."

"How's work?" she asked. Maria didn't know much about my undercover life, just understood that I had decided to become someone else for a living, to submerge my life in deception, to try and catch the bad guys by doing something very few agents had done before. Mostly, she just wanted to know that my goal, being an FBI agent, was going well.

"It's one of those nights," I said. "I had planned to come home, but something came up. I have to stay here at the office."

"Don't worry about it. I will hold down the fort," she said, her voice strong and firm. If she was disappointed, nothing in her delivery revealed it. A guilty silence filled the space between us, but then I heard the sound of small, faraway voices: my sons, bounding around the living room, waiting for dinner to be served and for their father to come home.

"How are the boys?" I asked.

"Hungry," she said, a sliver of mirth creeping into her tone, as if amused by the boys' incessant needs: food, clothing, shelter, affection. She had been mesmerized by them since the day they were born. She counted no behavior too frustrating, and no amount of doting too overwhelming, as she introduced them to the world. It was a trend that would continue as my absences grew longer, my dedication to being Manny became more pronounced, and the emotional equilibrium that held our family together became more precarious. "But do your thing," she said. "And be safe. Just make sure you're home for Christmas, so you can watch the boys open their gifts. I love you."

"I love you too," I said, and hung up the phone. My fake bedroom felt small and lonely just then, as if basked in disappointment. I pushed those thoughts out of my head, lay down, and tried to go to sleep. I kept a lamp turned on, a gun under my pillow, and my eye on the door.

* * *

**THE YEAR 1989 GAVE** way to 1990, the dawn of a new decade upon us, and the Medellín Cartel was even more eager to see if I really could handle a big load: three thousand kilos of 95 percent pure Colombian cocaine—with a street value of roughly $500 million. Since my team in Miami were the first FBI agents in history to actually receive a cash prepayment from Colombian drug lords, we were able to obtain authorization from the Department of Justice to use the money as the cartel directed it: to prepare for this massive shipment. If the operation was a success, we could create policy for future undercover cases. The cartel and I settled on a stretch of sea off the coast of Cuba as our rendezvous point. They were going to drop the drugs from the sky.

After buying more time with Pedro, we spent the next six weeks planning logistics. My fellow FBI agents and I needed this time so we could make sure, as soon as I delivered the load to the cartel's receivers in Miami, that the drug squad was ready to make one of the largest seizures in the bureau's history (at least up until that point). We also needed to ensure that the operation was completely disguised. This would protect my cover and deflect blame after the raid, but also force the cartel's hand: We wanted them to try and offset their loss by hiring me to transport more drugs, thus creating a chain of destruction that would both prevent dope from landing on the streets and keep me integrated within the cartel's machinery. With each load seized, the cartel would take another bite off its own tail.

This is what I told the cartel we would do: the drop would come in the dead of night. I'd park my smuggling vessel—an inconspicuous, hundred-foot-long lobster boat—at specific coordinates off the coast of Cuba. I also enlisted a thirty-six-foot Mako fishing vessel. This was our runner: I'd use the Mako to grab the bales and bring them back to the lobster boat. The two boats were outfitted with radios and satellite phones, so I could communicate with the Colombian pilot and his crew. After dropping anchor on the lobster boat and readying the Mako, I'd wait for the cartel's pilot, coming straight from Colombia, to fly over me. From there, the plane's crew would open the doors and drop the cocaine into the ocean, where I would pick it up. But I wouldn't go straight to Miami just yet. I told the cartel I wanted to hang out in the Caribbean for a week, tamp down any suspicion in case I was spotted by law enforcement, and then haul the drugs back to Miami. From there, the product would be unloaded, securely packaged, and transported to the cartel's stateside distributors. And then I would be ready for the next shipment.

This is technically what went down but, unbeknownst to

the cartel, a lot more happened behind the scenes. First of all: I obviously didn't need to hang out in the Caribbean for a week because I thought I'd be surveilled. The FBI would secretly transport the cocaine to Miami immediately, and they needed sufficient time to catalog the drugs and plan their raid. Moreover, the lobster boat and the Mako were covert FBI assets carefully disguised as legitimate smuggling vessels. The lobster boat also acted as our command and control center, outfitted with high-tech surveillance gadgetry. Large-scale drug trafficking investigations are tricky: We had to prove that the drugs seized in the United States actually came from Colombia, were being delivered by the Medellín Cartel, and were the same drugs that fell from the plane, hit the water, and were retrieved by me and my men. We had to document the entire process, or the impending prosecution could fall apart. (It did help, however, that the kilos were stamped with the cartel's logo.) It was the first time that the FBI had executed an operation of such immense scale. Dozens of agents and all the top brass were involved. No one wanted to screw it up.

For complete operational security, we stashed the boats at a covert site on the Cayman Islands. A team of FBI agents and I flew from Miami to retrieve them and start the mission. We spent three days on Grand Cayman waiting for the cartel to prepare the delivery. I was the only deep-undercover agent on the team, the guy who actually met with the cartel bosses and cemented their belief that I was a legit smuggler, but all of the agents involved in the mission posed as my smuggling associates and assumed undercover personas. In the cartel's eyes, my operation was so involved I enlisted an entire team to transport their cocaine.

After a last-minute maintenance check on both ships, we tethered the Mako to the lobster boat and set out for the rendezvous point, a three-day trek past Jamaica and through the Windward Passage that bisects Haiti and Cuba. By the end of the third day, we had arrived at our destination. As darkness settled on the Caribbean, I went into the belly of the lobster boat and ate a steaming hot cup of chicken fricassee. It was slated to be a long night. After I ate, two other agents and I transferred from the lobster boat and onto the Mako. We detached ourselves and made our way just over a mile south, to the drop location. The wind and current was such that, as the plane flew over us and dropped the bales of cocaine, the cargo would theoretically stay in the general area between where I was stationed in the Mako and where our mothership was anchored. From there, we could pick up the bales one by one on our way back to the mothership, Pac-Man–style. It sounded simple on paper, but in the pitch-black sea, anything could happen.

We settled down at the predetermined coordinates and waited. Having previously served in the Navy, I felt comfortable on the water. It had become a second home for me. A sense of adventure filled my chest, knowing that no one at the FBI had previously been able to orchestrate an airdrop from a Colombian cartel. But darkness soon settled firmly over my little boat and the sea began to roil violently. As the swells grew and the troughs sunk deeper, an ominous feeling settled upon us. Ten-foot swells rose up and sent our boat reeling. We grabbed on to anything we could to keep our balance. If one of us went overboard, the entire operation would be blown, and if the boat took on too much water, all of our lives would be at risk. Within minutes, a slick, three-inch-deep puddle of seawater coated the boat's deck. I tried to hold my balance, but I slipped, nearly rolling my ankle before catching myself. I prayed for the cartel to show up so we could grab the drugs and get the hell out of there, but I also found solace in my discomfort. To me, it was a gift not only to witness such a brazen smuggling operation, but to be an actor in this play, and to know I was pushing myself to my limits in order to achieve a massive goal.

An hour later, we received a garbled, static-filled call over the radio: the plane was one mile away. I asked the pilot to flash his headlights, so we could see him. Two short bursts of white light shot from the horizon. They were close. I radioed the mothership and told them to flash their lights in return. A great whooshing came from overhead, the rippled squealing of a plane. The cartel had arrived. And then I heard the sound: *BANG! BANG! BANG!* When a forty-five-kilogram *tula* of cocaine falls from an airplane and hits the sea, it sounds like a Mack truck crashing, a refrigerator being tossed off a building. And they were landing dangerously close to my boat. I went out onto the Mako's deck, lit a bright red flare, and waved it over my head. I grabbed my radio: "Don't throw on the flare! Don't throw on the flare!" If one of the bales hit our boat, we'd sink; if one of us got hit, we'd be killed instantly.

My smuggling vessel thrashed violently back and forth, swamped to the point of sinking, with the bilge pumps set to overdrive. My eyes shrunk to slits, trying to spot the glow sticks that the Medellín Cartel had affixed to their bounty, which slowly lit up the water's surface like fluorescent fireflies. The pilot doubled back and dropped more bales, each impact more violent than the last, like bombs in a war-torn battlefield. At the bottom of a swell, total darkness surrounded me, as if I had fallen into a bottomless pit. And then the sea sent the boat shooting upward again, to the crest of a wave, the sky a blanket of stars.

After a few passes, I knew that over two thousand kilos had

likely been dropped already. I grabbed the radio again: "*¿Acabastes? ¿Acabastes?*" Are you done? Are you done? The pilot responded: "*¡Una más!*" One more pass. He circled back for the final drop, engine screeching. The last batch of bales fell from the sky. The pilot jumped on the radio: "*¡Okay, muchachos, hasta la proxima!*" Okay, guys, until the next one! And then the plane sped off into the night, back to Colombia. I gazed out at the sea, the bales floating in the distance, in awe that we had made it this far.

I told one of my undercover counterparts to drive the boat while I grabbed the cocaine. Unlike retrieving large, deep-sea fish, I couldn't use a gaff hook; it would puncture the bales, let salt water seep in, and ruin the drugs. I had to do it by hand. I leaned awkwardly over the gunwale and hauled the hundred-pound bales into the boat as fast as I could. Back then, I was strong enough to bench-press three hundred pounds, but this was by far the most grueling physical exercise I'd ever experienced. My back seized up, my mouth was caked in dried spit from dehydration; my entire body was exhausted from being at sea for days. The swells rocked the boat violently, sent wave after wave over the stern, threw us sideways, and nearly tossed all of us into the ocean again and again. We took on so much water that the bales floated onboard and nearly washed back out to sea. We spent the next six hours grabbing bales and searching for stragglers brought out of line by the ever-shifting Caribbean current. The cartel was depending on me. If I wanted to infiltrate deeper, I couldn't leave any of their drugs behind.

We finally gathered the last of the load. It was just after sunrise, the sky brushed in a soft pink glow, the water reflecting the morning's first light. My legs were gooey and useless, my arms burned, my lungs begged for oxygen. I fell to the floor, panting. I closed my eyes and tried to breathe, my brain toggling between consternation and anticipation. I knew we were doing the right thing, but it took so much out of me, physically and emotionally, to get the job done. At that moment, my body heaving, the Mako pitching up and down within the aggressive Caribbean swells, I thought of my two sons asleep in their beds—and Maria in ours, the empty space next to her cold and bare from my absence.

We drove the Mako to the mothership, tethered to its stern, and climbed aboard. We then linked up with a sister agency (whose collaboration with the FBI is highly classified), which was slated to take legal custody of the drugs and transport them to Miami for the next phase of our operation. I couldn't help with transferring the cocaine onto their ship, however; I had to keep my identity a secret from everyone except for a core team of FBI agents, who were the only people on earth who knew I was undercover. If there was a leak of any kind, I could be killed. I stayed on the mothership, obscured in shadow. As I watched from a distance as ten other FBI agents transferred the $500 million worth of cocaine onto the second ship, I felt immensely proud. I had secured the cartel's trust. I had made this happen. It was history in the making.

After they departed with the cocaine, we made our way to Grand Cayman. I checked into an inconspicuous hotel—exactly what a smuggler would do after picking up a load. Four other agents accompanied me, all also operating undercover. I posed as their boss. We acted as if we were legitimate smugglers, treating ourselves to lobster and champagne, whiskey and steaks. Other patrons saw us with cell phones—an immense luxury at the time—and steered clear of us. We had to keep up appearances. When you're deep undercover, you're always on. You never know who might have eyes on you.

## INSIDE THE CARTEL

The following day, after my land legs were back to some extent, I called Pedro to share the good news. "We went to the dance. The musicians were fantastic," I told him, speaking in code. "There must have been thirty girls, and we danced with all of them." "Girls" meant bales of cocaine, and the fact that we danced with all of them confirmed that we retrieved the entire load without issue. "I was so drunk," I said. "It was such a good time." More code: The mission was a complete success.

"*Bacano*, Manny," Pedro said. "The musicians are planning another dance in Miami. You must go. I will send you the details soon." The transfer of the drugs was on.

I flew back to Miami. By the time I arrived, the cocaine had already been secretly transported into the United States. Once it landed on shore, the FBI picked it up in an array of nondescript vans and took the load to the drug vault at the Miami field office. I was still operating undercover, so I couldn't help catalog the dope as evidence, but after the team of FBI agents took photographs of the drugs and wrote a detailed report, a team of different agents, operating undercover as my associates for this phase of our operation, took custody of the cocaine and brought it to my warehouse. Now, the fun began. I had given the agents clear instructions for what to do next: They drove a box truck to an industrial supplier and purchased a dozen fifty-five-gallon metal drums. They broke down the bales, packed the bricks of cocaine into each barrel, tack-welded the lids on top (you'd need a plasma cutter to open them, all part of my plan), and loaded the barrels into the truck. This was overkill in terms of normal packaging procedures, but we needed it to be as difficult as possible for the dope to be taken out and broken down for the next phase of shipment. If it was truly a pain in the ass, the grunts would call their bosses and other associates for help. That way, instead of a handful of low-level criminals getting arrested during the raid, we could take down an entire trafficking cell in one shot.

After packing the dope into the box truck, our team made their way to a remote parking lot for final delivery. The cartel's men received the truck and drove it back to their secret warehouse. I was driving around Miami in my Porsche during the handoff. I needed to be mobile, just in case I had to meet with the cartel or my case agents as the raid progressed. Moreover, this was a safety precaution: If the operation went sideways, I wasn't a sitting duck at my office. It's hard to hit a moving target. I kept my cell phone close, knowing that Pedro would quickly get word that the barrels were welded shut and call me. As I careened down the highway, my phone buzzed, right on cue. Now we knew that they were in the process of unloading the drugs.

"Manny," Pedro said, "my men told me that they are having a hard time opening the barrels."

"That's not my problem," I said. "My job is to get the load to you safely. I didn't want any of your product spilling out or getting damaged during transport."

"Right, right," he said. "I understand. I will let my men know."

I hung up the phone. Although the underlings complained about my methods, the cartel leaders, like Pedro and El Viejo, were on my side. I had gone above and beyond to make sure their dope was secure, after all.

It took the cartel's men hours to unload the drugs. The FBI had set up robust surveillance around the warehouse. A few surveillance agents took down license plates, and other agents followed some of the men to their homes or other meeting places. As soon as we were sure that we had intelligence on as many members of the cell as possible, the raid began. Dozens of FBI agents in full tactical gear burst through the door, machine guns at the quick, and busted the entire operation—with nearly $500 million worth of cocaine seized. And yet, this was only one group of stateside traffickers that received dope from the Colombian cartels. By my count, there were at least a dozen more cells in Miami alone. Each was eager to receive as much drugs as Colombia would send, ready and willing to risk their freedom for a hefty payday.

After this monumental raid, I was able to sneak into the Miami field office to discuss the operation. All of the top brass attended this meeting, and everyone involved credited my partner Ricky and me as the masterminds behind the massive seizure. "You did good, Suarez," my supervisor Pete Paris said. "You did good." It felt great, after months of planning, the dangers at sea, and the risks we were all taking, to be given reassurance that my instincts were correct.

We feasted on a delicious catered lunch, but no seizure of this size would be finished until we had a memento for our hard work. My fellow agents and I stacked the bales of 95 percent pure Colombian cocaine into a tower, climbed on top, and posed for a picture, shit-eating grins plastered across our faces. But seawater had seeped into the outermost layers of the bales; after I sat on one of them for a while, the water-and-drugs mixture soaked through my jeans and into my skin. When I stood up, my ass was completely numb.

CHAPTER 2

# MI AMOR

**BAYAMÓN, PUERTO RICO, SITS IN A FERTILE VALLEY JUST** outside of San Juan, where the foothills of the Cordillera Central mountain range stretch north through the coastal plains to the Caribbean Sea. A bustling suburb, it is home to many middle-class Puerto Ricans, of which my family was a part. In the 1940s and 1950s, my parents lived in Long Island, New York, where I was born. My father had just left the military, having served in the Second World War, and worked at the local Veterans Affairs hospital. We soon returned to Bayamón, where both my parents' families lived. As they raised my siblings and me, the city and our extended family became a supportive network.

My mother worked as a dental assistant and an office manager for a heart surgeon. She was also a promising artist and a soprano in the church choir. Growing up as the second-born, I had a lot of freedom to roam the island, which instilled in me a sense of adventure. I'd routinely climb cliffs in the mountains, spend hours at the beach with my cousin away from the eyes of our parents, or ditch school at the urging of more defiant kids. We'd explore abandoned buildings in downtown San Juan or snatch fruit from trees in strangers' front yards. Although I straddled the line between good and bad as a child, I always made sure to never do anything so over the line as to get me into any sort of legal trouble.

As my yearning for exploration blossomed, my parents started calling me "the Roamer." As I entered my teenage years, I especially enjoyed going to festivals and block parties in different towns throughout the island. Each region had its own dialect, its own mini-culture. I would constantly meet new people, some of whom were criminals mixed in with regular society. I was intrigued, not nervous. This was the late 1960s, after all, and it wasn't uncommon in Puerto Rico to rub shoulders with unsavory characters. I would talk to them, play it cool, and learn a lot about their lifestyle. This doesn't mean that I avoided confrontation. One time, a group of kids stole my clothes and money off the beach while I was swimming. I found them in an abandoned house and had to fight them to get my stuff back. I won. I walked out with my clothes and my money, every cent accounted for.

In Puerto Rico, at least back then, class wasn't as strictly segregated compared to regions in the United States, and in general the island boasted a smaller, tighter-knit community. It was much easier to experience all walks of life simultaneously and with little effort. (Moreover: just because someone was wealthy didn't mean they avoided crime; many well-off families back then blurred the line between the legal and illegal.) I was a naturally smart and observant kid and, as a roamer, I gained a lot of intangible knowledge by meeting people from different walks of life—a kind of master's degree in psychology. I learned how to read people, to understand their motivations just by the look on their face. Over time, it became an instinct—and the most valuable asset I brought with me when I went undercover for the FBI almost twenty years later.

I kicked around Bayamón the summer after high school. I played water polo, hung out with my friends, took some shifts as a lifeguard, and enjoyed one last stretch of being a kid before the real world came calling. It was 1975: the salsa band El Gran Combo dominated Puerto Rican radio, disco was just starting to gain traction, and a sense of carefree liveliness permeated tropical San Juan. My youngest brother worked as a bagger at a local supermarket, and he and his friends kept gossiping about their coworker, a girl named Maria who ran the cash register. I knew who they were talking about; I had seen her in the store when I popped in to grab a few things for my mother. She was stunning—and just my type. Her strawberry-brown hair flared out like a lion's mane. Her skin was sun-kissed, eyes big and brown, teeth glowing. And her curves started at her ankles and didn't end until her neck. The next time I walked into the store to do some shopping, I went into her line. When I got to the register, she smiled. I smiled back.

"I hear you play water polo," she said, scanning the items for which my mother sent me to the store. "I'd like to watch one of your games sometime."

*Oh shit*, I thought to myself. *She's hitting on me!* There was only one problem: I was broke. I couldn't afford to take girls out on dates. My job as a lifeguard was sporadic and paid a pittance; I didn't have a car; and although my family was middle-class by Puerto Rican standards, my parents didn't dole out spending money. Maria must've caught on because, after I fumbled through our first conversation, she pitched that maybe we could just take a walk on the beach together. A cheap date? I readily agreed. She must've really caught on that I was broke because, when we met at the bus stop that weekend, she held up a bag of fried chicken for us to share. She even bought us Cokes from a vendor on the beach. We spent the afternoon together, traversing the coast and falling into easy conversation, but when it came time to hop the bus back home, I realized I didn't have enough money for two tickets.

"Hold on," I said, thumbing pitifully through the coins at the bottom of my pants pocket. The bus stop sat in front of a bar, so I sprinted inside and ran up to a guy drinking a beer. "I'm on a first date, and I have no money for the bus," I told him. "I need twenty-five cents. Please help me." The man reached into his pocket and handed me a dollar bill. I thanked him profusely, ran back to Maria, and tried desperately to hide my embarrassment. She just smirked, clearly amused that I would go through all that to make sure we didn't have to walk back home. Maybe this small gesture showed her the lengths I would go, even with slim resources, to provide for her in the future. We climbed aboard the bus and took our seats.

"I obviously have no money," I said, feeling like a failure. "Do you still want to date me?"

"Yes, Martin," she said. "You'll have money one day." We smiled at each other as the bus chugged along, taking us home.

\* \* \*

MARIA AND I WERE still dating the following year when we both enrolled in college. She studied math and accounting at Inter American University of Puerto Rico, while I chose to pursue biology at Pontifical Catholic University of Puerto Rico. She flourished while I floundered, mainly because I had to hold a job while in school. After a year, in 1978, I dropped out and enlisted in the Navy. Maria came from a military family, had lived in the United States and Germany, and understood my decision to join the armed forces—to follow in my father's footsteps and serve my country. She stayed behind in Puerto Rico to finish her studies when I shipped off to boot camp. Our status morphed from steady to in limbo; we were unaware of when we would see each other again or what our future might hold. I hung a photograph of her above my bed, face gleaming in the sunlight, her pose showing off her slender legs. I'd stare at her every time I climbed into bed, fantasizing about the life we could have together and brooding over how the Navy might tear us apart. One night, my bunkmate peered over at the picture and asked, "Is she a nice girl?" I told him that she was gorgeous, funny, smart, hardworking—all the trappings of a future wife.

"Man," he said, "you have to marry her, then."

"Really?" I asked.

"Yes," he said. "A girl like that, you can't let her get away."

I lay in bed and couldn't get out of my mind how stupid I would be to have my enlistment allow Maria to find someone else. I made my decision right then and there. I didn't tell my parents or my brothers or anyone else what I was about to do. The next morning, I picked up the phone and called her.

"Maria. *Mi amor.* I love you. Marry me."

She said yes. A few weeks later, during my first break from basic training, I flew back to San Juan. We eloped, didn't tell a soul: rushed to the courthouse, stood in front of the judge, and said, "I do." After tying the knot, the judge asked me, "What will you do to support her?" I looked at Maria, those brown-sugar eyes staring back at me. I thought back to our first date on the beach: the fried chicken and ice-cold Cokes she'd bought, the bus fare I scrounged embarrassingly from the bar patron.

I addressed the judge: "We will support each other, Your Honor."

When I was a boy, I'd walk the main beach along San Juan Bay and gawk at the fancy hotel that anchored the strip. I even got to go inside once: crystal candelabras hung over the foyer, all the furniture was made from rich mahogany, the dinner menu was expensive, and a lot of well-dressed Americans stayed there. I told myself that one day I'd book a room there for a special occasion—which is exactly what I did for our honeymoon. I used my first few checks from the Navy for the suite, which didn't leave me much cash for dinner and drinks. We opted for a hole-in-the-wall burger shack, and I bought a bottle of cheap sparkling wine. It didn't even have a cork. I unscrewed the cap and poured two glasses. We toasted to the rest of our lives, all that we would do as a team, the dreams we hoped to accomplish. We curled up in bed together, made love, and fell asleep to the sound of rushing waves and swaying palm trees. It was true happiness. And yet, our parents were upset at our elopement. Maria's father had always wanted to throw a lavish wedding for his daughter, as a reward for her good behavior growing up. My parents, for their part, thought that we weren't established enough for marriage. Neither side disapproved of our love, but had reservations for their own reasons. But I knew I had to do it. I didn't want to lose her.

Just as quickly as I had committed my life to Maria, I was back in the grip of the Navy. I became quite the promising sailor, to the point where the Navy sent me to finish college at the University of New Mexico, where I studied engineering. Upon graduating in 1984, I became an engineering and missiles officer, specializing in large-scale projectiles, including Tomahawk, anti-submarine, terrier, and harpoon missiles. My first son was born on the Kirtland Air Force Base in Albuquerque that same year. It was a hard birth; Maria was in labor for nearly thirty hours. I held her hand the entire time. The doctors believed in holistic methods, so Maria squatted down in the shower and muscled through breathing exercises. She pulled me in with her. I stood under the hot water, holding my wife, fully clothed and sopping wet.

Finally, the baby came, that little head poking out. The room started spinning and I nearly fainted—not because of the blood, but because I realized that I was part of bringing a new human into the world, the understanding that he was mine for the rest of my life. I felt like crying, but I held my tears. I wanted to be strong for my son. And Maria: she was always a kind and loving woman, but I saw her, when the doctors placed our baby into her arms, expand into an elevated version of herself. I knew then she would be a natural mother, as if it was her calling to have a child. The birth of my first son changed me as a man, as it should have, but just as quickly as he came into the world, I was off again, patrolling the high seas and protecting my country. It broke my heart to leave them.

The Navy relocated us to Newport, Rhode Island, where I enrolled in officer candidate school. The curriculum centered primarily on how to handle the responsibilities of overseeing hundreds of men working within the catacomb of a Navy ship. These vessels operated like miniature cities, with complex machinery that kept the ship alive. We were also taught that every officer should be a leader, and our teams should respect us. I was first placed in naval aviation, tasked with chasing Soviet submarines from the air, and eventually became a surface warfare officer (I graduated with honors) on a guided missile cruiser. My job was to use the ship as a weapon.

Then the Navy relocated us yet again, this time to Jacksonville, Florida, where I joined the USS *Dale*, a guided missile cruiser, as a lieutenant junior grade. It was 1986, and I had been in the Navy for eight years. My first son was coming up on his third birthday, and Maria was pregnant with our second. After Maria dropped me off for my next trip out to sea, my eldest son refused to get out of the car and go back into the house. Maria pleaded with him, but all he would say was, "No. Let's go back and get Dad." She drove my son back down to the dock, but my ship had already departed. Maria told him I had to leave to defend our country, and that I would be back soon. But my son knew the truth: it would be a long time before he saw his father again. Maria had no words of optimism to share with him—instead just held him in her arms, the sea stretching out before them—because underneath her role as supportive wife and loving mother, she too was filled with a deep longing for my return.

Maria went into labor that very night, not ten hours after I had set out to sea. I was at Guantánamo Bay by then. The Navy informed me, however, that in two months we would be docking back in Florida before making our way across the Atlantic to the Mediterranean. As soon as we arrived, I rushed off the ship to see my second-born son. But the stress of preparing to deploy to a hostile territory, the never-ending list of things to do to ready the ship and lead my men, overshadowed the joy of becoming a father again. When you're in the Navy, nothing is more important than the ship and the men on it. I couldn't fully enjoy the visit with my newborn son because the Navy consumed my mind. To this day, I don't remember if I even got the chance to hold him.

I knew this was no way to live. When I returned from deployment eight months later, the Navy had scheduled for me to go back to school to continue my education on advanced dynamics and rocket propulsion, to keep climbing the ranks to captain and eventually run my own ship. But, with two children at home, I decided to retire from the military. This was a decision I had been grappling with for some time, knowing that the longer I stayed in the Navy, the less time I would spend with my family and the less opportunity I would have to be a present father. Moreover, I wanted to take a shot at a dream that was born when I was a young boy: becoming an FBI agent.

Getting into the FBI is a long process. It can take up to a year to be officially hired. After I retired from the Navy and put in my application, I got a job as a systems engineer for Texas Instruments. I flew to Austin, Texas, to get settled before Maria and the kids were to join me. After my third day on the job, I called Maria to check in on the family and to let her know that I was almost ready for them to make their move.

"I was actually waiting for you to call," she said. "You got a letter in the mail today."

"A letter? From who?"

"The FBI. They hired you, Martin," she said. "You are to report for duty at Quantico in a week."

I was shocked. Out of the thousands of applicants, I had been chosen.

\* \* \*

I BECAME AN FBI agent in 1988. I was thirty-three years old. The War on Drugs was in full swing and federal law enforcement was dealing with their most powerful adversary to date, a global threat that became the impetus of my entire undercover career: Colombian drug cartels. These narco-empires, led by the Cali, Medellín, and North Coast cartels, had been gaining power and influence since the late 1970s, when drug barons switched from growing marijuana to refining potent, and highly addictive, cocaine. It quickly became the drug of choice for Americans in the 1980s, which supercharged production in Colombia and distribution into the US. This, in turn, increased domestic crime, which put a strain on local law enforcement and public pressure on the federal government. Presidents Nixon, Carter, Reagan, and Bush Sr. all labeled illegal drugs as America's most dangerous enemy. This directive obviously influenced how the FBI ranked their own priorities. When I first joined the bureau, it was made clear that our job wasn't to merely arrest street dealers, but to trace drugs back to the groups who worked directly for the cartels and oversaw large-scale importation and distribution of cocaine—and thwart their efforts. In essence, we were focused on the *people*. We let local law enforcement worry about the actual drugs once they were being sold by pushers on the street. It was a massive mission, almost too big to wrap my mind around, but it gave me a sense of purpose. I had a clear villain, and I would do anything to take them down.

Once I finished my orientation at Quantico, I was thrown into a fast-paced narcotics squad in Miami, where I worked alongside fifteen agents. We stemmed all manner of crimes related to the drug trade: weapons, homicide, smuggling, even human trafficking. During my first few months on the team, we tracked shipments and set up stings. It was thrilling stuff, and I loved it. But the drugs just kept coming. These cartels, and the men that ran them, were cunning, entrepreneurial, and hell-bent on making a shitload of money by any means necessary. Over time, it became clear that the FBI needed to infiltrate the international drug trade and take it down from the inside.

By the late 1980s, the majority of the drugs being smuggled into the United States from Colombia were being routed through the Caribbean. When the directive came down to infiltrate the

# MI AMOR

cartels, my naval training became hyper-valuable. I knew ships. I knew aircraft. I also had the perfect cultural background: I spoke Spanish, held Puerto Rican street smarts, had nerves of steel, and could easily master all the narco-lingo required of a smuggler. I also knew that evidence collected undercover—lived experiences alongside criminals, their own voices caught on the wire—is nearly unimpeachable in court. It was the gold standard of investigative techniques—and certainly the most difficult. My superiors at the FBI thought I was the perfect fit and asked if I would be willing to go undercover. I wouldn't be the first FBI agent to do it, but if I was successful, I would be the first to breach the cartels and make them believe I was one of them. I wanted to be the agent who made the prosecution's case airtight. I wanted to make history. I didn't hesitate.

I went back to Quantico, to the FBI's undercover school. It was an intense two-week training course where I was thrown into elaborate role-playing situations on soundstages rigged to look like grungy basements (for kidnapping reenactments), trap houses (drug buys), back alleys (international espionage), bank vaults (robbery), and white-collar offices (securities fraud). I was also tossed out into the real world, tasked with prying loose certain bits of information from unsuspecting strangers, with plainclothes FBI agents watching my every move. I barely slept, barely ate, the entire exercise running 24/7. I passed with flying colors. I was cleared to go undercover—to infiltrate the cartels.

*  *  *

ALTHOUGH THE FBI HAD been periodically employing undercover techniques for years, the policies, procedures, guidance, and resources that surrounded these operations were still in their infancy—especially for deep, long-term, continuously undercover assignments. When I joined the FBI in 1988, only one such operation had been conducted before, when Special Agent Joe Pistone became Donnie Brasco almost a decade earlier and infiltrated the New York City mob. No one in the bureau had gone that deep into a criminal organization since—especially a drug cartel, the culture of which was even more suspicious of newcomers than the Mafia. And only one agent before me had achieved that level of penetration for good reason: so much of an undercover agent's performance is contingent upon the culture of the criminal organization within which they embed. The safety precautions were the same across the board—working with a team of case agents, having cutting-edge technology and firepower at the quick, making sure an agent's legend is airtight—but specifically *how* the job is done is entirely different if an agent is tasked with infiltrating the Mafia versus a drug cartel. The norms for each organization are specific, the nitty-gritty of which can't readily be found in a how-to manual. This is why, when fighting the cartels throughout the 1980s, the FBI relied on more tried-and-true tactics, like tracking local cells and breaking up their distribution networks. It's fairly easy to pose as a smuggler for a weekend in order to conduct a bust; living as one for years at a time is a different animal, and there was no clear tutelage on how to cement that type of longevity. In essence, the FBI needed to find the perfect agent, at the perfect time, under the perfect political administration—and with the perfect enemy—to make a deep-undercover operation viable. Which is why, until I joined the bureau, infiltrating a cartel had never been done before. (And, to be honest, it's never been done since.)

In hindsight, after working undercover for decades, I've realized that this type of long-term, successful penetration can rarely be taught. In many respects, it comes down to the unpredictability inherent to deep-undercover work. Much like in a game of poker, you never know which cards will be dealt during any given hand, and all the training and conceptual strategy falls away in the face of an unexpected turn of events. It is these crucial moments, for which no one can ever be truly prepared, that separate a mediocre undercover agent from a legendary one—and dictates, with a supreme degree of accuracy, how deep said agent is able to go, whether his cover will be blown, and if he may wind up dead. I quickly realized that despite the fast-paced education I received at Quantico—which was merely a test to see if I would crack under the pressure—much of what I would be doing day to day would have to be learned on the fly and from sources within the cartel, who were better teachers than anyone in the bureau. In the end, though, my wits—and sticking to my invented backstory, never breaking cover—were the only things keeping me from being unmasked as a federal agent and killed on the spot. There was no rule book for the most important part of the job. I had to trust myself—and just do it.

I broke the news to Maria. She was in the kitchen, preparing dinner, having just gotten home from taking the boys to the park. I told her that I had to change my identity, turn into someone else, and essentially become a criminal for a living. I had only been in the FBI for a year by this point, and Maria and our boys were used to having me around—a long-awaited equilibrium finally captured.

"Is it dangerous?" she asked, apprehension threaded into her voice.

"Oh, no, no," I said, brushing off the question, unwilling to admit how treacherous going undercover actually was—especially within a cartel. "We do a lot of preparation before I get sent in."

# INSIDE THE CARTEL

"I want you to do what makes you happy," she said, her hand on my shoulder. "But just remember that we have two sons. I love you Martin, and if something happens to you, our world will collapse."

"Nothing will happen to me," I said, bringing her close to my chest. "Don't worry."

She pulled away and looked at me. "Well, I guess anything is better than the Navy, right?"

I smiled. "Yes, sweetie. This will be much better than the Navy."

It was never part of our plan to have me take on a job like this once I joined the FBI. The Navy, with its nine-month-long tours, was tough enough. I was away from her more often than we were together. What's more: Our sons were not yet five years old, and Maria was working as a middle school algebra teacher. We were finally settling down into a normal life, and here I was, ripping it out by the roots, taking this next step in my career. It was a big risk for all of us. But Maria acquiesced, knowing that I held a deep sense of duty for my country. This was a guiding light that she and I shared, and part of the fabric that bound us together. Of course, it is true that my ego was a factor, as well. I wanted to be at the center of the action, the cornerstone of the most important takedowns. Maria may have sensed this too, but she never gave any indication. We just agreed on a plan: she would look after the house and the kids while I went undercover—and became "Manny."

\* \* \*

MY FIRST ORDER OF business was to learn how to actually *become* a smuggler: duplicate how they think, how they act, their personality traits and culture. I had to know it all. The FBI arranged a meeting between Diego, our cooperating witness and a former pilot for José Gacha, coleader of the Medellín Cartel, and me. Diego had actually come into the FBI's orbit on a whim. He falsely believed he was being followed by the feds—acute paranoia, the hallmark of all prolific smugglers—and came to the bureau unprompted, hoping to cut a deal even before being arrested. The FBI was not, in fact, investigating him, but we took his offer to be a confidential witness seriously. It wasn't every day that a high-ranking member of a Colombian cartel volunteered to flip. After a diligent vetting process, the FBI agreed to make Diego an official source—and to have him work alongside me, the only agent in the Miami field office cleared to go deep undercover.

Two case agents drove me to Diego's house, just outside of the city. They needed to make sure that I wanted to work with him, and that we had chemistry. He lived in a gorgeous, two-story Mediterranean revival, filled with the finest Italian furniture, a far cry from what could be obtained on an agent's salary. We walked into the living room and found Diego sprawled out on his fine-grain leather couch. He was a clean-cut guy, with straight black hair and rich olive skin. I later learned, as we became close associates, that his heritage was mixed: South American Indian, white Spanish, and a slice of European.

"Manny, this is Diego," one of the case agents said, using my new code name. "He's going to teach you how to act like a smuggler."

Diego gave me a once-over. My father had a saying: *El hombre viste de los pies a la cabeza.* A gentleman dresses from his feet to his head. Diego was impressed. In the world of drug running, appearances were everything—especially the shoes. I always kept mine shiny and clean, a habit from my Navy days. This was a good sign to him: if anyone from a cartel saw that a smuggler was wearing scuffed or resoled shoes, they'd know immediately he was a cop. Diego stood and shook my hand. He turned to my case agents and said, "I think this guy will do just fine." His wife, Carla, a Dominican woman who would later become my secretary at the undercover warehouse, joined us. She was thin, with a model's face and a delicate sense of dress. She wasn't some trophy wife, however; Carla had been entrenched in the cartel for many years, having always hung around with smugglers and traffickers. For lunch, Carla served Cornish hens stuffed with rice. I sat down, began eating, and listened to everything Diego had to say about his life as one of the Medellín Cartel's most prolific pilots and smugglers. I had to ask him to repeat himself more than once, however, because he spoke an odd dialect of Spanish, full of garbled slang. This was hard for me to follow at first, but I soon caught on to his vernacular.

Diego didn't mince words, and gave me clear directives for while I was undercover. I barely got a word in edgewise among the onslaught of his directives.

"If you're in a meeting with someone from the cartel and don't know something, just stay quiet," he said. "And if you're at a restaurant with a bunch of cartel guys, don't be cheap. They spend money, so you have to spend money too."

"Well, we have to submit all of our receipts to the DOJ," I said. Diego didn't even entertain my response, just moved on to the next topic.

"The good thing about dealing with more senior members of the cartel is that there's a code of ethics, of sorts," he said. "No one will ask specifics about your full name, where you grew up, and all that. Extend them the same level of privacy. I know it's against your nature to not try to extract information, but be patient. Once they are comfortable with you, they will open up more."

"What about equipment for deliveries?" I asked. "What do they normally use?"

"A Piper aircraft is used for flyover drops," he said, "and an Aero Commander 1000 is used for bigger shipments where the plane has to land."

"Aero Commander 1000?" I said. "That's a million-dollar plane."

"Eh," Diego said, shoving his fork into the rice, "more like $1.5 million. But who's counting, right?" He took a bite and chewed. "Oh," he said. "I almost forgot. The vast majority of smugglers drink Johnnie Walker Black Label whiskey. And always on ice, with no mixers."

"I need to know those cultural things, the norms that are second nature to them," I said, "so I can immediately blend in."

"Well, they do love crude humor," he said. "Instead of saying 'son of a bitch,' they would say, '*triple hijo de puta.*'" (Rough translation: triple son of a whore. It doesn't make much sense when you say it in English, but it was how they spoke, I guess.) "You can't get offended at the things they say to you," Diego went on. "They might say, 'Manny, go get your girlfriend, three other whores, and let's party.' It doesn't mean they don't respect you. It's just how they are." He chuckled, thinking back to his one-liner. "That's actually a good one, Manny. You should use it in the future."

The most important thing to remember, Diego told me, was this: When all hell breaks loose after the loads with which I am involved get seized by the FBI, the Colombians are going to point fingers at each other for who's to blame, and a meeting will be called by the cartel leader. It could be El Viejo, one of the Ochoa brothers, or even Pablo Escobar himself.

## INSIDE THE CARTEL

"It's very important, Manny," he said, "that you go to these meetings. We always know that whoever doesn't show up for the meeting is guilty of something. From there, well . . ." He clenched his jaw and dragged his thumb across his throat. He took another bite of his hen and shrugged. "That's just how it goes." Almost a decade later, I became acutely aware of the murderous control that the cartels had over their employees: an army of sicarios murdered one of the FBI's sources. They drove a wooden stake through his heart and fed his body into a woodchipper. His DNA was found scattered throughout a field; his blood drenching the soil like rainwater.

After we were done with lunch, Diego sent us on our way. I felt so in awe of all that he shared with me, but I also knew that his tutelage served other means. First, it allowed him to become comfortable with working for the good guys. The mindset of a smuggler—of any criminal, really—is normally so entrenched that it's difficult for them to use their knowledge for a selfless cause. I hoped my willingness to listen to him made that transition easier. Secondly, I had to remind myself that thinking like a smuggler, understanding their point of view, would greatly enhance my covert technique. If I truly became Manny, I would succeed. Now I just needed all the gear to accompany my budding persona.

I stocked up on the finest European linen, Italian slacks, high-quality denim, cowboy boots, and tropical fedoras. To complete the vibe, I put more swagger in my step. I ratcheted up my cockiness. I grew a thick mustache. For good measure, the FBI hooked me up with a diamond-studded Rolex and a thick gold bracelet. They also handed me the keys to a few vehicles: a gold Porsche 928, a black Porsche 911 Carrera S, and a Bentley Continental. I rented an undercover apartment and adopted an undercover dog. A female FBI agent—who was pregnant at the time—even volunteered to go undercover as my girlfriend whenever I was invited to formal cartel gatherings. She was a great partner, her ears always tuned in, seeking valuable intelligence.

After I secured my undercover warehouse, Diego and Carla began posing as my employees. I quickly started meeting with men from the Medellín Cartel, all of whom were under the impression that I was a smuggler. I wouldn't offer my services to just anyone, though; as with any great con, I played hard to get. I'd tell them, "Man, why would I bring you in? I have been doing this for twenty years. I don't know you, and I have a good thing going here." After my rebuff, Diego and Carla would keep them interested by continuing to boast of my prowess. After this initial tease, the cartels were begging to work with me. Sure enough, I began moving hundreds of millions of dollars' worth of cocaine into the United States by sea and air, the full weight of the FBI behind me. Not a gram of those drugs ever made it to the streets, and we funneled every payment given to us by the cartel back into the government's coffers. In essence, our investigation into the cartels was being funded by the cartels themselves.

Although I reveled in the theatrics required for any undercover operation, especially one as high stakes and demanding as drug smuggling, I found it even more thrilling to chisel away at my undercover persona, to make Manny more and more believable, and carve a new version of myself out of stone bit by bit. It was artistry within the world of law enforcement, a dance between my two personalities. As time went on, I was Manny more often than I was Martin. This dance turned into a tug-of-war until I eventually became the most prolific undercover money launderer in FBI history.

## CHAPTER 3

# ¡ESTÁN TIRANDO COCA!

**I UNSPOOLED MY ROLL OF TRANSCEIVER WIRE AND TRIED** to catch a signal. I had to make contact with the Medellín Cartel, who were about to send nearly $200 million worth of cocaine to my private airstrip in Puerto Rico. It was late 1990, and I had done a few more runs for the cartel since our airdrop off the coast of Cuba (and our monumental raid in Miami), and they were becoming desperate to make up for their perceived loss in revenue.

After the success of that operation, my supervisors at the FBI began to trust my instincts. Still, we wanted more operational control over the smuggling. Setting up two boats in the middle of the Caribbean and collecting dope dropped from planes was dangerous, costly, and time-consuming. So, I made my pitch: Let's build an airstrip in Puerto Rico. The cartel trusted me now, and I was convinced that, if I built a landlocked pit stop, they would use it—and then the FBI would have complete control over their midpoint between Colombia

## ¡ESTÁN TIRANDO COCA!

and the United States. This would also allow me to enhance my undercover legend and infiltrate even deeper. But most importantly: no more barfing at sea. No more salty bales of coke. No more loads falling down on my head.

My bosses in Miami told me that if I could get the San Juan field office on board, I could give my plan a shot. When I spoke to the island's team, however, they nearly fell out of their chairs laughing. "You will never get Colombians to land here," they told me. "You can't possibly be that far in with them." They had no idea that I had been negotiating shipments with the likes of Pedro, El Viejo's top deputy, not to mention that Diego, a former pilot for the coleader of the Medellín Cartel, José Gacha, was my cooperating witness. They stopped laughing when I shared all that I had accomplished so far, and agreed to lend me a team of their agents to help my vision come to life.

I brought a handful of agents, including Ricky, with me from Miami. We dressed up in our undercover gear, in case anyone affiliated with the cartel spotted us, and scoured the entire island in a Black Hawk helicopter. We needed the perfect spot. We settled on a defunct sugarcane field near the island's western coast. We built a mile-long runway the width of a football field, and parked cars at the head and foot to signal its location from the air. It took us nearly a week to carve out our makeshift airport. After I returned to Miami, I asked Pedro out for a drink.

At the bar, we chatted for a while about the similarities between Puerto Rican and Colombian culture, especially their shared love of horses, before turning the conversation to business. "It's too bad our big load got fucked up," Pedro said. "But you're a gentleman. You did your part."

"Why do you think I chose to get paid up front?" I answered. "I'll always take the sure thing. I'm in this for the long run, you know." I took a sip of my whiskey. "But if you want to rake in some real cash, and make up your losses, I can help you."

"What do you have in mind?" he asked.

"Why don't you just fly a plane into Puerto Rico? I have an airstrip in the sugarcane fields." I grabbed a napkin off the bar, took a pen out of my pocket, and drew a map of the miniature airport. I explained how it would all go down: fly from Colombia, land on my airstrip, unload the cocaine, and let me take care of the rest. "It's foolproof," I said.

Pedro stared at the napkin, obviously impressed. He took a matchbook from atop the bar, grabbed my pen, and started scribbling on the inside cover.

"Call this number when you're there and ready," he said, sliding the matchbook over to me. Placing my prize into my pocket, we shook hands. It was on.

\* \* \*

A FEW MONTHS LATER, I made my way to Puerto Rico. As the FBI prepared for the load to arrive, my team and I stayed at a fancy beachside resort, playing our roles. We dressed the part, put swagger into our step, and projected a nonchalant confidence. The hotel staff scowled at us, convinced that we were the bad guys. Honestly, I loved it. I was getting so good at being Manny that, as soon as I walked into the hotel lobby, the look on their faces said it all, a mixture of fear and disdain: *This guy works for a cartel.* If Pedro's men came around the hotel asking about me, the staff's assumptions would enhance my credibility. I was even subtly pushed to leave when I was told that the hotel wouldn't accept my American Express credit card. I didn't want to come across as aggressive and cause a scene, and have the cartel hear about it. I finessed the clerk and convinced him that I meant no harm. He ran my credit card. It cleared without issue. The staff's suspicions grew the following morning when the maid came into my room and found a gun under my pillow. She glared at me, but didn't say a word.

A few nights before the load was supposed to arrive, I spent a few hours at the hotel pool with two undercover Puerto Rican agents from the San Juan field office. We swam, ate dinner on the deck, and made passes at pretty women. We acted as if we had done this a thousand times—that lounging by the pool while we waited to pick up hundreds of millions of dollars' worth of dope from a Colombian drug cartel was just another day's work for us. In this moment, deepening my tan at a five-star resort, I was so enamored by the turn my life had taken that I almost didn't see the three men across the way, whose eyes were burning a hole in my chest.

One of the Puerto Rican agents tapped me on the shoulder. "Hey man, see that guy over there? And that guy? And that guy?" he said, his eyes darting toward the three men. I nodded. "They are all Customs and DEA," he said. "They think you're the real deal." *Shit*, I thought to myself. Did the hotel rat us out? Could these guys sabotage the operation, wrongly thinking that they were taking down a big-time drug lord? This had happened to me before: Other federal agencies, unaware that I was undercover, tracked me as if I was a real criminal. Not only did I have to worry about being unmasked by members of the cartel, but also by my own government allies. In these situations, I would never break cover, even to let the other agency know that I was a good guy. Moreover, the higher-ups at the FBI never told them, either. My role as an undercover agent was that secret. In fact, I would've rather gotten arrested by the DEA or Customs than break cover. If that happened, we would deal with the fallout. It was just part of the job: I couldn't keep my cover without occasionally being chased by the good guys. It was proof that we were doing things right.

"Let's get out of here," I said, standing up and tossing my towel onto the chair. "We have to make contact with Colombia anyways, to check when they are bringing in the load."

We made our way upstairs. In total, a dozen agents were part of the operation, and our rooms adjoined one another down a long corridor near the top floor. I went into my room, unlatched my suitcase, pulled out my high-frequency radio, fired up my transceiver, and tried to connect to Colombian airwaves. No luck. But I had an idea. I gathered the other agents, and we proceeded to string a long-wire antenna from balcony to balcony, as if we were decorating the building for Christmas. I connected the wire to my transceiver, which sat on the dining table in my suite.

There was only one problem: hotel security was watching our every move. The resort boasted two tall towers next to one another, and the security guards stood across the way, peering at us through binoculars. Now they knew, without a doubt, that we were smugglers. I spotted them, but I continued trying to catch a signal anyway. I turned a couple knobs and hit a few buttons, but it still didn't work. I switched to my satellite phone and finally got on the line with Pedro, whose men would be doing the run. I explained that the airstrip was ready to go. I shared the coordinates and told Pedro we would be waiting for them in two nights to receive the dope. Pedro confirmed that they would be there. I hung up, respooled my wire, broke down my gear, and put everything back into my suitcase. Just as I was zipping it up, someone aggressively knocked on my door. I walked over, peered through the peephole, and then opened up. In front of me stood two huge men in suits: hotel security.

"There's a lot of partying going on up here," one of the men said. "A lot of people are complaining."

I turned around and gestured to the empty room. "Do you see a party going on in here?"

The security guards peered inside. "Do you mind if we come in?"

"Sure," I said, acting as if I had nothing to hide. "Please, come in."

The two men looked around my room suspiciously, and then walked out onto the balcony. No satellite phone, no transceiver, no wire. Nothing.

"What seems to be the problem?" I asked. But before they could answer, I switched gears and put the blame on them. "You know what," I said, my tone firm, my body language tense, "I have been given a hard time ever since I set foot in this place. I'm spending ten thousand dollars *per day* here. I'm going to call the regional manager and tell him that I am not being treated fairly, despite all the money I am putting down here with my crew."

The guards were clearly taken aback. They knew their jobs could be on the line if a big spender like me made a complaint. We even gambled in the hotel casino to further enhance the ruse. "Oh, that won't be necessary," one of them said. "We're sorry we bothered you. It won't happen again."

"Look, I pay my bill on time. My credit card doesn't get declined. I am a model guest, aren't I?" I said, my tone softening from anger to exasperation. "Why are you invading my privacy like this? You're embarrassing me in front of my guests."

"We're sorry," one of the men said. "We didn't mean to

offend you. We'll be going now." And with that, they walked back out into the hallway.

"That'd be great, but let's make sure this doesn't happen again," I said. I flashed them a smile and gently closed the door.

* * *

MY MEN AND I spent the next day hanging out on the beach, at the bar, and in our rooms. We acted as smugglers would, except we never drank more than a few sips, and were always on high alert. After nightfall, we loaded into the five vans I had rented, and made our way down to the airstrip so we could accept the drugs and bring them to Miami. It was a long drive, a few hours into the mountains, and we all had to pee—badly. We pulled over in a remote area, near to what appeared to be an abandoned house, and unzipped our flies. It turned out that the house was not, in fact, abandoned: As we peed, an old man burst through the front door and came running toward us wielding a machete. He screamed at us at the top of his lungs, saying his wife was on the porch and saw all of our business. We quickly buttoned our pants, ran back to the vans, and skidded out of there, leaving a cloud of dirt in our wake. I peered into the rearview mirror. The man was still standing there, waving that massive knife.

The dirt road weaved down the side of a mountain, around a creek, and through the central valley's sticky marshes. We kept going, hours and hours of driving, until we entered Cabo Rojo, a small seaside village on the western coast. A few miles farther down, the tree line opened up and the flattened sugarcane field came into view. We finally arrived at our airstrip. It was well after midnight, the sky illuminated by stars. I unpacked my satellite phone and pointed the antenna toward the sky. The dozen other agents milled about, fueled by adrenaline, ready for the cartel to show. Antonio, a longtime agent on our team, ran down to a nearby beach shack and grabbed some roasted pork and plantains for us to eat. We quickly devoured the food. It was delicious.

Our contact at Customs, who was monitoring radar air traffic for the FBI, called me. He explained that he had picked up a low-flying aircraft just north of our location, near a lighthouse that looked very similar to the one that was used as a landmark for our airstrip. I immediately called the pilot and asked him to describe what he saw. I knew he was at the wrong lighthouse, but I couldn't give myself away, no matter how much I wanted this delivery to succeed. He said that he saw two lighthouses: one close, and one farther south. I directed him to the correct location and prepared my men for the handoff: Be cool, let me take the lead, don't speak unless spoken to. They probably wouldn't have time to talk to the Colombians, even if they wanted to; cartel pilots aren't really down for chitchat during a big delivery. Every second they are on the ground increases their risk of getting caught. For them, the plan was always the same: land the plane safely, unload the cocaine as fast as possible, and hightail it back to Colombia. But we did bring them a few cases of Budweiser to present as a gift, as was customary within the cartels. We were so close. All we needed to do was make sure the plane landed safely.

The pilot came screeching overhead. He made one pass over us, circled around, and made another. I had a feeling something was wrong. I called the pilot, and he gave me the bad news: He wasn't going to land. He saw police lights in a nearby village. This was unrelated to our operation, but he thought it was a setup. Of course this delivery was, but just not in the way he thought. I immediately called Pedro and told him that the pilot wasn't landing. "Manny, tell the *malparido* that if he doesn't deliver, upon his return *va a quedar mamando*." Which roughly translates to: If the pilot doesn't do the job for which he was hired, he's going to be sucking dick when he gets home. "And tell him that we won't turn on the lights back here," Pedro said. "He'll have to land in the dark jungle, so he better fucking deliver." I hung up, called the pilot, and relayed the message.

The pilot made two more passes over us and then, all of a sudden, bales of cocaine started falling from the sky. Those goddamn refrigerators. *BOOM! BOOM! BOOM!* The crew unloaded the cargo indiscriminately, drugs careening through the darkness like bombs. As they fell, we heard men yelling in the nearby village: "*¡Están tirando coca! ¡Están tirando coca! ¡Están tirando coca!*" They are dropping coke! They are dropping coke! They are dropping coke!

My fellow agents were shocked that the cartel was just tossing the bales out of the plane. But I didn't care. To me, this was controlled chaos. We were prepared, and I was confident we could handle any curveball pitched our way, including massive bales of coke falling from the sky. All of us scrambled to grab the drugs. Some were so deep in the swamp they were hard to find. It was a mad dash. We didn't have time to load them up into our vans and head out, knowing we could be stopped by the local cops—who were likely made aware of the falling drugs and didn't know we were FBI agents—before we could escape. Instead, we quickly shuttled the cocaine into a barn on the outskirts of the airstrip we had previously secured as a staging area. It was filled with every slithering critter imaginable, from rats to salamanders to snakes. As we huddled together in silence, drugs stacked all around us, we heard the squeal

## ¡ESTÁN TIRANDO COCA!

of sirens, the whooshing blades of helicopters. The Puerto Rican police had descended onto the field with a barrage of dogs. They were looking for the smugglers. They were looking for *us*.

Helicopters beamed their searchlights up and down our airstrip, into the swamp, and near the barn. A procession of cops fanned out across the field and scoured both for drugs and smugglers hiding in the weeds. A cloud of dust enveloped the area, the rumble of trucks shook the ground, and the sound of barking dogs radiated throughout the woods. I lay down inside the barn and tried to relax, but as with the pickups at sea, I felt like I was in a warzone. For some reason, the cops never searched the barn. All they found were two bales of cocaine that we had left behind in our haste. That was presumably good enough for them; it would make for a great press conference the next morning. And between us and the local cops, no drugs were left unseized, which was a plus. We lay there for over six hours, not moving a muscle, until we were sure that they had left. I feared the local cops almost as much as the tropical beasts slithering around the dark barn.

As the sun crept over the horizon, at just before six in the morning, the coast was clear. We loaded up the drugs and headed out. We originally came out in five vans, but two were now stuck in the swamp, so we all had to cram into the remaining three vehicles, stuffed to the brim with just under a thousand kilos of cocaine. After loading the last bale, we rushed out of the field and back into the mountains, speeding as fast as we could, hoping we weren't driving into an ambush set up by the local police—or a gang of criminals who might've heard of our operation. An hour into our drive, my stomach started to lurch, twisting into a knot.

"Man, my stomach is killing me," I said.

# INSIDE THE CARTEL

Ricky looked over at me. "Mine too."

The pressure dropped from my stomach and into my intestines. "It was that fucking pork!" I yelled. I turned in my seat, writhing in pain. And then it hit me: I had to go to the bathroom *immediately*.

"Pull over," I said, trying to hold it in. My case agent, Dean McCarthy, was driving the van. He looked at me like I had two heads. *Here? In the middle of nowhere? With $100 million worth of blow in the back?* "I don't care if we have the coke! I have to take a shit!"

"It's too risky, Martin," Ricky said from the back seat.

"Do you want me to do it here in the van?" I screamed. I was desperate now. "Pull the fuck over! Now!"

The van skidded to a stop at the edge of a sugarcane field. I jumped out, ran down a ravine, squatted within a cluster of cane stalks, and relieved myself. My boots sunk down into the mud, the watery waste splashed on my legs, and spiders and centipedes fell off the sugarcane and onto my shoulders and chest. It was miserable. A few other agents followed me. The pork had done them in, too. (Thankfully, we had toilet paper in the van.) After a hellish ride to our covert warehouse, where we stashed the drugs under armed guard, we finally made it back to the resort. We all walked in, covered in mud, reeking like a swamp. It was almost lunchtime, and it was clear that we had been up all night. Right on cue, the hotel staff glared at us. *Goddamn smugglers.*

\* \* \*

THREE DAYS LATER, THE FBI securely transported the drugs to Miami, where they stashed the bales in the drug vault, recorded them as evidence, and prepared for us to hand them

## ¡ESTÁN TIRANDO COCA!

off to Pedro's receiver. I was already back in Miami by then and, while the drugs were being processed, I met with Pedro at a bar in Biscayne Bay, near the ocean. I told him about the bungled drop-off, reiterated how his pilot refused to land, and explained that we had to bust our ass to recover as much of the cocaine as possible. To give credence to my story—and deflect blame from me and my men—I showed him a clipping from a Puerto Rican newspaper, which detailed the event from law enforcement's point of view: a smuggling plane dropped cocaine into a sugarcane field, the cops were alerted, and they recovered a good chunk of dope. Pedro was still upset, chiding me for leaving some of the drugs behind.

"Man, your guy should have landed," I said. "Instead, he dropped the load all over the place. One bale even fell right in the middle of the village square! Now my airstrip is burnt. I can't use it anymore. And all of my guys almost got busted. Tell El Viejo that he owes me a million for the airstrip. It's nonnegotiable." I came up with the $1 million demand on the spot; that kind of money could support our undercover operation for years to come. But to the cartel? It was chump change.

Pedro mulled it over, elbows on his knees, kneading his palms together. He relented. "All right, Manny," he said. "One million for the airstrip. I'll add it to your fee. No problem."

I switched tack and smiled, placing my hand on his shoulder. "Hey, it could've been worse, right? At least we got the majority of it back here for you."

He grinned. "You're right, Manny. You're right. It's still a win in the end." We sipped our drinks, comfortable in our partial victory. "You know," he continued, "I actually have to bring this load to Houston. The guys you are giving it to are driving it there for me."

Bingo. This was the perfect stroke of luck. As I went deeper and deeper undercover over the past two years, I quickly learned to always seize upon an opportunity presented to me on the spot, to always be on the lookout for ways to further the FBI's goal of understanding, and breaking up, large-scale drug distribution networks. We hadn't yet learned how, and by whom, Miami was linked to other major cities. If I could weasel my way into this section of delivery, it would prove highly valuable and, as always, help deepen my cover within the world of cartel smuggling.

"Pedro, come on," I said. "That's pretty risky—me, dropping off the load to a guy in Miami, only to have him hit the road to Texas? Why pay someone else to bring it? Throw in another thousand per kilo and I will get it to Houston for you. It's safer for you and your product."

"My western route is one of my most valuable," he said. "I can't take any unnecessary risks with it. Are you sure that you have the resources to do that?"

I smiled. "Of course I do."

I was going to the Lone Star State.

\* \* \*

I TOLD PEDRO THAT I was going to stash the dope inside of a box truck and drive it to Houston. But of course, the FBI had other plans. A few days later, the drugs were securely transported by plane to Texas and stashed at the Houston field office while Ricky, a few agents from Texas, and I set up a plan for the drop-off. Pedro had already introduced me to his Houston connection, a big-time trafficker with enormous, bushy eyebrows, one of which was completely white. His name was *La Cejilla Blanca*, the White Eyebrow. He came from Buenaventura, seventy miles northwest of Cali, but also did business out of Barranquilla, on Colombia's northern coast, a hotspot for cartel activity. Home of the North Coast Cartel—for whom I would soon become a money launderer—it was a bustling hub of drug exportation. The region was seen as the little brother to the major drug hubs of Cali and Medellín, and their sense of competition and strive for control resulted in some of the most ruthless traffickers in the world.

La Cejilla Blanca wanted us to transfer the dope from our box truck into the back of a pickup truck. He told me that the truck would be waiting for us in the parking lot of the Galleria, a shopping center in uptown Houston. Jimmy Padilla, one of the Houston case agents who would eventually work with me in Puerto Rico when I became a money launderer, picked up the old, beat-up Toyota without issue. The only problem was that the truck didn't have a cap; its bed was exposed. When we loaded the duffel bags full of cocaine into the back of the pickup, we knew that we had to cover them up, so we used garbage pulled from a nearby dumpster. We topped everything with a recently discarded Christmas tree. The truck looked prepped for a run to the local dump.

I then called Cejilla and told him I was ready to discuss our delivery logistics. We agreed to meet at a restaurant inside the mall. Ricky and Jimmy came with me. We walked into the restaurant, and I spotted Cejilla sitting in a corner booth with two men—dudes that I immediately assumed were professional hitmen. It was customary to bring protection when dropping off money, after all. I kept my face buoyant, my posture upright, but I knew that these situations could get dicey in a second. We prepared for such things: the FBI arranged for three surveillance agents to hang out inside the restaurant and watch the meeting. If anything went sideways, we'd have backup at the ready. But there was another twist to this situation: I was wearing a wire. We needed to have this crew on tape talking about the shipment, and if the sicarios decided to pat me down, I'd be in a world of trouble. I took a deep breath and tried to keep my cool. I told myself that it was highly unlikely we would be shaking each other down in such a public place. We were vetted business partners, after all, both here for a common goal. There was no need for suspicion. Ricky and I sat down in the booth across from the three men. Cejilla had just finished a plate of barbecue ribs. He licked his fingers clean.

"Is it ready?" he asked.

"We are getting it ready now," I said. "I will call you later to tell you where to pick it up, but I'm waiting on an up-front payment first, and then the rest after." Cejilla had already gotten the memo from Pedro. He nodded at one of his men, who pulled four thick stacks of cash—about $40,000—out of his jacket and proceeded to thrust it toward us under the table. The restaurant was packed, waiters milling about, the tail end of the lunch rush.

"What the fuck are you doing, man?" I asked. "Just put the money in my car. Don't give me the money here!" But it was too late. Ricky and Jimmy grabbed the bundles from under the table and haphazardly stuffed the money into their jackets. We peered around the restaurant, hoping no one spotted us. We stood up, Ricky and Jimmy looking damn near pregnant with the money filling their leather coats, and stormed out. We then handed the cash off to the case agents for processing, and went back to our hotel. I kept in touch with Cejilla throughout the night and told him the load would be ready for him the next day. In the morning, I called him again, and told him to meet me at the ice-skating rink in the center of the Galleria at 1:00 p.m.

## ¡ESTÁN TIRANDO COCA!

"Once we are together," I said, "I will tell you where the load is going to be."

"Not a problem," he said. "I will be there."

Ricky, Jimmy, and I decided to park the dope truck at a local Holiday Inn. The parking lot was busy, so our surveillance team could blend in seamlessly with the other cars. Jimmy volunteered to drop off the truck and hand over the keys to Cejilla's driver, while Ricky and I met up with Cejilla at the Galleria. He was waiting for us at the ice-skating rink, as promised. We walked back to my car—which was bugged—and got inside.

"The merchandise is at the Holiday Inn," I said. "It's ready to go." I explained the different markings stamped onto the kilos, to prove to him that I really had the drugs and wasn't trying to rip him off. He was more than satisfied.

"*Perfecto*," he said. "Let me call my driver." Cejilla's man was on his way, so I called Jimmy to relay the update.

"Man," Cejilla said, smiling, "once we do this, we will have a partnership for a long time."

"Let's see how it goes," I said, knowing full-well that he would be indicted soon enough. Jimmy called me back a few minutes later: Cejilla's driver had shown up, the keys had been handed over, and he was driving away in the truck. What Jimmy didn't say on the phone, but which I knew, was that our surveillance team was now following the truck to locate their stash house and plan our seizure. Ricky and I offered to take Cejilla out to lunch. Jimmy also joined. After we ate, the four of us drove around Houston, killing time, waiting for Cejilla's men to call him and confirm that they had gotten to the stash house.

A few hours later, Cejilla's phone rang. It was his driver. Everything was square.

"We got the merchandise," Cejilla said. "It's all good to go."

"All right, he confirmed that you have it. Now, where's my money?" I asked.

"I don't have the money here," Cejilla said. "We have to go get it."

"I thought you had it close by?" I asked, a mere inquiry, no edge in my voice, acting like I trusted him completely. We were partners now, after all.

"That would be very dangerous," he said. "I need to go get the money and bring it to you. It's getting late. Why don't we meet here tomorrow morning? I will have it then."

I shot a look at Ricky and Jimmy. This was sketchy. On one hand, a veteran smuggler would never let a payday wait, especially from a guy like this. Us being with him was our insurance policy that he wasn't going to take the cocaine and renege on our deal. On the other hand, I was the cartel's smuggler, and therefore his ticket to a huge payday. Without the drugs I could deliver, he couldn't make any money. He obviously didn't have much of an incentive to screw me over. Plus, if he did, he would have to answer to Pedro and El Viejo. The response was clear: We could wait. No problem at all. As always, these relationships were built on trust.

"Sure," I said. "I don't have any issues with that."

Once we parted ways, Ricky, Jimmy, and I checked in with the surveillance team who had followed the driver.

"We lost them," Trent McKentyre, the lead case agent, explained.

"You lost them?" I asked. "What happened?"

"They went joyriding on the highway, looping all around the city, probably to make sure no one was following them," he explained. "We kept up, but they turned into a residential neighborhood, and that's where we lost them. There's got to be two hundred houses here, but they're in one of them."

"We have to find them," I said, "or we're in deep shit."

"Hold on," he said. "I think we found them. I'll call you right back."

Thirty minutes later, my phone rang. It was Trent. "We got it, Martin," he said. "We got the load." He explained that he and his team scoured the neighborhood, looking for a needle in a haystack, when one of the agents spotted the tip of a Christmas tree through a garage window—the same Christmas tree we had plopped on top of the load when we loaded the truck. They staked out the place for a few minutes, and then five dopers, all young guys, came out of the house. They piled into another car and sped off. A covert surveillance vehicle tailed them to a nearby nightclub. Although they were supposed to stay at the house and guard the drugs for the next week, never leaving it alone for a second, they broke the rules to go party. The agents simply picked the lock on the garage door and seized the cocaine. In its place they left a crisp piece of white paper: a search warrant, signed by a federal judge. It might have been the easiest seizure in FBI history.

"Trent, that's incredible," I said, laughing, after he told me the story. "Maybe it was actually smart of them to leave the dope behind, so they weren't there when you all seized it."

"We're taking the load back to the field office now," he said.

"Great," I said. "I'm meeting up with Cejilla in the morning. I will keep you posted on how things go."

The FBI staked out the house all night and into the next morning. The dopers didn't return. The cartel didn't yet know that we had seized the load. Cejilla called me and told me to meet him at the Galleria. He had my money. I met up with Ricky, who was nervous.

"We shouldn't do this," he said. "We already made the case. We have them dead to rights. Who cares about the money?

Plus, what if they know we seized the load, and it's a setup? They'll kill us."

"If I don't show up, then they'll think it was me who stole the load when they find out later," I said. "It could blow my cover. I have to go."

"I don't know about this."

"Look, surveillance told us that the kids haven't been back to the house," I said. "There's no way any of them know that we took the load."

"All right, Martin," Ricky said. "I trust you."

We picked up Jimmy and made our way back to the Galleria. Cejilla was once again waiting for us inside the restaurant, perched at the bar, having a drink. "Let's get you your money," he said. "It's in the trunk of my car."

We walked over to his vehicle together. He took out his key and threaded it into the trunk's lock. My mind spun: What if Ricky was right? What if there was a sicario lying inside, holding a shotgun, ready to blow a hole in my chest? The air was sweltering, and my clothes were soaked in sweat. Although we had already made our case by seizing the load, I still had to play the part, to keep my cover intact. Plus, receiving the rest of the payment could help fund future operations. It was always the mission, making sure everything went smoothly and no one got hurt, that sent my blood pressure through the roof. But in that moment, waiting to be handed a bag full of money, I kept my mind alert and my hands steady.

When Cejilla opened the trunk, all I saw were two black duffels, filled to the brim with cash. "It's all there," he said. "One million dollars."

"Looks good," I said. Jimmy drove our car over. We loaded the money into our trunk and left. With the money secured, we raced to a nearby hotel, where I had already booked a room. I went inside and waited for Ricky, who was sweeping the area for cartel men with a team of surveillance agents. The coast was clear. He came into my room, and the other agents entered the adjoining room, which they rented under their name. I transferred the money to them through the connecting door, to be taken back to the Houston field office for processing.

I fell down onto the bed, exhausted, adrenaline still coursing through my body. We got the drugs. We got the money. We logged invaluable evidence. It was over. I could go back to Miami. I told myself I would see Maria and my boys as soon as I landed. But I also knew that all hell would break loose once the cartel figured out that another one of their loads was gone. I would certainly have some explaining to do. Luckily, Ricky broke my train of thought.

"Should we get some dinner?" Ricky asked.

I lifted my head off the pillow and looked at him. "I guess that's what smugglers would do, right?"

CHAPTER 4

# I KNOW NOT TO SAY A DAMN THING

**BY 1991, I HAD SMUGGLED NEARLY $1 BILLION WORTH OF** cocaine into the United States for the Medellín Cartel. My run undercover in Miami still stands as one of the most successful narcotics investigations of all time. We had gathered more intelligence, seized more drugs, and started the process of indicting more criminal targets than had ever been done before. No one in the history of the FBI had been able to infiltrate a Colombian cartel's smuggling operation, much less break up numerous core groups. My work was set to become the basis of how future undercover agents would do their jobs—but at this moment, all I cared about was staying alive.

In the 1980s and 1990s, less than 1 percent of FBI agents worked undercover, and the majority of those who did so only lived as their alias for a few weeks at a time—what we now call "light undercover." In many respects, I molded the role of a covert agent into a new model that could exist continuously for years within the criminal underworld and enamor even the most street-smart bad guys. And yet, I never felt gleeful in my success in deceiving these men. To me, it wasn't personal. I wasn't out to get them individually, but what they represented. My job was only a means through which I could alleviate the harm that drugs cast onto society. I came to realize that finding success while working deep undercover is based, more than anything, upon using a target's firmly held biases and belief systems against them. As an undercover agent, I was able to create an alternative reality for drug lords, but only because they had already become blinded by greed. In effect, a successful undercover case is a magic trick whose spectator doesn't know they are on a stage. Many years later, when I sat in court testifying against the criminals with whom I had previously collaborated, they refused to believe I had been a federal agent. Their cardinal sin wasn't stupidity, but confidence.

And yet the War on Drugs dragged on. This was the Achilles' heel of federal law enforcement at that time: No matter how much dope was seized in America, no matter how many international distribution chains were broken, the drug lords in Colombia just kept manufacturing more cocaine and finding new ways to smuggle it into the United States. Theoretically, I could've thrown away my life as Martin Suarez and *become* Manny, and I still would have been just chipping away at the cartels decades later. I never, however, let any sense of short-term tedium or abstract futility of my job get in the way of the mission I set out for myself. I convinced Maria that I could achieve something noble, and I told myself that, despite the stress thrust upon me by my work as an undercover agent, I needed to prove to her and to my two sons that their father could make a difference in the world.

On top of that, the FBI was keen on keeping their prized

covert agent embedded within the world of international drug trafficking. I became a ghost in the Miami field office, an agent who never came out of the shadows. My colleagues taped a picture of my face to the back of my desk chair, which sat empty week after week. When I heard about the joke, I was told, "It's so we can remember who you are." With all this in mind, I made my way back to Miami after the Houston sting. I was still Manny, still a dirty smuggler, still stationed at my undercover warehouse. I was ready for the next mission from the cartel. And what a mission it was.

I was sitting in my office at the warehouse when my phone rang. It was Pedro. He and I had already discussed what had happened in Houston. It turned out that the young guns who were supposed to be watching the dope didn't realize it was gone until a week later, when it was set to be transported. Once they found out, they disappeared. No one ever discovered the search warrant, and El Viejo assumed that the youngsters either got robbed or just stole the cocaine. This allowed my cover—and the Medellín Cartel's trust in me—to stay intact. Now, Pedro had a new problem. And he needed a solution. Fast.

"Manny, I'm screwed," he said. "My guys are stuck in Mexico. I can get them across the border, and then here, to Florida, but can you get them back to Colombia?"

I was confident that my superiors at the FBI would find the necessary resources to pull off Pedro's request. "Come to my office and we'll figure something out," I said.

I thought that this could be a great opportunity to leverage his desperation for our benefit, to twist the screws and gain more access into the cartel's inner workings. Up until that point, I had only been able to gather intelligence on the logistical details of their smuggling operation. Now, his predicament would allow us to put faces to names, and to dissect the cartel's personnel structure and hierarchy. When Pedro showed up at my office, I told him to get his men here, and that I would make sure they made it back to Colombia.

Pedro rented a couple of cargo vans and shuttled his men to a safe house in Miami Lakes, near a mansion that he owned, so he could keep an eye on them. Once the cartel employees arrived, I lured them to my office under the guise of letting them use my phone to call their families back in Colombia. In reality, we had hidden cameras in the ceilings and microphones in the walls to document my meetings with the underworld, and now we had an entire smuggling team speaking amongst themselves and with their Colombian contacts. It was an intelligence jackpot. During their many calls, we learned that a $250 million shipment of their cocaine had gone sideways. It was a massive operation, complete with twenty-one cartel-employed pilots and mechanics. The route was circuitous, but their mission was to fly seven planes into Mexico, unload the drugs, and then have Mexican smugglers take the load by truck over the US border, following a route that came to be known as the Mexican Trampoline. There was only one problem: Mexican law enforcement—working on behalf of a rival Mexican cartel—intercepted the planes the moment they landed. The Mexican authorities stole the drugs and gave the Colombians a macabre choice: walk to the US border or be executed.

This was a problem with which the cartels had been dealing for years. When narco-dollars prop up an economy, as they do in Colombia and Mexico, the entire geopolitical system turns corrupt to find equilibrium. But this became a double-edged sword: The cartels needed widespread public corruption to bolster their power, but the duplicity they so heavily relied upon also opened them up to risk. You never knew to which cartel a branch of law enforcement had pledged their allegiance, especially outside of Colombia.

Truth be told, the majority of Pedro's men were scared shitless. They had found themselves in a nightmare situation: drugs confiscated, planes seized, and forced into the United States with no paperwork and no idea on how they would return home. Moreover, two of the pilots were El Viejo's grandsons. Now, it wasn't just Pedro calling me, begging for my help. Other high-level associates of the cartel called me day and night, urging me to get their men home. Their trust in me was palpable, and further confirmed that the tactics I had used to get this far were immensely successful, even if the loads for which they hired me to transport were eventually seized. This raised the stakes for the FBI immensely. If I could get El Viejo's own flesh and blood back to Colombia, I'd be woven into his inner circle forever.

Although Pedro had his safe house in Miami Lakes, a few of the men refused to leave my warehouse once they showed up, terrified they would be arrested. Their encampment in Miami morphed into a strange, cartel-themed sleepover. We plied them with pizza, snacks, and beer. We hoped by placating them, making them comfortable, they would talk. And talk they did. We were able to use all of the phone numbers they dialed, all of the names being mentioned in conversation, and all of the details spilled in our presence to set up a half-dozen wiretaps, which strengthened our case and gave us even more access into the nexus between their domestic operation in Colombia and their international distribution networks.

While the men used my office as their de facto headquarters, I scrambled behind the scenes to figure out how we could get them back to Colombia. Luckily, my fee had already been established. El Viejo promised to pay me $500,000 for my services. That much money could sustain our investigation for a year or more. After solidifying a plan with my superiors, I called a meeting at my undercover office with Pedro and his men. I wanted the entire scene recorded on video. If we were to bring conspiracy charges against these guys in the future, the tape would prove invaluable in court. Pedro brought the men staying at his safe house to my warehouse, and they joined their comrades who were sleeping there. We rounded them up to announce our plan. Ricky and I sat them down as if I was about to lead a college lecture. The men fidgeted and bickered among themselves. They were on edge. Their lives were in my hands, after all. And I wasn't even Colombian.

"*Oigan, oigan,*" Pedro said. Listen, listen. The men quieted down. "We're going to take care of this for you." He turned to me. "What's the plan, Manny?"

"Half of you have passports, yes?" I asked. About a dozen men nodded their heads. "All right, the first part of the plan is for you. I'm going to buy you tickets and you'll fly back to Medellín on a regular, commercial flight. My connections in the government will make sure you don't get stopped at the border." This was a total lie: I didn't have any secret connections helping these men out. It was comical: When we spoke with Immigration, they explained that the men with passports didn't technically commit any crimes on American soil, so the proper course of action would be to simply deport them. I was charging the cartel half a million dollars for a service that the United States government would've happily done for free.

"And what about the rest of us?" one of the pilots asked. "How are we getting home?"

I folded my arms and paused for dramatic effect: "I'm going to smuggle you out." The men glanced at each other. A hushed silence filled the room. "We're taking you to Grand Cayman, where El Viejo and Pedro will have a plane waiting," I said. "From there, you're home free."

After Pedro's driver brought some of the men back to the safe house, I pitched Pedro on adding another layer to the plan: "If you're sending a plane to pick these guys up anyway, why not fill it with merchandise and I'll smuggle it back to Miami?" He couldn't see it, but I had the twinkle of another massive seizure in my eyes.

"*Bacano. Perfecto*," he said. "It is, um, how do the Americans say, *Kill two chickens with one rock*?"

I laughed. "That's right, Pedro. You're exactly right."

\* \* \*

THE FBI ARRANGED FOR an undercover plane at a small, smuggler-friendly airport in South Florida. A couple days later, in the middle of the night, Pedro drove the cartel crew to the airstrip. A team of FBI agents, posing as my drug-running employees, waited for them on the tarmac. The pilots and mechanics boarded the plane. The FBI's pilot turned on the engine, its propellers whirring, and flew them to a private airport in Grand Cayman.

I had already traveled to Grand Cayman the day prior. I needed to work with our surveillance team so we could document the entire exchange. A team of Royal Cayman Islands Police agents hid all over the airport, snapping photographs for us. (I brought them a side of American-raised beef as a thank-you gift, as well as a duffel bag full of cash to cover their expenses.) I hung back at a local hotel and used my cell phone to keep in touch with Pedro, my men on the tarmac, and a cartel representative back in Colombia. I needed to act like a boss, the conductor of this orchestra; a true leader would never thrust himself into the middle of the action for an escape like this. The plane carrying the crew landed in Grand Cayman and, a few hours later, just before sunrise, the cartel's plane arrived from Colombia. It skidded to a stop, the agents pulled out the cocaine, the cartel staff boarded, and the plane took off back to Colombia, with a few cases of celebratory beer we threw in for good measure.

The on-site FBI agents loaded the cocaine into our covert plane, but the cartel brought more drugs than we had anticipated—nearly eight hundred kilos, with a street value of roughly $100 million. Yes, the extra drugs showcased their level of greed, but also their trust in me. They knew I could handle it. But the plane was overweight; our pilot could barely make it off the tarmac. He juiced the power, pushed the propellers to maximum velocity, and still, he couldn't gain proper altitude. Just as the plane was about to crash into the sea, its wheels literally skimming the water, the pilot yelled for the six agents inside—including Ricky—to run toward the nose, near the cockpit. That balanced the weight. The plane climbed into the night sky, and they made it back to Miami safely.

Once the drugs landed in Florida, we prepared the load for delivery as we normally would. I crammed in meetings before the drugs were set to be handed off, both with Pedro and my case agents. Pedro would tell me how he wanted everything to go down, and then I would secretly relay that information to my team so surveillance was in place and the bust would go off smoothly. I also met with Rocky, a Colombian courier who would be delivering the drugs to New York City for the cartel. He gave us a nondescript Volkswagen van in which to load the cocaine. We congregated at Diego's Italian-themed mansion to go over the details. When I arrived, Rocky was watching a soccer game in the living room with Diego's children, all of them sprawled out on Diego's luxurious leather furniture. Rocky fidgeted in his seat. Sweat coated his brow. I could tell he was under a lot of pressure. Stateside transportation was always the most stressful part of a trafficker's job. He could be arrested, robbed, kidnapped, or killed.

Hoping to project an image of prowess and calm, like I was part of the family and had been here many nights before, I sauntered over to Diego's son and placed my hand on his head. "Hey buddy, how's the game?" I asked. He glared at me distrustfully. I had met Diego's children before, but I was the least-close with this boy. I kept my eyes on Rocky, who didn't see the exchange. If he did, he would've known that something was amiss. It was a quick lesson that I never forgot.

After discussing the pickup plan with Rocky, I sent Diego and Carla to meet him the following day at Haulover Park in North Miami Beach. The old Volkswagen van was packed to the gills with cocaine. My covert colleagues handed him the keys, told him the gas tank was full, and sent him on his way. As we loaded up the van, however, we made sure that one of the taillights was busted. Within a few hours, a Florida state trooper who collaborated with our squad—and knew the van was full of drugs—pulled Rocky over in a "routine" traffic stop. With the faulty taillight, he had probable cause, after all. Rocky immediately jumped out of the van and hightailed it into a nearby neighborhood, giving the cop the perfect excuse to search the vehicle and seize the cocaine. Not only was the blame placed squarely on Rocky, but the Florida State Police took sole credit for the seizure. Publicly, the whole thing was chalked up as just another regional drug bust, and no one knew that the FBI was behind it all.

## I KNOW NOT TO SAY A DAMN THING

After Rocky admitted to Pedro what happened, Pedro called me.

"We lost the load," he told me, panic threaded into his voice.

"Really? What happened?" I asked, playing along.

"Rocky got stopped by the police," he said. "As soon as they pulled him over, he ran."

"He ran? The cop didn't ask to search the van or anything?" I asked. "That sounds like his problem, not mine. Why are you calling *me* about it?" Deflect blame. Put him on his heels. Play the role. Stay in control.

"Well, Manny, this is one of many loads that have been lost. El Viejo wants to hold a meeting in Bogotá to discuss what we should do." El Viejo wanted me to come to Colombia? This wasn't good. I thought that this might be the end of our relationship, that I could go no deeper without being labeled a problem by the cartel. And yet, we had carefully orchestrated crucial details (like the taillight) that squarely placed the blame on other people. We had spun them around so many times that they didn't *want* to believe that we were the culprit. Even if I could talk my way out of this latest seizure, however, the FBI would never let me travel to Colombia. It was too risky. I could be kidnapped, interrogated, tortured, or murdered. But Diego's words echoed in my head, his thumb cutting across his throat: *If you don't show up to the meeting, you will be blamed.* In a situation like this, there were no good options on the table.

I pivoted. "Look, Pedro, you know I'd come, but I have other clients who are giving me great business and don't give me a headache like you do. Hell, how do I know that you don't have surveillance on you all the time? That could bring heat onto my operation. If they really want to talk to me, they can come here to Miami."

Pedro relented. "I understand, Manny," he said. "I will let El Viejo know."

I told Diego about El Viejo's directive, and how I wiggled out of going to the meeting in Colombia. But Diego was connected to me now. In his mind, one of us had to show up or we would *both* be blamed. I pleaded with him not to go. I told him I couldn't protect him if he left the States, but he was steadfast in his conviction. Diego held a lot of sway within the Medellín Cartel; if anyone could keep us out of harm's way, he said, it would be him.

A few days later, Diego boarded a flight to Colombia. He arrived at a mansion in the foothills of Bogotá, one of the many homes that El Viejo owned in the region. It was a farming estate, complete with a veranda that wrapped around the house, ornate furniture, marble floors, and ultra-wide hallways. Hand-carved crown molding outlined every doorway. One of El Viejo's deputies then told Diego that the meeting was actually taking place at an apartment in the city's center. A sicario drove him to the location and led him into a large dining room. A table anchored its center, with a VHS camcorder pointed at one of the chairs. The interrogation would be recorded, and a runner would bring the tape to El Viejo, who was in a secret location. No one was allowed to leave Bogotá until the Old Man gave his word on who he thought was to blame.

Diego took a seat at the dining table. And then the door opened. In walked Lulu, a razor-sharp Colombian lawyer—and El Viejo's COO. In her forties, she was tall, blond, and projected an icy stare. She wore designer jeans, high heels, and a silk blouse, with her hair pulled back into a tight ponytail. Gold hoop earrings dangled alongside her clenched jaw. Lulu's reputation preceded her: intelligent, conniving, and emotionless. All it took was one snap of her fingers and Diego would be dead. Diego tried to keep calm. He waited for her questions.

Pedro called me just as the meeting was about to start and explained that El Viejo had two sicarios at the quick, and that they would "squeeze Diego's balls to make him talk" if they thought he was guilty. My heart jumped into my throat. I couldn't let them harm my star cooperating witness. "You want Diego? You know where to find him—and me. We aren't going anywhere. If you ever intend on doing business with us again, you need to consider that." Pedro said he would relay the message to El Viejo.

One of Lulu's sicarios placed his pistol on the table so Diego could see it, and she began her interrogation. The camera lens pointed at him like the barrel of a gun.

"We have lost a lot of product recently," Lulu said, "and someone has to pay for it. Someone either slipped up, or is working with the cops. The Old Man wants to know what happened."

"It wasn't us, Lulu," Diego said. "We had nothing to do with it."

"There won't be any more loads until we find out," Lulu said. "And remember: All of your friends and family are on the hook, too. When you speak, remember that you are speaking for all of them."

"Yes, Lulu. Of course."

"Where is Manny?"

"Manny is busy with other commitments that have already been paid for."

"I see." Diego could hear the tapered heel of her shoe tapping against the hardwood floor.

"Do you think Manny would really come here?" Diego said. "He was thinking you would kidnap him and not let him leave the country until the issue was resolved. He can't afford to be away from his operation for that long. If you want to meet with him, he said you are welcome to come to Miami anytime."

Lulu dismissed the offer with a *click* of her tongue. "Tell me what happened," she said.

And so Diego did: He reiterated, in detail, all the aspects of the delivery. He explained how we packed the cocaine, how we secured it in the van, how it was delivered to Rocky—and what Rocky did when the cop pulled him over. Neither Rocky nor his direct boss in New York City came to the meeting, and Diego attacked them relentlessly. "Let's think about this simply," he said. "Conventional wisdom, right? The person who is not here is at fault." Diego slumped in his chair and softened his tone. "It was just dumb luck that Rocky got pulled over, Lulu," he said. "If he didn't run away, none of this would've happened."

Lulu tapped a single acrylic nail on top of the VHS recorder. "We will see what the Old Man thinks about your story," she said. "My men will bring you back to the house, and we will let you know his decision." Diego was held in Bogotá for a few more days until a verdict was rendered: El Viejo spared his life. He thought Diego's explanation was logical, that he wouldn't have shown up to explain his case if he was guilty, and that I wouldn't have helped his crew get back to Colombia if I was working with law enforcement. Diego was allowed to return to Miami. Ricky and I picked him up at the airport. When he sat down in the back seat of my Ford Bronco, he began to cry.

\* \* \*

**AFTER THIS OPERATION,** I wanted to stop. I had been working deep undercover as a smuggler for almost four years, and I was burned out. Ricky, too. The constant juggling of reality, the mingling with smugglers, the late nights. The stress gave me splitting headaches and threw me into a persistent state of hypervigilance. When I was able to see my family, I was constantly looking over my shoulder, convinced that cartel men could be watching me. If I saw someone suspicious, I'd follow them until I was sure they were clean. The danger forced me to always be Manny, even when I was Martin. I could never let my guard down. A constant river of stress coursed through my body like a low hum, burrowing its way deeper and deeper, the tether to my true self slowly fraying. I did a great job hiding my feelings from my wife, however, who had no idea how much pressure I encountered through my job. And yet, a few months later, she got a front-row seat into the secret life I had been leading.

Every June, Puerto Rico celebrates *Noche de San Juan*, a night of prideful revelry in which residents flock to the beach, spend the day drinking and eating, and party well into the night. At the stroke of midnight, everyone rushes into the ocean and falls backward into the warm tropical water. It's a ceremony that's supposed to rid one's life of all negativities. The FBI wanted me to lay low after the heated meeting with Lulu in Colombia, which meant that I could spend some much-needed time with Maria and my two sons. God knows I was dealing with a lot of negativities. It would feel nice to wash it all away, if even in spirit.

Still, I couldn't just throw caution to the wind. The cartel knew my face, and I was becoming well-known in certain circles of the narco-trade. The truth was, there were eyes everywhere. I rented a condo on the beach in San Juan. We lounged by the pool for the day, our boys splashing in the shallow end, their floaties keeping their heads above water. Maria's brother came too, and one night he offered to watch the boys so we could go for a walk on the beach together. Maria and I gazed at the sunset, and after nightfall, watched thousands of partygoers make their way to the ocean's edge. Maria and I appreciated the luxury of this personal time. I felt comfortable within a crowd, almost anonymous. I assumed it would be hard for anyone to spot me here. Martin was struggling back to the surface.

Then, a voice came from over my shoulder.

"*Caballero*?!" the voice said, using a more formal greeting. "Manny, is that you?"

I turned around. It was Alejandro Gomez, a high-level money launderer who worked for the Cali Cartel. I had met him many times before. He obviously remembered me. My growing reputation as Manny was morphing from an asset into a curse. Luckily, his mood was buoyant. He wore a loose-fitting linen shirt and a bathing suit, his black hair was slicked back. His wife, a skinny Colombian woman, followed him. She wore a blue satin dress, her feathered hair dancing in the seaside breeze. The majority of my psyche was already Manny, so it didn't take much for me to smile, shake his hand, and fall into my alternate persona.

"I didn't know you took days off," he said, trying to make a joke. He glanced at Maria, and I saw a flicker in his eye. I had never mentioned to him that I was married, or even had a girlfriend. I looked at Maria who, hearing his Colombian accent and seeing his fancy clothes, froze in fear. When I first started working undercover, I told Maria that something like this might happen. I explained that she just had to act natural, follow my lead, and trust me. She accepted my instructions gracefully, even though she never fully understood why. I kept the majority of the details regarding my work away from my wife. I wanted to protect her as much as I could. But now, on the beach, she could tell what I had gotten myself into. She knew this guy worked for a cartel. Maria forced a smile, playing a part for which she had not auditioned.

"Oh, well, you know," I said, turning back to Alejandro. "It's such a beautiful night. We thought we would enjoy it."

"We're doing the same," he said, grabbing his wife's hand. "We're heading to dinner, so I'll leave you to it. Enjoy the night." He turned to Maria and tipped his head in a show of respect: *"Encantado. Un placer conocerle,"* he said. I'm enchanted—a pleasure meeting you. "Manny is a respectable man. You're in good hands." I watched them saunter over to the boardwalk. I always expected to run into cartel men in public, had prepared my mind to not be easily shocked or rattled, but never with Maria. I turned around and looked at my wife.

"Manny, huh?" she said. "Now I see why you spend so much time away from home." I didn't know what to say. I felt ashamed, as if I had been keeping a secret from the person I loved most. Which of course, I was.

She grabbed my hand and looked into my eyes. "Don't worry, Martin. I know not to say a damn thing."

At the stroke of midnight, we both ran into the ocean. I let the waves come crashing down onto me. At that moment, I allowed myself to feel vindicated, not stressed. I reminded myself that I was born to do this job, that danger was far away from me, that the sacrifices were worth it, and that nothing bad would ever happen to me and my family.

\* \* \*

PEDRO COULDN'T LEAVE ME alone. Not even a month after Diego's near-fatal meeting with Lulu in Colombia, he called me. "Manny, I have a big party lined up," he said, speaking in our well-rehearsed code. "There's going to be the most beautiful women in attendance—at least thirty. It's going to be a huge feast. Will you come?"

"I can't do it," I told him, breaking our code talk and cutting to the quick, so he knew I was being serious. "You guys are so heated up. It's only a matter of time before I get busted."

"Manny, *por favor*, just listen to me. I can explain—"

"I really can't have you calling me anymore," I said. "I'm changing my number. I think I might move to Puerto Rico. Miami is a tough place to do business now, because of everything that has happened. I have to take a step back for a while. Maybe I'll start laundering money instead. This isn't personal," I continued, getting ready to hang up. "It's just business."

## CHAPTER 5

# GOING HOME

**THE MOST CONVINCING LIES ARE ALWAYS THREADED WITH** truth. Although I didn't have any plans to start laundering money for Colombian drug cartels, I did want to move back to Puerto Rico. Maria and I hadn't lived there for fifteen years, and we yearned to go home. It was 1991, I had just turned thirty-six years old, and my two sons had blossomed from fumbling toddlers into rambunctious little boys. I also needed a break from working undercover. I missed the camaraderie of office life, the holiday parties, the high-fives after a slam-dunk case. I didn't want to be the guy with my picture taped to the back of my chair anymore. It felt like I was bonding with the bad guys, not the good guys.

I scheduled a meeting with Special Agent in Charge Bruce McNeil, the big boss in Miami, and told him that I wanted to transfer to Puerto Rico. He was shocked. By the early 1990s, Miami had become the nucleus of the FBI's undercover operations. In fact, our statistics were so astounding that the top brass in Washington, DC, instantly approved our budget requests. We also established the new technique of using trafficker-directed funds to further an investigation, rather than merely seizing it and handing it over to the US Treasury. The seizures we conducted and forfeitures we secured more than made up for the cost of our investigations. Because of our team, this soon became a nationwide standard implemented by the Department of Justice. Moreover, we amassed a host of usable assets using the cartel's money, inadvertently closed unsolved homicides for local cops, and trained agents in New York City, Houston, and Los Angeles. We were the rock stars at the FBI. McNeil demanded to know why I would give all of that up.

"I want to spend some time with my father," I told him. "And to let my sons see where I grew up. But maybe I can transfer to San Juan, and then come back to Miami at some point?"

"I would take you back in a heartbeat," he told me. "You always have a home here, Agent Suarez. But what are you going to do about Diego and Carla?"

I explained that Ricky would handle them while I was in Puerto Rico, but that I also wanted to keep them on my team, so to speak, so that I could collaborate on cases with the Miami field office. Puerto Rico had become one of the cartels' midpoints between Colombia and Florida, and I knew that Miami would be better off with the San Juan field office working the same angle. "We can share assets, our money will go further, and we can do better work," I said. McNeil didn't hesitate. He told me to get my ass down there.

My colleagues threw a going-away party for me a couple weeks later in a small banquet hall at the Police Benevolent Association in Miami. The entire drug squad came and we feasted on barbecued chicken and ice-cold beer. My immediate supervisor, Pete Paris, gave a short speech about my work, and presented me with a parting gift: a plaque that labeled me "the Cartel Buster." As I walked off the small stage with the plaque under my arm, Ricky pulled me aside. He was sad to see me go; we had become like brothers over the past few years. "I'm going to miss you, Martin," he told me, "but I know you'll be back."

I put my hand on his shoulder. "I'll find something for us to work on together in Puerto Rico," I told my dear friend. "Don't you worry."

In Puerto Rico, Maria and I bought a house in a nice neighborhood on the edge of a golf course and just steps from the beach. As we packed up our things in Miami, my eldest son started crying. He told Maria he was going to miss our home. Maria knelt down and wiped the tears from his eyes. "As long as we are all together," she told him, "we will be home." She was right, of course, but it was more than that. As we moved into our new house on the island, I thought back to the vows Maria and I exchanged when we got married, how we promised to always support each other, and how it was our teamwork that got us this far, into this wonderful house, and back to our homeland safe and sound.

The San Juan field office assigned me to their terrorism unit. Although I still did short drug-related undercover stints when necessary, including back in Miami, I was not assigned to a long-term, deep-undercover role. This freedom gave me ample time to play sports with my kids, man the grill at cookouts, and be the family man I had missed. The true reason I wanted to return to Puerto Rico, however, was to be close to my father. He had just turned sixty-six years old, and I wanted to give him as much time as possible to get to know his grandsons—and to show him that I was a man now, someone with a family of his own, and that I had put into practice all he had taught me.

Although I visited him as often as I could while I was working in Miami, I hadn't lived on the island since I enlisted in the Navy over a decade prior. My father was thrilled at the proximity we now enjoyed, if not for me, then surely for his two budding grandsons. After Maria and I got settled in our new home, my father and I spent the day together at his house. He inquired about my transfer to the San Juan field office, and I explained that I had been assigned to the terrorism squad. His eyes lit up. "Are you investigating the Macheteros?" he asked, referring to the militant group that aimed to liberate the island from outside control.

"Ah, come on, Dad," I said. "You know that's classified." But it was obvious that the FBI was looking into them; they were the most prominent terrorist organization in Puerto Rico, after all. He held this assumption even as I went back undercover and became a cartel money launderer later that year. As we caught up, I inquired about his time in the armed forces during the Second World War. Now that my Navy career was behind me, and I had a few years of being a special agent under my belt, I felt I would understand his own service with more clarity. Subconsciously, I wanted to extract details as a way to compare my own experiences to his, a subtle confirmation that I had tried as hard as he did, that I was becoming the man he had envisioned. His words would be a mirror against my own progress.

"Being a soldier was a rough life," he explained. "We were expected to perform at the highest standard, and at the top of our abilities, at all times. The pressure to succeed—to excel—was constant."

I nodded along. I knew what he meant. I inherited my work ethic from him, and I hoped my physical strength rivaled his own. My father was a tall man, fair-skinned, with a face that resembled both John Wayne and Abraham Lincoln, chiseled and sharp. Whenever he got injured, it seemed to not affect him. He always recovered easily, defying expectations. Once, when I was a boy, he was hit in the arm with a metal pipe during an attempted robbery on the streets of San Juan. His arm was mangled. The doctors performed emergency surgery, and installed rods and pins. They said he would never use his arm the same way again. Within a few months, his arm was back to normal, as if nothing ever happened. All that remained from the incident was a thick scar that ran down the length of his arm. Over the years, whenever I would see the scar, it reminded me of how strong of a man he was.

* * *

IN THE LATE 1950S, before my family moved from Long Island to Puerto Rico, my father brought a brand-new television home for us. Every evening, he and I would sit next to each other and watch movies and television shows depicting brave Naval officers and cunning FBI agents. We gorged ourselves on *The F.B.I.,* starring Efrem Zimbalist Jr., and *Combat!* Bathed in patriotism, these characters always put their lives at risk to chase down the bad guys. Watching these shows reminded my father of his time as a machine-gunner during the Second World War. He valorized these noble men, and he told me that, if he could go back in time, he would've tried to become an FBI agent himself.

"It's the most fantastic law enforcement agency in the world," he told me. "They are protecting the entire United States. And you see their logo?" He pointed to the television as the show's title sequence flashed across the screen, the bureau's insignia beaming blue and yellow. "It stands for honesty, fidelity, and bravery. That's what it's all about."

"I want to be an FBI agent!" the six-year-old me yelped.

He leaned in close and smiled at me. "Martin, if you study hard, you just might be."

After we moved to Bayamón in 1961, my father and I spent many hot summer nights together fantasizing about what it would be like to be a Navy hero or a special agent for the FBI. These were the J. Edgar Hoover days, however, and my father was aware that very few, if any, Hispanics would ever be admitted into the world's premier law enforcement agency. Or to the rank of Navy officer, for that matter. He knew, from his time in the armed forces, that racism and segregation still ran rampant in the military. His entire unit was Puerto Rican, and they weren't allowed to be in the same platoon as white soldiers. One time, he was heading back to base on a military bus. He sat in the back with the Black soldiers. Although my father was Puerto Rican, his complexion was light compared to other Hispanics. The bus driver, after calling him "a n-word lover," told him to move to the front of the bus. Despite putting his life on the line for a country he loved, my father felt the sting of reality. If his time fighting the Axis powers gave him apprehension about what was possible for me, he never showed it. He just wanted me to have a noble career, making a difference in the world. He made it seem like anything was possible.

My father taught me nobility in ways beyond television, too. He was dedicated, through the limited means that he had, to help Puerto Rico's less fortunate. On Friday nights, he would take a projector to a local housing project and set it up against the side of the building. He played all types of classic movies for the residents, many of whom didn't have enough money to go to the movie theater: *The King and I*, *Lawrence of Arabia*, *Casablanca*. When I joined him, I was in awe at how much these impoverished people adored him for his kindness. As Christmas approached every year, he would lobby private companies in San Juan to chip in and buy toys for poor children. Being there, as he helped the less fortunate, made me feel like I was part of something bigger, a mission with a strong moral foundation. It inspired me to join the Boy Scouts, which held a similar philosophical purpose. My favorite outing with him, however, was when he would help the elderly with home renovations. He and I would routinely rebuild bathrooms to accommodate wheelchairs for the aging Puerto Rican population. I'd hand him materials as he laid tile, and he'd use this time to teach me lessons about life.

"There are many people who have time on their hands," he said once, "and instead of hanging around at home drinking beer, they should be out here, helping people in the community." He'd also remind me to visit my grandmother, who was in the hospital at the time, and to always look out for our family and my fellow man. "You can make a difference in the world, Martin," he told me, "but only if you take the time to do it."

As the years went on and I became a teenager, those nights watching television with my dad, and our excursions into the community, instilled in me a sense of determination. I never forgot the dreams my father had for me. He was a stern, taciturn man who grew up in poverty, was a champion boxer in his youth, and never spoke of emotion—a man who never said, "I love you." Once, when I was eight years old, my father took me crab hunting in the coconut jungles that stretched along the Puerto Rican coastline. It was thick terrain, and he used a machete to hack a path for us. As I followed him through the brush, I fell into a massive hole and landed atop a giant turtle, who was nesting. The creature started flopping around, trying to buck me off its shell. I was terrified, and started crying. My father pulled me out, stood me up, and said, "Martin, it's okay. You're all right. Toughen up. We're on an adventure, and brushes with danger are part of it." I was comforted by his directive and quickly regained my composure. In another instance that same summer, I accidentally fell into a swimming pool fully clothed. I couldn't swim yet. My father was near the pool, but a family friend, a teenage girl, jumped in to save me. I had gotten water into my lungs, and was coughing violently. My father slowly walked over to me and bent down. His voice was calm, his eyes and hands steady, just like with the turtle. He said, "Are you okay?" I nodded, still coughing up water. "Good," he said. "Let's get you a towel and we'll head home."

In these moments, he never coddled me, never treated me like the child that I was. But the fact that he pulled me from the turtle's hole, and got me a towel by the pool, showed me that he loved and cared about me, even if he never verbalized it. I came to understand his being as it related to showcasing emotion: His actions, not his words, would communicate how he truly felt. As I got older, I realized that I didn't need the words to understand what his heart was saying. He was always there for me, but from a distance. In his mind, his lack of outward emotion was a tool that allowed life to teach me lessons. And yet I knew, deep down, that he would never abandon me, that he would always be there if I ever needed him.

All the lessons he shared pushed me to become a Navy man and then an FBI agent. I knew that he would always support me in my ambitions, whatever they may be, but I also understood that the only way I could make him truly proud of me was to achieve what he could not. I stopped at nothing to do this. I wanted my dad to live vicariously through me, his eldest son. As I became older, his actions, and the words of wisdom he bestowed, never left me. In fact, they played on a constant loop in my head as I geared up to enlist in the Navy—and then again as I applied to become an FBI agent. I realized much later that my father wasn't merely being kind in showing movies, gathering gifts, or remodeling a shower for the island's lower-class residents, but rather trying his best to unburden people from suffering. I wanted to do the same thing, even if I chose a different way of approaching that goal.

I wrote my father letters often while I was in the Navy. I couldn't share operational details, who we were hunting or why, but I did write about the places that I had visited. When my father was in the military, stationed in the Pacific in anticipation of invading Japan, he docked in Alaska between deployments. He loved the majestic beauty of the snowcapped mountains and rugged terrain, which could've been another planet coming from Puerto Rico. When I was a boy, he would regale me with stories of the northern frontier. I never got to go to Alaska, but I did visit other places where he was stationed. Every time I went, I'd write to him and describe what I saw. I'd also take photographs, which showed some of the same places he himself had been decades before, and mail them alongside the letters. One time, I was even able to find a bulky VHS camcorder and record a few short videos. I visited him in San Juan just after. We sat in the living room, in the same position as when I was six years old gawking at the naval officers on television, and watched my own exploits on screen.

My entire family traveled to Rhode Island in 1984 when I graduated from the Navy's Officer Candidate School. A marching band, fifty musicians strong, introduced us as my fellow officers and I, suited up in our dress blues, strode across the stage. With my sword in my hand, I was full of pride. After the ceremony, I went to my father and we embraced, his athletic frame pulling me close. When he let go, he held me at a distance and inspected my uniform. "It looks good on you," he said. "You've already accomplished more than I ever could."

Years later, I didn't tell my father when I applied to be an FBI agent. But I did bring him with me when I went before the hiring panel. Wearing a well-tailored suit was part and parcel for this stage of the application process. We were all applying to be G-men, after all. But I wanted to show the FBI who I truly was. I didn't want to be a carbon copy of every other agent that had come before me. I strutted into the room in my naval officer uniform, ribbons affixed to my chest, surface warfare pins polished to a mirror shine. To me, these accolades meant everything. They proved that I knew how to defend a ship—to defend America. I was proud to have been in the Navy, and I wanted to showcase that dignity to them; if they hired me, I would execute my job in the FBI with the same level of dedication. I wanted to exude nobility, just as my father had taught me. After the interview, a recruiter from the FBI told me that the panel kept bringing me up. "The guy in uniform, what was his name again?"

When the call came that I had been hired, the first thing that ran through my mind wasn't the training I was about to undertake, where I would be stationed, or the type of work I hoped to take on. I thought of my father. But I waited to call him until after I filled out the final hiring paperwork at the recruiter's office a few days later. I sat down on the bed in my hotel room and dialed his number. "How's Texas?" he asked.

I cut right to it: "I've been offered a job at the FBI." He didn't respond. "As a special agent," I continued.

"A special agent?" he asked, his voice cracking.

## GOING HOME

"Yes," I said. "Not an administrative position, but a special agent."

He went silent once more. The only noise that came into my ear was his breathing. "Wow," he said. "I am living my life through you."

A few months later, I visited Puerto Rico and met up with my brothers. They said that our father was so overwhelmed with emotion after I told him I'd become an FBI agent that he got into his car and drove up to his plot of land in the mountains where he grew fruit, to be alone with his thoughts.

"*Subistes como la espuma*," my brother then said. You rise like the foam of a beer: fast. He was proud of me, too. "No matter what we do," he added, "you are always going to be the one that dad believes accomplishes the most." It was true. My brothers had both become accountants and my older sister became a doctor, but our father was, overall, prouder of me. This could be chalked up to favoritism for his eldest son, a tendency in Hispanic culture that my siblings did not resent, but I knew the truth: He was most proud of me because I was fulfilling the dreams he once held for himself. A few months later, when a family member dismissed my new job as merely acting as "a source," my father instantly corrected him.

"No," he said. "Martin is a *special agent*. Never, *ever* forget that."

\* \* \*

I DIDN'T LAST LONG in the San Juan field office's terrorism unit. The drug squad had been following myriad narco-trafficking groups that used Puerto Rico as a transshipment hub, and they kept asking me to lend a hand with their cases. My deep knowledge of the cartels' inner workings proved invaluable for their investigations. It was only a matter of months before they asked me to officially join the drug squad—and go back undercover. I have to admit that the itch had been coming on ever since I transferred. I couldn't escape its pull. Moreover, San Juan had become rich with high-level targets, and Manny was still very much alive in the minds of the Colombian cartels for whom I previously worked. To them, I was just taking a break. If I came back into the fold, they would think I was just like any other smuggler, letting greed get the best of me.

My Puerto Rican pride also influenced my thinking. I held a strong allegiance to my home country, the island that made me who I am, the place where I'd met my wife. It was a core part of my identity; even as Manny, I stuck to the truth and always boasted about being Puerto Rican. I knew my time roaming around the streets of San Juan helped me become a successful undercover agent. I had mastered the skill of interacting with people in high-wire situations, and I could think on my feet better than other agents who came from more traditional backgrounds. Let's be real: American suburbs and Ivy League schools aren't the best at teaching street smarts. I felt proud to be home when I made my transfer, but I knew my sense of moral duty would be heightened if I went back undercover. Puerto Rico had always been plagued by drug violence. The best way, in my mind, to rid the island of its evils would be to try and dismantle them from the inside out. So, less than a year back in my home country, I pulled the trigger. I became Manny again.

I rented an undercover apartment on the sixth floor of a high-rise building in San Juan. It was luxurious but not too flashy, with a large balcony that overlooked the bay. It came furnished, but I also bought a cutting-edge TV and stocked the bar. I needed to make the place feel lived in, just in case I had guests over. I stuffed drawers with papers and knickknacks, made sure to have a half-full bottle of laundry detergent in the closet, and kept plenty of food in the cupboards. I also reupped my wardrobe. Honestly, projecting the aura of a cartel man had become second nature to me. I didn't even feel like I was preparing for a role. It felt like the real me.

I moved in and slowly made friends with my neighbors, none of whom had a clue I was an undercover FBI agent. I helped old women with their groceries and made sure to greet people when I saw them in the hallway or parking garage. I did not want them to know that I was working undercover, but I also didn't want them to think I was a smuggler either. I recruited a couple female agents from the field office, who would come to the apartment and pose as my girlfriends. I didn't want the Colombians, if they were watching me, to have any reason to think I had been secretly working against them while I was stationed in Miami. I had to ease right back into my role, and back into the game.

It wasn't hard to get noticed. On the dope-running side of things, we created a honeypot, a way to have the island's smugglers approach me, lured by the sweet smell of a new way to make money. I purchased a few high-end fishing boats, drove them around to different marinas on the island, and presented them with our cutting-edge communications antennas exposed, so mid-tier traffickers with whom I hadn't previously interacted would think I was a legitimate smuggler. To seal the deal, I'd tow my boat behind a luxury truck, hang out at the marina bar drinking my Black Label whiskey, and subtly flash my $30,000 Rolex. It worked out beautifully. The Puerto Rican crooks double-checked my references from El Viejo's clan, and Diego vouched for me, too. I even brought Ricky, my co-undercover agent from Miami, down to the island to help bolster my story. I met higher-ranking cartel bosses from different core groups on the island, and provided services for larger jobs, including building secret compartments in boats and cars for smugglers at my new undercover warehouse. This time, I had a drug-running body shop. I also used seized funds to purchase a hundred-foot yacht complete with six bedrooms and four bathrooms. I used it to host lavish soirees for smugglers and drug lords. I was back to my old ways, and over those first few months, I transported tens of millions of dollars' worth of cocaine into the United States from Puerto Rico—all of it eventually seized by the FBI.

* * *

**THE MEDELLÍN CARTEL QUICKLY** heard about my exploits in Puerto Rico. Pedro put the word out to Diego and Carla, who were still living in Miami, that El Viejo wanted to work with me again. During one of our near-daily calls, Carla told me that Pedro wanted to see me the next time I was in Miami. We had survived Lulu's interrogation, after all, proving we were to be trusted. El Viejo wanted us back in his operation.

I flew to Miami later that week and scheduled a dinner meeting at Diego's house. Ricky came, and Carla again made her famous Cornish hens stuffed with rice. We agreed that bringing Pedro back into the fold would be a wise move, and we could use Puerto Rico as our center point. Plus, we now had the entire San Juan field office's drug squad to assist us. With my transfer, we essentially doubled our available manpower. The following night, the four of us met Pedro at a bar for drinks. He was thrilled that we wanted to work together again and said he would come to Puerto Rico the following week to scope out the scene and formulate a plan. Ricky, Diego, and Carla agreed to come down too.

## GOING HOME

I held back at a luxury waterfront hotel while Ricky drove to the San Juan airport to pick him up. Instead of Pedro walking out to the curb, however, Ricky was greeted by a man we had never met before: Dante. He walked with the same swagger as Pedro, and wore a loose-fitting shirt made from Italian cotton, fancy shoes, and black jeans. A straw fedora perched atop his head, and oversized aviator sunglasses shielded his eyes from the sun. He was a cartel man, through and through. I waited at the hotel bar for them to arrive, unaware that Pedro had been replaced by Dante. When they strode into the hotel, Ricky shot me a look, a bit of eye contact that was part of our well-rehearsed code: *I am just as surprised as you are right now.* I introduced myself to Dante and offered him a drink. I excused myself and paged Pedro, who called me almost immediately.

"*¿Ay, malparido, dónde estás?*" I said. Hey, buddy, where are you? "You're supposed to be here. I thought we were going to party and talk business." I acted confused, but in reality, I was thrilled to have access to another core member of El Viejo's organization. All I needed to do was act unbothered, to see Dante's visit as just another part of doing business. Working undercover always required embracing spontaneity. And it made sense why Pedro and El Viejo sent a proxy: After all of their loads with me had been seized, they needed to make sure I was clean. Trust—but verify.

"Manny, it's all good," he said. "Dante is going to work with us closely now that you are in Puerto Rico. You treat him like you'd treat me, *¿listo, hermano?*"

"*Seguro que sí, Pedro*," I said. "*Como si fuera tu.*" Of course, Pedro. As if he was you.

I brought Dante to my seaside villa. I had just sourced the house a few weeks ago. I approached a realtor, who assumed

I was a drug smuggler and who clearly didn't care where my money came from. I rented it—in cash—as Manny. It was one of the most luxurious homes on the coast, with white marble floors throughout. Two large French doors opened to a rear patio boasting a jungle of tropical plants and a staircase that led directly to a private beach. I gave Dante a tour. He took in its luxury with a quiet reserve.

"You can stay here, if you'd like," I said as he inspected the marble floors.

"Thank you," he said, "but I think I prefer to stay at the hotel." I didn't really care if he stayed there or not; I just wanted him and Pedro to not feel like I was hiding aspects of my life from them. I even had pictures of my fake family framed and hung around the house. And of course I was wearing my wire, capturing every conversation that I had with El Viejo's Caribbean proxy.

I spent the entire week with Dante. He wanted to see my new fleet of boats and my import station, but I demurred, hoping to squeeze more cash out of them so we could continue funding the operation with the cartel's money. "You see the boat, you buy the boat," I told him. What I meant was: If you want to see the asset I use to move drugs, you have to purchase equity in it. This gave us an equal stake in the risk of investing in such equipment. If it became compromised by a screwup, we'd both lose out. My excuse made sense; the cartel used this type of negotiating tactic all the time. It protected their investments. I offered, instead, to show him some of my "burned" boats: assets that had already been compromised and which I wouldn't be using for future deliveries but were very similar to what I would use for a real smuggling run. He agreed, and we made our way to the marina.

I showed him my fifty-six-foot Defender boat, which boasted

a two-ton storage compartment, and gave him a tour of my undercover apartment. I explained that I used it as a home base during deliveries. I didn't have any burned points of entry for smuggling, so I just drove him to two beaches that other smugglers used and explained that they sustained my operation last year. It was a great fib. I also took out a map and showed him where I used to pick up airdrops at sea that came from Saint Martin, which were actually used by Dominican smuggling crews. He was impressed, nodding along as I shared in great detail how I did what I did. I was a gracious and transparent host. He bought my story hook, line, and sinker.

We drove through remote mountains and tropical forests on joy rides around the island. Like El Viejo and Pedro, Dante was a rich landowner in Colombia, and he appreciated the landscape of Puerto Rico. "It's so lush and green," he said. "There's a lot of places for us to stash our loads here."

"Well," I said, "when I get the loads onto the island, I don't stash them. I just hand them off or bring them into Miami."

"But look at all this," he said, pointing out the car window. "It shouldn't be a problem to stash for a while."

"It's too risky," I said. "I have been doing this for almost twenty years, and I don't depart from my best practices. It could ruin my entire business model."

Dante glared at me, clearly upset. I knew I could never deliver on a promise to stash their drugs. If the cartel had a stash spot with me, they would use it to keep thousands of kilos there and only pull out a couple dozen at a time. In the eyes of the FBI, that doesn't help our case at all. For one, we couldn't seize the drugs if they were under my supervision, because it would signal to the cartel that I couldn't protect their product, thus sowing distrust and even potentially blowing my cover. Secondly, the FBI would have to assign agents to pose as my musclemen who oversaw security of the drugs. We didn't have those types of resources. Moreover, it's incredibly dangerous to have drugs in your possession for any length of time. Not only did this type of arrangement not further our operational goals, it opened up the FBI to an immense safety risk. But, Dante: he didn't like my answer. That was clear. I pivoted.

"Fine," I said. "I will stash for you, but it will be done my way. If you want something from the stash, I will need five days' notice. And every day that I keep the stash, it will cost you $1,500 per kilo." This was an exorbitant sum, something I knew he would never agree to. It was the perfect line to get him off my back.

"Why so much?"

"I have to hire a team of guys to guard it twenty-four/seven," I said. "You get what you pay for."

He rubbed his chin. "Okay, it's fine," he said. "Let's keep it the way it is."

"I just want this to be easy, you know?" I said. He nodded in agreement.

By the end of the week, Dante's visit was over. I decided to have a little fun with him before he flew back to Colombia. I told him I saved the best adventure for last: a ride on my fifteen-hundred horsepower, forty-five-foot-long Scorpio race boat, which was so fast that it could hit speeds of nearly a hundred miles per hour. We climbed on board and I went for it. I juiced the engine to full throttle and pushed the boat to its top speed. We hit waves and literally jumped the boat completely out of the water. I looked back and spotted Dante gripping the handlebar that stretched across his seat, a terrified look plastered across his face. When I finally slowed the boat down, he looked like he was on the verge of passing out.

The next day, Diego, Ricky, Carla, and I made our way to

## GOING HOME

Dante's hotel in my Dodge Caravan so we could take him to the airport. I rolled down the windows, filling the cabin with a warm Caribbean breeze. We swung down by San Juan Bay and looped around to the hotel. Diego went up to grab him. Dante was in the bathroom but called Diego into the room. He'd only be a minute, he said. Diego walked over to the bed to take a seat, but then he spotted a little black book on the floor. He picked it up. Before he could flip it open, however, Dante walked out of the bathroom. Diego secretly stuffed the book into his pocket and turned to Dante.

"Need help with your bags?" he asked, smiling.

"Sure," Dante said. No side-eye given, no grit in his voice: he hadn't seen Diego snatch his book. They grabbed Dante's luggage, took the elevator down, and made their way out to my van. Dante clutched his lower back as they approached.

"You all good, Dante?" I asked, smiling, knowing he was still hurting from our boat ride the previous day.

"*¡Ay, Manny, hermano, me puso a parir, me sacaste la piedra!*" he said. You made me give birth to a kidney stone!

I helped him load his luggage and we pulled out of the parking lot. Halfway to the airport, I snuck a glance in the rearview mirror and saw Dante, wedged between Ricky and Carla, patting down his jacket pockets. He leaned forward and tapped me on the shoulder.

"I think I forgot something," he said. "We have to go back."

"Are you sure?" I said. "You might miss your flight."

"I'm sure," he said. "I can't leave this item behind."

I returned to the hotel, and Dante ran back inside. "What did he lose?" I asked, eyeing Diego.

"I'll tell you later," he said.

Dante came running back to the car and hopped in.

"Find what you were looking for?" I asked.

"Yes," he said, forcing a smile. "All good to go." I knew he was lying, but I played along. We made it to the airport, and he hustled through check-in to board his flight back to Colombia. Once he was gone, I again asked Diego what Dante left behind, knowing by now that he swiped something from his room.

"This," Diego said, pulling out Dante's little black book. We raced back to my undercover apartment and, once we got there, scoured the pages. Inside, Dante had written down every address associated with us; every phone number we used; places in which we hung out; names of associates, ranging from hotel employees to local bartenders with whom we were friendly; VIN numbers for all of our cars; detailed notes of everything we did during the trip; maps of our entry points; and our boats' registration numbers.

The next day, I handed over the book to one of my case agents. I told him that I wasn't worried about its contents, but that we should double-check what he gathered, just to be sure. He took it back to the field office and ran all of the information through the FBI's computer system, to see what Dante's due diligence would've revealed. Everything checked out, all of the data pointing back to my cleverly disguised legend—except the boat. When my case agent punched the registration number into the computer system, it showed who clearly owned it: United States Customs, from whom we borrowed it.

I was with Diego and Ricky when I heard the news. I turned to them and said: "We must be doing God's work. He is protecting us."

CHAPTER 6

# WEARING THE WHITE HAT

**THE IRS GOT A TIP. IT WAS AUGUST 1992, AND A BANK IN** San Juan submitted a report to the agency detailing a suspicious man who was swapping large amounts of cash for cashier's checks—a sign of "smurfing," in narco-talk. It was a practice that began in response to the Bank Secrecy Act of 1970, which required financial institutions to file reports for currency transactions above $10,000. The smurfs, however, always obtained cashier's checks for under that amount, which normally kept their true intentions concealed. The IRS contacted the San Juan field office and asked if we could investigate. I was still working undercover as a smuggler, so a few other agents started tracking the guy, which revealed the contours of what appeared to be a secret money-laundering ring.

Santo Sanchez, a longtime FBI case agent stationed in Puerto Rico, led the investigation. He discovered that the man appeared to be picking up cash and, after smurfing it at various banks, dropping off the cashier's checks at a house in one of San Juan's upscale suburbs. Additional surveillance revealed that a man named Tony lived there, who was likely running the operation. Santo eventually approached one of Tony's associates, who, it turned out, was feuding with him. She ratted him out immediately and began feeding Santo information on when he would be bringing money into the house, when he would send grunts out to swap the cash for checks, and when he might be throwing out evidence in the trash.

Santo and a few other agents began rooting through his garbage cans. This isn't the most glamorous investigative tactic, but you'd be surprised at what kind of evidence is tossed out. One night, Tony's mother, who was at the house, took out the trash. Inside the bag lay the evidence the FBI needed: receipts for millions of dollars in cashier's checks made out to Colombian-linked companies. It confirmed that someone—likely a Colombian cartel—was somehow getting cash to Tony, he was having his employees exchange it for cashier's checks, and then Tony, or someone else, was somehow moving the money off the island and back to the cartel. The FBI, armed with probable cause, obtained a search warrant. A couple days later, they busted through the front door, found $250,000 worth of checks and $150,000 in cash, and took Tony down to the San Juan field office.

While Santo was searching Tony's house, I was three hours away, in Cabo Rojo, doing routine maintenance on one of our covert smuggling boats. This is another area where my naval expertise was useful. All seagoing vessels have to be properly maintained, but we couldn't just have a bunch of FBI-hired mechanics take on the task. It would blow our cover. It became my job to care for my fleet as needed. I was nearly back in San Juan when my cell phone rang. It was Santo.

"Martin, I've got a cartel money launderer in custody, but he doesn't want to flip. Can you come talk with him?"

"I'll be right there," I said. I changed my route and made my way to the field office. I realized that Santo had a bigger vision at play here: He could easily just arrest Tony, but Santo thought that we could convince him to become a cooperating witness—and to work alongside me, the only deep-undercover agent on the team. This might be our chance to see how a cartel's money machine actually worked.

They held Tony in an unmarked car, the windows tinted to a midnight black, at the rear of the field office parking lot. I didn't have my badge on me and wasn't wearing one of those classic blue windbreakers with big yellow FBI letters on the back. I was in my drug smuggler garb—always undercover. I climbed into the car. Tony looked at me like I had two heads. "Are you an agent?" he asked.

"Yes, I am," I said. My tone was friendly, honest. I didn't want to come across as patronizing or judgmental. I had one shot at making him work for us. I needed him to feel valuable—and to trust me.

"I'm talking to an FBI agent, just like them?" he asked.

"Yes, you are," I said. "Tony, I'm sorry to say, but you're in a world of hurt right now. My fellow agents found a lot of evidence at your house. Now, these guys would love to just arrest you, put you in jail, and be done with it. But I have a better idea. You could work alongside me. I'm an undercover agent." He resisted, making every excuse he could think of, but I pressed him for close to an hour. After making my case, Tony looked at me, knowing full well that his options were thinner than the silk shirt he was wearing.

"I have a lot of responsibilities with the cartel," he said. "If they find out I'm working with you, they will kill me."

"You have the opportunity to wear the white hat," I said. "You and I are going to be partners. We will stick together. But you can't lie to me."

He looked up at me again. "If you give me a hundred percent, I'll give you a hundred percent. Deal?"

I smiled. "Deal."

* * *

**TONY'S WIFE WAS NOT** happy that her husband had decided to become a cooperating witness for the FBI. She put up with his money laundering in exchange for the wealthy lifestyle provided by the cartel. But now, with Tony in the federal government's grip, that well had run dry. The FBI was only willing to pay him a small stipend for his services, a sliver compared to what he made laundering drug money. And yet she kept her mouth shut, a silent hub in the wheel of this sprawling investigation.

I quickly realized that Tony wasn't some street cat. He was well educated, a savvy businessman, and had a firm handle on the logistics necessary to run a money-laundering enterprise. He cut a striking figure, too: tan, blue eyes, a full head of salt-and-pepper hair. He was, however, a chronic chain-smoker, and had lost all of his teeth due to gum disease. He had recently gotten dentures, but continued to hide them behind a close-lipped smile, the instinct to conceal his rotten teeth overriding his new pearly whites. He lived in a modern, two-story house in Cupey, with an open-concept kitchen grounded in white tile and a spacious family room lit by expansive bay windows. He always wore a freshly pressed suit or button-up shirts made from the finest Italian silk. Tony explained that, before he became a money launderer for the cartel, he was a law-abiding CPA with a finance degree who worked for a wholesale grocery and alcohol distributor. A few years ago, he began socializing with a few men linked to the cartel, and they swooned him into the business with the promise of a low-risk, high-reward role that never involved touching drugs. Tony accepted their offer and stepped over the line into the underworld.

Tony was terrified to double-cross his cartel bosses, but I always treated him with compassion and tried to understand his position. I coached and motivated him in his role as a cooperating witness, but always told it to him straight. We were engaged in dangerous business, and we had to be on our toes. This wasn't a game, but rather a life-or-death mission. And because of this level of transparency, Tony and I became close. I knew that extending Tony respect was the only way he was going to put me inside the heart of the cartel's money-laundering machine.

It was great timing for this new development in our work. By the early 1990s, the Department of Justice had come to realize that the nucleus of the War on Drugs wasn't actually drugs. It was money. But all that money posed a problem for the dons of the drug trade. The hardest part of running a cartel isn't getting your drugs *into* the United States. It's getting your money *out*. A hundred million dollars weighs over eleven thousand pounds—more than an elephant. Imagine trying to transport that back to Colombia. It required multiple trips, posed security concerns, and was expensive and laborious. (In fact, during a raid early in my career, I discovered $7 million in an underground vault owned by the cartel. The cash was rotting. It had been there for months; they hadn't yet found a way to move it.) The cartels needed a reliable, and secretive, way to get paid. Enter: money laundering.

And yet, the FBI had no idea how the cartels completed the

economic loop that sustained their business. It was a black box, the keys to which were only given to the most trustworthy of associates—guys like Tony. What we did know, however, was that Puerto Rico was quickly becoming a hotbed of laundering activity. The island was legally part of the United States and therefore within the US banking system. It was also relatively close to the northern coast of Colombia, and getting to and from Miami took just two hours by plane. It was clear that the only way to stop the flow of drugs into the United States was to take down the money-laundering apparatus that sustained the cartel's business model. If drug lords had no way to get paid, they'd theoretically stop importing drugs. In the hourglass of the drug trade, the pinch point is money laundering. With me at its center, much of its sand would pass through my fingers.

Once Tony was on board, the FBI officially transitioned me into my new undercover role. We slowed down the smuggling operation, and I distanced myself from El Viejo, Pedro, and the Medellín Cartel. (I did, however, keep in touch with Diego and Carla, who continued to act as my sources in Miami whenever I needed them.) I told Pedro, quite simply, that smuggling had become too risky, and I was moving into money laundering. He tried to convince me to keep working with him, but I stood my ground. "You guys have some problems," I told him. "You called Diego down to be interrogated by Lulu. I don't need that. Plus, I don't want to go to jail, and I think it's just time for me to move on. I want to make money, not problems." We slowly drifted apart until he was indicted for drug trafficking less than a year later—and realized that I was an undercover FBI agent the entire time.

But I didn't have time to worry about Pedro: it was all about the money now. Santo Sanchez continued to lead the investigation as case agent and act as my tether to the outside world. Jimmy Padilla, an agent with whom I had worked in Houston, had recently transferred to San Juan. He came on board, assisted Santo, and acted as our whip-smart logistics whiz. Santo looked out for me, kept track of all the details, and Jimmy made sure I had the resources I needed. They were the only people inside the FBI with whom I was supposed to communicate on a regular basis.

I have to give Santo credit: if I was on call 24/7, so was he. We were the same age and made a great team. He was good-looking, a great singer, and women adored him. He loved to do karaoke whenever he got the chance. But this operation was always his first priority. As the months went on, he wrangled hundreds of agents into the investigation, from technical minds to surveillance gurus to light undercovers to paper pushers. And he always made sure I was safe, that I'd make it home to Maria and my boys.

There was another heavyweight in my corner: Dick Sanders, Special Agent in Charge (SAC) of the San Juan field office, the big boss on the island. He made sure, with Santo on the ground alongside me and Jimmy handling details at the office, that we had all the resources we needed. Dick knew this was a once-in-a-lifetime chance to truly understand how the cartels worked—and to bring them down from the inside. He ran interference for us with FBI headquarters and the Department of Justice in Washington, DC, both of whom wanted constant updates. Alongside Santo, he also kept the US Attorney's Office apprised of our investigation, so they could brainstorm the best way to prosecute once we were finished. All I needed to do was learn how to launder money.

I spent two weeks practicing under Tony's tutelage. I needed to know every detail, every nuance, and we spent hours talking through the ins and outs of cartel money laundering. Tony explained that I must come across as an expert. Once I started meeting the cartel bosses back in Colombia, specific aspects of the operation would be discussed, and I had to know what I was talking about. Moreover, if anything went wrong, or if they wanted to switch up procedures, I had to be on top of my game to act accordingly. If I started making decisions on the fly, I would surely run into trouble.

The first thing we had to invent was my money-laundering legend, the backstory that would support Tony's pitch to get me involved. We agreed on a résumé as close to the truth as possible: I was a highly successful smuggler with nearly twenty years' experience, who now wanted to move into a less physically demanding line of work—and a role with less risk. If I got caught with a bag full of money, I wouldn't necessarily go to jail. But a boat full of cocaine? Thanks to the War on Drugs, I'd be locked up for life. The career shift made sense. To enhance our pitch, I gave Tony an accelerated master's degree in smuggling and filled him in on all my connections and procedures. We wanted his bosses to think we had known each other for a long time.

Tony and I met every day at bars around the island. This didn't have to be cloak-and-dagger like my meetings with Diego when I first started out. Men on the island who worked for the cartels knew me as a smuggler and Tony as a money launderer, so it wasn't suspicious that we'd be out in public together. I'd keep my drinking to a minimum during these meetings, but Tony always ordered a rum and Coke. "But no lemon!" he'd shout at the bartender. "*¡El limón hace daño!*" Lemon is bad for your health!

During our first meeting, he laid out a few important topline points. "By nature, we have to be quite cagey," he told me.

"We never talk about the money's connection to drugs. This helps insulate us from risk. You have to think of this like running a bank. We are just picking up the money and making deposits, no questions asked."

"Is that the most important thing to know?" I asked.

He shook his head. "The most important thing is to know how to drive," he said, smiling. "Let's go. I'll show you." I followed him out into the parking lot, and we hopped into his Chevy Camaro. He explained that operational security is key while doing money pickups with drug lords, and knowing the streets of San Juan like the back of your hand would be the only thing between making it out safely and getting killed. I had been through training at the FBI's Tactical Emergency Vehicle Operations Center, but Tony was on another level. We drove around San Juan, dodged traffic, cut down alleys, and sped past landmarks. He showed me ingenious shortcuts, including through a few parking garages.

"You have to *memorize* the entire city. It all has to be up here," he said, pointing to his head.

Tony also drove me to a nondescript building in downtown San Juan. He pulled up to the curb and parked. "You pick up money inside there?" I asked.

He shook his head solemnly. "No," he said. "*Es la casa de la muerte.*" This is a kill house. "Manny, it's a bloodbath in there. People get chopped up and put into plastic bags, and then the cartel dumps them in the river." He looked at me. "The cartel, they are very serious people. You don't want to end up there."

"I won't," I said. "And I'll make sure you won't either."

"Thank you, Manny," he said. "Next, I'll teach you about how we handle our money. We'll start tomorrow. Just bring a fake ID."

"Good thing I've got plenty of those."

## INSIDE THE CARTEL

That's when Tony taught me how to smurf. We met up with Santo and Jimmy, and they handed us $75,000 in cash from the FBI's budget. Tony knew every single bank in San Juan, which cashiers were the least suspicious, and which managers were on the take. I stuffed $10,000 into my bag and Tony drove me to the first bank.

"Remember," he said. "Give the teller the money and do as she tells you. It's easy."

I nodded and got out of the car. I was nervous, not because I felt like I couldn't play it cool while swapping the cash for checks, but because if I did somehow set off red flags, I'd be tossed out of the bank and humiliated in front of Tony. But my reservations were for naught: I handed over the cash, the cashier gave me the checks, and I walked out. It was simple. This, too, was pre-9/11, long before the American government discovered that terrorists were using the American banking system to recruit, train, and deploy enemies of the state. Back then, everything was much laxer, with very few safeguards or regulations. For drug smugglers, the US financial system was ripe for exploitation.

I came out of the bank and smiled at Tony, signaling that I'd succeeded. I climbed into the car. "See?" Tony said. "Not so hard, right?" The rest of the banks followed suit, and I easily got the checks. We went back to his house and he showed me how to package them for handoff to the cartel's couriers, or for delivery through the mail. Tony grabbed a stack of newspaper and a roll of tape.

"Now," he said, unfurling the newspaper to the funny pages, "you must only use the comics when wrapping the checks. And only color comics, not black-and-white. If they receive the checks in any other wrapping, they will know that they have been tampered with. Plus, X-ray machines can't see through newspapers. The ink blocks their vision."

"Uh," I said. "I don't think that's true, Tony."

He shrugged. "That's what the Colombians say, at least," he continued, wrapping the checks in a sheet of newsprint. "Once they are wrapped, we use this special tape. It is reinforced with fiberglass, and the only way to remove it from the paper is to cut it. It's another security measure." He finished with the package and held it up for me to inspect. "You can fit around $2.5 million worth of checks into one envelope, if it's being mailed, but my contract is only for $700,000 per week."

After we ran through the basics of how to launder money, Tony sent word to his boss in Colombia that he needed a right-hand man on the island whom he could trust—and that I would be the perfect fit. He referred to his boss only as *El Toro Negro*. The Black Bull. Tony didn't know his real name, the breadth of his connections, or the complete ecosystem of his international scheme. Toro was smart that way: He heavily compartmentalized his business, and only let his associates know just enough so they could do their jobs correctly. Everyone knew there was much more to Toro than what they were privy to. We just needed to keep digging until we figured everything out.

I went to Tony's house and we waited for the call. He paced around the room, clearly on edge, realizing that his decision to flip on the cartel was real.

"Would you just sit down?" I asked. "There's no need to be nervous, Tony."

"We have to be very careful, Manny," he said.

"I've been doing this for years. How do you think I got this far?" I asked. "We'll be fine. I'll be polite and let you take the lead. Just trust me." And then the phone rang. Tony picked it up.

"Toro, I want to introduce you to Manny, my new partner," Tony said. "With your blessing, he's going to be working with us in Puerto Rico. Like I said before, Manny and I are old friends, and have done much business together in the past."

"*Señor* Manny, *mucho gusto*," Toro said.

"*Un placer*," I replied. It's a pleasure. "Thanks for bringing me on board."

"From what Tony has said, you will be a good partner."

"I hope so," I said.

"Previously, with only Tony working the island for me, our capacity was limited," he said. "But I am thinking of having you both come to my big party. You'll be able to dance with at least a hundred beautiful women. Do you think you can handle that?"

*Holy shit*, I thought to myself. *$100 million?* What the hell had I fallen into? My mind raced with the implications. I hadn't yet laundered a single dollar, but I knew that men who dealt with this kind of money weren't bit players in the international drug trade. They were at the center of it all.

"Yes, *jefe*, we definitely can," Tony said.

"Good," Toro said. "Manny, I will have you meet my other associates soon, but for now, *¡pilas y mosca!*" Get ready, be alert, and don't make any mistakes.

"Of course," I said. "I take my work very seriously."

"I'm glad to hear it," Toro said. "And Manny, always remember that I can reach across the world, at any time, and touch your shoulder."

Translation: *Don't mess with me, or I'll have you killed.*

I knew this all too well.

CHAPTER 7

# I CAN SMELL A COP FROM A MILE AWAY

**TONY HATED MY SPORTS CAR. WHEN I FIRST WENT UNDER-** cover in Puerto Rico as a smuggler, I purchased a glittering gold Nissan 300ZX coupe with 225 horsepower (not much by today's standards, but it was plenty of juice for such a small island). I brought it into our new operation. To me, it was a reliable vehicle that could zip through heavy traffic well. To Tony, it was a liability—too flashy, too easily spotted by shady characters who might want to steal the money that we had just stuffed into the trunk. I eventually won the argument after we picked up $1 million from a drug lord in Tony's beat-up jalopy, which he claimed helped disguise our illegal activities. As we were about to leave, the car broke down. He cranked the key and the starter whined. No luck. It was dead. The traffickers who just handed over the cash laughed at us, but luckily, they had jumper cables and gave us a hand. We were back on the road in a few minutes.

"That was a major fuckup, man," I said as we cruised down the highway, the car's rusted-out shocks creaking over every bump. "We're not driving this piece of shit anymore. We're using my Nissan from now on."

Tony laughed, clearly amused. He slapped the steering wheel. "Look at us!" he said. "We're fine!" I glared at him. Not a chance in hell, especially considering that we had just started laundering together. I didn't want this operation to blow up before it even started. So: the Nissan it was. We spent a lot of time in that car together. We cruised to pickup locations, down to his house, and parked at my apartment. (We always switched cars, however, for meetings with Santo and Jimmy, who weren't working undercover.) Tony loved telling me how to navigate San Juan. The first time we took the highway together, he shouted, "Manny, always drive in the far right lane! It's the fastest lane, in case we have to escape!"

"Tony, there's a lot of traffic here," I said, pointing at the swarm of cars in front of us.

"Man, trust me," he said. "I know this island like the back of my hand. Stay on the right!"

I did as he told me, just to shut him up. I hit the throttle, beelined for the right lane, and zoomed past a line of cars. We made it to our exit in a flash. He cracked a smile, his fake teeth sparkling in the tropical sunlight. "I told you so," he said.

\* \* \*

EL TORO NEGRO, THE mastermind of this international criminal ring, lived in Maicao, the money-laundering capital of Colombia. The city is situated on the edge of the Gulf of Venezuela, on the country's northern coast, and is strategically located near many offshore banking jurisdictions that had become havens for drug cartels: Aruba, Curaçao, the British Virgin Islands, and Panama. Tony explained to me that Toro had launched his money-laundering business in the mid-1980s and, with Puerto Rico as his go-between, had made inroads into the continental United States. He had a partner stationed in Miami, who acted as Tony's second boss. "You'll meet him soon enough," Tony told me.

Although Toro laundered money for any cartel or one-off drug baron who requested his services, his largest client was the North Coast Cartel, helmed by Alberto Orlandez-Gamboa, also known as *El Caracol*, a reference to a famous Colombian beach by the same name. It technically means "the shell," but when he rose to prominence in the English-speaking world, his nickname got translated into "the Snail," which, although technically inaccurate, stuck. Although North Coast had for years operated in the shadow of the Medellín and Cali cartels, the Snail would eventually be revealed as one of the leading individual cocaine exporters in the world. He first got his start in the late 1970s, in the coastal city of Barranquilla, about two hundred miles southwest of Toro's stomping grounds in Maicao. Barranquilla was the perfect place to be a drug lord. It acted both as an export station to the Caribbean and the headquarters of the coca cultivation jungles that stretched south toward Medellín.

At first, the North Coast Cartel was aligned with Pablo Escobar, who had installed José Silva, the fifth in command within Medellín, as North Coast's leader. But after Silva was indicted on drug-trafficking charges and extradited to the United States in 1987, a power vacuum formed. The Snail used his regional prowess to take control of North Coast and fill the void. By the early 1990s, with Escobar's power dwindling, the Snail flipped his predecessor's alliances and partnered up with the

Cali Cartel, who was quickly overtaking Escobar as the most powerful criminal organization in Colombia. (The Cali bosses even formed a suborganization, Los Pepes, who helped dismantle the Medellín Cartel by carrying out targeted assassinations of Escobar's inner circle and feeding intelligence to the Colombian authorities.) As the Snail's alliance with Cali blossomed, an agreement was made: the North Coast Cartel would control all distribution routes in the Caribbean. This savvy coup d'état slowly shifted the country's narco power balance from the south, with Escobar at the helm, to the north, with the Snail leading the charge. In the coastal strongholds of Barranquilla and Maicao, power was now consolidated.

The Snail collaborated with the northern bloc of the United Self-Defense Forces of Colombia (AUC), a violent paramilitary group that controlled much of northern Colombia. They helped protect his turf. He also formed alliances with many regional politicians, who turned a blind eye to his exportation of drugs along the northern coast. In 1992, when I first began infiltrating Toro's money-laundering operation in Puerto Rico, the Snail had become one of Colombia's premier drug lords—and certainly the most creative. He routinely packaged his cocaine in crates filled with mustard or cough syrup, which masked the smell and made it easier to avoid detection at the US border. The Snail was also prone to violence; he employed a rotating cast of sicarios who carried out kidnappings and assassinations at his behest. (The AUC also assisted in this regard.) All in all, he was a bad dude—and very powerful.

As the Snail's narco-empire grew and gained power, Toro emerged as the final piece of the puzzle that allowed the North Coast Cartel to expand exponentially. He made sure the cartel's drug profits were routed successfully through a complex web of financial transfers, so it landed safely back in their coffers in Colombia. His operation was so good, Tony explained early in our partnership, that Toro was able to clean over $500,000 *per day*. "He is a genius," Tony said during one of our first drives around the island. "And very powerful. Everyone in Colombia is in his pocket—and I mean *everyone*."

After Toro gave me his blessing, Tony and I were responsible for picking up roughly $1 million per week from various drug traffickers. Toro would call my cell phone and speak in code as to whom I was scheduled to meet, with each counterparty given a specific number. For example: "Pick up at six p.m. with number forty-five." Each smuggler from whom we received money had mapped out a rotating cast of spots around the island, including lavish hotels, gas stations, secluded parking lots, restaurants, forest roads, or private airports. After picking up the money, I would drive to a predetermined location, normally a controlled area behind a Pueblo supermarket or a Toys "R" Us, where my FBI colleagues waited to collect the cash.

We also decided to abandon the smurfing operation. It was too unwieldy, too risky, and too time-consuming. The FBI made an agreement with a local bank manager, who was vetted and trustworthy and had machines that could count a large amount of cash quickly. After it was counted, we'd log the amount into our evidence binder, and then I would call Toro and tell him how much money I received. And I had to be honest. Everything is a test: If I received more than I was supposed to, I had to claim it, because Toro could've fed me misinformation on purpose, to see if I was skimming off the top. From there, the bank manager would swap the cash for cashier's checks, solidifying our carefully orchestrated ruse. At that point, the checks were wrapped and ready for the next leg of their laundering journey, where it was secretly transported by Toro's courier to bank accounts in Aruba, Panama, Venezuela, Colombia, or Miami.

I quickly realized how dangerous this operation actually was once I started doing money pickups. In the world of cartels, drugs aren't super special. Cocaine is just an instrument through which the end goal is achieved: money. You're much more likely to get ripped off for $1 million than you are for a truck full of dope. And by "ripped off" I mean ambushed by a half-dozen cars full of sicarios carrying machine guns. These men don't leave witnesses behind. Moreover, everyone handing over their cash is on high alert. They don't want to get ripped off by me either, so there's a mutual degree of skepticism inherent in this business. And for good reason, I suppose. But when you're a deep-undercover FBI agent, this can quickly turn into paranoia, thinking everyone is onto you, that you're one slip of the tongue away from being discovered. I was on the edge of exposure every day. In fact, I was nearly unmasked my first month in this new role.

* * *

TORO ORDERED TONY AND me to collect $250,000 from Gustavo, a high-level trafficker for North Coast who went by *El Loco*. His public front was that he was a local businessman who owned a series of gas stations. Toro gave us the directive that morning over the phone: "Pickup from number twelve," he said, using Gustavo's code name.

"You got it, boss," I said. I called Gustavo to confirm the details of where, and when, he wanted to meet: Casa de la Luna, around lunchtime. I turned to Tony, who was sitting next to me in my undercover apartment. Toro normally called at the same time every morning. Tony would make his way to my place so we could take the call together and show Toro that we were ready to go. He came to enjoy these little kickoff meetings, and always brought with him coffee and pastries from a bakery down the street. He bit into a doughnut as I explained our mission.

"La Luna?" he said, chewing. "The socialist hangout, where all the separatists get together?"

"I guess so," I said. Puerto Rico had always been a hotbed of political unrest, and underground rebel cells had popped up over the preceding few decades. They hoped to reestablish the island's sovereignty from the United States. They were also violent dudes who themselves engaged in illegal activities. In the 1960s, the FBI had even investigated the groups as part of COINTELPRO, a covert operation that infiltrated a host of political organizations, but the operation did little to halt the separatists' growing influence on the island. They were skeptical of everyone—but absolutely hated the United States government. We had to be careful.

"I don't know, Manny," Tony said. "That's a sketchy place."

"What other choice do we have?" I asked. "We have to follow Toro's orders."

Tony shrugged, resigned to the plan. I walked into my bedroom and grabbed my recording device from the closet. It was just like you'd see in the movies: a thin wire with a microphone at its tip that plugged into a sleek receiver. I usually kept it in my handbag with my pistol. It wasn't uncommon for cartel men to carry small satchels, to hold both guns and other important items, so the fact that I had such a bag never raised any suspicion. Plus, high-level cartel members—smugglers, money launderers, or otherwise—never searched a colleague's satchel. It was a disrespectful move that wasn't good for business. This professional code of conduct helped me tremendously. During meetings, I'd simply place my bag on the table and record the conversation. The audio was clean and crisp. Getting the cartel on the wire was always the most dangerous part of the job, but also the most necessary. It shook my nerves whenever I waltzed into an unfamiliar situation with the wire at my side, all the more now because we were dealing with so much money and with such frequency. And yet, if we wanted the evidence required to bring the cartel to justice, the wire was mandatory. I tried my best to carry it with me for every pickup, every meeting, every single time I interacted with a kingpin. It was part of the job. And yet, if anyone ever searched my bag, the jig would be up. Finding that wire was a death sentence.

I walked back out into the living room and stuffed the wire into my bag. I glanced at Tony. He looked like he was about to puke, his face white and slicked with sweat. He knew the wire was our greatest liability, and if it was discovered, I wouldn't be the only one getting a bullet in the head. "You ready?"

He swallowed the last bite of his doughnut and nodded. "As ready as I'll ever be," he answered. "Let's go."

* * *

**WE MADE OUR WAY** to the restaurant just after noon. Tony and I had made contact with Santo before the pickup, and he assured us that surveillance would be in place. The bar, made from rich caoba wood, anchored the main room, and small tables filled the rest of the space. Gustavo rose from his seat at the far end of the restaurant and waved us over. He was tall, with reddish hair, a trimmed beard, and green eyes. At first glance, he looked Irish. He wore a four-pocket shirt with custom embroidery, a fancy style customary in the Caribbean at the time. Next to him sat a gorgeous Colombian woman, elegant and understated, clad in a cream-colored blouse, wide-cut skirt, and high heels. She looked like a model. I led the way, Tony trailing behind me, and shook Gustavo's hand.

"This is my wife, Ella," he said, turning to the woman.

"*Mucho gusto*," she said, her formality a clear signal that she was approaching this meeting with caution.

We sat down, ordered some food and a round of drinks, and got into the details of the money.

"I have $250,000 for you," Gustavo said. "It's in my truck. I know I was supposed to deliver $600,000, and I am sorry about that, but I will have the rest for you shortly."

"No problem," Tony said, sipping on his rum and Coke. "We know you are good for it."

"I appreciate that. I just have so many things going on. This, but also my real estate and gas station businesses. And I also got into something new," he said, pulling a bundle of lottery tickets out of his bag. "These are winning tickets. My friend at the lottery knows which ones are winners, and then I buy the tickets from him at a premium. It's a great way to clean money."

"Oh, really?" I asked, playing along, hoping he would explain more. "Maybe I can use them to launder my own proceeds."

Gustavo laughed. "Of course!" he said. "It's tough to handle all this money. My shipments come from El Caracol directly. He sends so much, I sometimes need to make my own plans in order to handle all of it. And *los puercos*"—the damn cops—"are everywhere nowadays. I've had to bury my loads at the beach or tie them to an anchor and sink them down onto the reef. Sometimes, we have to wait for days to retrieve them. That's why I don't have the full $600,000 for you today. The rest of the merchandise is still down by the beach!"

As we ate and talked, Ella kept looking around the restaurant, her eyes forever wandering. She interrupted the conversation and pointed to two men at the bar. "We should get out of here," she said. "Those two guys, over there, they are feds. I can smell a cop from a mile away."

It always surprised me how much more perceptive—and resolute—women were than men, especially in the world of drug smuggling. In fact, some women that I met during my work as an undercover agent actually revealed themselves to be far more powerful and cutthroat than their male counterparts. During one operation years later, I met a female Colombian drug kingpin at a hotel in Panama. She just had a baby and arrived pushing a stroller. As we talked shop about how I could help her secretly import hundreds of millions of dollars' worth of cocaine, she took the infant out of the stroller, unbuttoned her blouse, and began breastfeeding. The baby suckled for the rest of our meeting. When we were done and the woman walked away, one of her bodyguards turned to me and said, "She might look beautiful in that skirt, but when she bends over, you can see her *balls*."

After Ella's comment, I put my drink down and turned around. The two men she identified were *my* men, running surveillance. Hell, one of them was Santo! This could've been a bad sign for how difficult this operation was going to be, but I viewed her paranoia as just another indication of her criminal culpability. By admitting her concern regarding law enforcement, she implicated herself. I could hear Santo talking to the bartender in a terrible Colombian accent; it was clear that he was acting. But I told myself to just stay calm, keep a straight face. As with any game of poker, there's always another bet to make, a way to bluff yourself out of a jam.

"I see what you're saying," I said to her, trying to act comforting, "but I'm sure it's nothing. No one knows we're here."

"Baby," Gustavo said, placing his hand on her knee. "It's fine. Just chill out."

Ella glared at Santo and the other agents for the remainder of the meeting, but she kept her mouth shut. After we finished eating, Gustavo said, "Well, let's go get the money." We walked out together, past Santo and my men. I wanted to shoot him a dirty look, for being dumb enough to come in here and act like he was Colombian, but I just waltzed by as if we didn't know each other. In the parking lot, Gustavo dropped the tailgate of his Toyota pickup truck and pulled out two duffel bags. He handed one to me, and one to Tony. They were heavy.

"Sorry about the small bills," he said.

"We will take what we can get," Tony said.

"It's not a problem," I added.

"The next one won't be like this," Gustavo said. "I promise." He rooted around in his bag. "And take this," he said, handing me a stack of lottery tickets. "They're all winners."

After loading the money into my car, Tony and I eased our way out into the street. I looked over my shoulder at Ella, who stood in the parking lot with her arms crossed, staring at us until we were out of sight.

\* \* \*

**AFTER LOGGING THE MONEY** with a team of agents, I switched cars and drove to a remote parking lot on the edge of San Juan to meet with Santo. I pulled up next to him, got out of my vehicle, and jumped into his. When I opened the door, he had a paper bag shoved over his mouth, breathing heavily in and out. His eyes bulged out of his head, sweat poured down his face, and his hands shook as he tried to keep the bag in place. He was having a panic attack.

"Where did you get that awful Colombian accent from?" I asked, ribbing him. "You didn't fool anybody."

Santo pulled his mouth away from the bag and smirked. "Sorry," he said. "I messed up. Ella was staring a hole through my chest."

"I took care of it," I said. "Calm down. We're fine."

He gulped down three more large breaths and removed the bag from his mouth. "We could've been made," he said.

I put my hand on his shoulder. "But we weren't," I said. "They have no idea that I'm undercover. The operation is still intact." I opened my bag, took out my wire, and shook it in Santo's face. "And we have this."

# CHAPTER 8

# THE WIRE

**I HADN'T SEEN MY FAMILY IN ALMOST EIGHT WEEKS. IT WAS** August 1993, and the investigation into the North Coast Cartel had been barreling ahead nonstop for the better part of a year. The close call with Gustavo's highly perceptive wife didn't slow us down one bit. In many respects, the fact that I got out of the situation unscathed kicked the operation into an even higher gear. Throughout the summer, I made dozens of money pickups for Toro, and helped launder over $15 million. He was so happy with how well Tony and I were doing that he sent us on more and more missions. It was a strange, sad seesaw. The better I became at my job, at money laundering, at being Manny, the further I was pushed from my reason for doing this job in the first place: my wife and sons.

Maria never forgot our run-in with the cartel man during Noche de San Juan. It hung over us like a dark cloud every time I was able to visit for a night or two. The beach near our home was private, quiet, and unkempt. I'd take my boys down there and play catch whenever I had time to see them. But Maria always stood off to the side, her arms crossed pensively, looking over her shoulder. Her vulnerability was palpable, even if she never verbalized her apprehension—and it was because of me, and the line of work that I had chosen. The stress of potentially being spotted again while I was with my family also kept me hyper-prepared. Whenever I transformed back into Martin, I still kept a loaded pistol stuffed into my waistband and an undercover driver's license in my pocket. I never knew if cartel soldiers would confront me on the street and demand proof that I really was Manny. The cartels murdered thirty cops a year in Puerto Rico. If they even suspected I was a federal agent, I'd be dead. My life became a room of funhouse mirrors in which my psyche was reflected and distorted. A piece of my mind always had to be Manny, even when I was with my family as Martin.

We still did our best to raise our sons together. Maria and I had access to a getaway bungalow on the far edge of the island, a piece of property that had been in my family for years. She brought our sons there often, and my parents sometimes joined. Maria would wake up in the morning and watch my father and his grandsons walk down the beach, hand in hand, scouring for seashells. We both knew that her taking them there was a weak attempt at distraction, a way to show our sons a good time to make up for how often their father was gone. And yet my boys knew our circumstances were not normal. My eldest son was especially affected, never forgetting the day when I had boarded the Navy ship and sailed away. If you asked him now, he would tell you this was a devastating time. A young boy, he just wanted his father around. My youngest son also showed his frustration. When I was gone, he'd take my clothes out of the closet and throw them onto the front lawn, a tantrum projecting his grief at my absence.

The truth is, I would constantly break promises to my sons. I'd tell them that I'd be home in three days but disappear for two weeks or more. Many years later, after my youngest son became a man, we sat down and watched a televised boxing match together. Somehow, we got to talking about that time, and he told me, "The man I loved was never around." When you're working deep undercover, the bad guys dictate your schedule. It's just how it works.

I carried this hard truth with me every day. Despite the thrill of our new, expanded investigation, my heart ached. I missed my family dearly, but I knew it was too dangerous to go home as often as I wanted. Between money pickups for Toro, I'd try to clear my mind, to trick myself into believing that I was doing the right thing (for me, or them, I could never decide), and that this immense sacrifice would be worth it in the end. My father owned some land up in the mountains, a different property than his beachside bungalow. It was a safe and secluded place. He grew lemons, mangoes, grapefruit, and bananas. I went up there alone a lot that summer. I'd bring *The Epic of Latin America*, a thick history book about the origins of my people. I also read a lot of Puerto Rican literature, such as *El Jibaro* or *La Resaca*, two tales of heroes who overcame the abusive reign of the Spanish. I'd sit under the trees' shady canopy and thumb through the pages, hoping to get lost in the larger-than-life tales, trying to forget how consumed I was by the story of Manny, how he was forcing his own abusive reign over me. My escape never lasted long, however. Right when I got to the point of forgetting, my phone would ring, and I'd have to return to the mission, to a story I had to finish.

\* \* \*

### INSIDE THE CARTEL

FOOTBALL SEASON STARTED IN September. My boys loved the sport and played on a local team. I wanted so desperately to be there for them in the bleachers, but it was too risky. I couldn't put them in harm's way. I couldn't be selfish. For their first game, however, I drove out to the field and parked far enough away so that they couldn't see me. I stood in the shade of a palm tree and watched my boys run down the field, dodge tacklers, and reach for a touchdown. I spotted Maria on the sidelines, cheering them on. I felt so helpless, so alone, at that moment. I looked down at my money-launderer outfit, my fancy watch and shiny shoes. I glanced at the sports car that I drove to nail down my alter ego. *Look at me*, I thought to myself, *a ghost even to my own family*.

I stayed only for a few minutes. I got back into my Nissan and started driving to my undercover apartment. I careened through downtown San Juan and came to a stoplight. I looked to my left, a decrepit building towering over me. To any normal person, it was just another structure that had fallen to disrepair on an island struggling to survive. But Tony had divulged to me the true nature of this place: a cartel torture facility. I'd see it almost every time I conducted a money pickup, if I was dropping Tony off at his house, or even if I was driving down to a beachside restaurant for some dinner. If I were ever unmasked as an FBI agent, Toro would surely have me brought here. I pictured it every time I drove by: me, strapped to a chair, beaten to a pulp, a machine gun pressed into my head. And if I didn't talk? Everyone who got on the wrong side of the cartel received a similar treatment: a group of sicarios would burn off the tips of your fingers with a blowtorch, electrocute your testicles with a high-voltage battery, scoop out your eyeballs with a spoon, cut off your tongue and, finally, chop you up into tiny pieces with a chainsaw, your body unrecognizable, never to be found again. This process allowed the cartel to invent their own verb: disappeared. It was the ultimate fate.

A car honked behind me. The light had turned green. I shifted my Nissan into gear and kept driving.

After watching my sons play football from afar, Maria rooting from the sidelines, I contemplated if, many years from now, I would come to regret doing this type of work. And yet, at the same time, I felt there was no other place for me within the FBI. I couldn't think of anything else I would rather do with my life. I knew that working undercover provided the greatest positive impact in thwarting crime. I knew I was good at it. Conversely, it produced the most negative impact on a stable family life. I had become skilled at dismissing this tug-of-war. Still, during my most vulnerable times, I couldn't completely remove my family from my mind. I'd be having lunch with Tony, on the phone with Toro, or going over back-end details with Santo, and all I could think of was my wife and sons.

One night shortly after watching my two boys play football, I returned to my undercover apartment. I nodded to one of my neighbors as I climbed the steps to my front door, and I realized how totally alone I was as an undercover FBI agent, that no one truly knew what I was sacrificing to be here. My neighbors just thought I was another bachelor who lived alone. I walked into my apartment. Although this place was the nucleus of my case, of my identity as Manny, it lacked the soul of a real home. It felt cold and foreign to me, no matter how much time I spent in it. I had future missions for which I needed to plan, but I wanted nothing more than to hear my wife's voice.

I brought my cell phone out to the living room and plugged it into my portable recording device. I knew that this operation was far from over, and I needed something that would keep me tethered to my family. I needed their voices, even when I couldn't be with them. I dialed my home number and brought the phone to my ear.

"Hello?" Maria said.

"Hey sweetie," I said. "It's me."

"Hey!" she said. I could tell that she was in a good mood. "We just got home. How's work?"

I didn't want to talk about work. I wanted to talk about them. "Where did you go?" I asked.

"I took the boys to see *Batman versus the Joker*," she said. "There was a live-action play in the park." And then: a yelp in the background. It was my youngest son, who had quickly figured out that I was on the phone. He had just celebrated his eighth birthday. I had missed it. I wasn't able to call him for another three days. Another small abandonment in this years-long betrayal.

"He wants to talk to you," Maria said. "Hold on."

"Dad?" he said, his voice rising with excitement.

"Hey buddy," I said. "Mom says you went to the park today?"

"Yeah! And we saw Batman! And the Joker! And Batman beat the Joker!"

"Oh, he did?"

"Yeah! Batman is good, and the Joker is evil, and Batman beat him!"

"You like Batman, don't you?" I asked.

"Yeah! When they were fighting, I was yelling, 'Get him, Batman! Get the Joker!'"

"So, the good guys won in the end?" I asked.

"Yeah, Dad. The good guys always win!"

"We always hope that's the case, son," I said. "We always hope that's the case."

I hung up the phone and thought about how fast my sons

were growing up. At such a crucial age, how would my being away come to affect them? Was I doing the right thing, accepting such a demanding and dangerous job? Would I regret this decision years down the line? I thought then, of how I could do better as a father, given the life that I had chosen, and how I could be there for them as time passed. But then the phone rang again, and Manny came back into focus. The cartel needed me, and I had to answer.

*  *  *

MY PHONE BECAME MY greatest enemy. Whenever it rang, I knew that I'd have to pick up more money for Toro and the cartel. The phone became a constant reminder that despite being a member of the most powerful law enforcement entity in the world, I had very little control over my life. Its incessant buzzing gave the FBI valuable evidence, but it pushed me even further away from my family. It was always the phone, with the voice on the other end of the line, a bodiless specter telling me what to do, tugging invisible strings as if I was a marionette doll. And I always had to obey.

The morning after I spoke with my son about seeing *Batman* in the park, Toro called with details for the next pickup. He instructed me to meet with a Colombian named Melenudo, who had most recently worked as an underling in Gustavo's smuggling group. Melenudo had branched off, however, and started working for himself by cementing his own team of men. Now, he wanted Toro to launder his money. This pickup was the start of their one-on-one relationship.

"This is more of a favor than anything," Toro told me. "You'll only be receiving $47,000."

"Not a problem," I said.

"Melenudo will call you to arrange the details," he said. "And once you have this last batch of checks, I'm going to have you meet with my courier so he can take the money off the island." My ears perked up: I had never met Toro's secret courier before. It was a massive opportunity. It would allow me to move closer to the ultimate goal of any undercover operation: capturing the leadership. With each level I climbed in the hierarchy of any criminal enterprise, the more damage would be done to the organization as a whole. And yet, the deeper I went, the more likely I was to get into harm's way. It's the double-edged sword of doing investigative work. But I had to keep meeting new players, if not as an asset to the case, then as a measurement of how well I could do my job. If all went to plan, I would have an image of another gear in his laundering machine.

"You got it, *jefe*," I said. "*Hecho*." It's done.

"Good, Manny," he said. "You'll be meeting with him a lot from now on."

Perfect.

\* \* \*

I GAVE MELENUDO A call to confirm the details given to me by Toro. "My associate, Appa, will give the cash to you," he told me. I was directed to meet Appa in a remote neighborhood near Barrio Shanghai, between San Juan and Santurce. It was a really sketchy place, all run-down shanties, busted-out streetlights, and stray dogs. Tony wasn't with me on this pickup. Toro had come to trust me so deeply that I was going at it alone.

"You want me to meet him there?" I asked Melenudo. "It's

crawling with police. I'm driving a nice car. I'll be seen." I didn't really know if the place was teeming with cops. I just wanted more control over the setting, to protect myself. You never know what could happen in a poor, isolated slum.

"You'll be fine, Manny," he said. "Don't worry about it."

The meet was set for later that evening. I called Jimmy and filled him in on the details. He passed the information along to Santo, who then called me. Santo explained that Appa was the lead suspect in a recent murder, and the US Attorney's Office wanted me to get further evidence for his identification.

"You're going to have to wear the wire," Santo told me. "If it's in your satchel, it may not pick up the conversation well enough to be used in court."

"I'll see what I can do," I said.

"We have to make sure that we get him on tape," he said.

I swallowed his directive like a dirty stone. "All right," I said. "I'll do my best."

I climbed into my Nissan and made my way to the rendezvous spot. I crept down the grimy, narrow street and saw Appa and his men waiting for me. Appa was wiry, with dreadlocks that hung past his shoulders and a deep scar cutting across his face. He looked like the Predator. I popped my trunk and one of Appa's men deposited the cash inside. I was about to peel out of there when Appa's second enforcer answered his cell phone and quickly muttered something in Appa's ear. Appa's eyebrows shot up in surprise. The man with the cell phone nodded to another man, who walked over to a nearby retaining wall, and retrieved an AK-47 that was hidden in the brush. Another man pulled a pistol out of his waistband. Appa followed his two enforcers to a nearby car, got in, and left. A fourth man gripped his pistol and stepped in front of my car. I had no idea what was going on. Two thoughts crossed my mind: I could hit the gas and run over the pistol-wielding enforcer, which could cause a whole host of additional problems, or I could play it cool, wait, and hope that none of this had to do with me. I stayed put, kept my heartbeat steady, and waited for Appa to return.

Santo later told me what happened next: Appa and his men drove around the block and discovered my surveillance. Appa pointed his gun at them and demanded to know who he was, and what he was doing there. Thinking quick on his feet, the agent told him that he was with the DEA, and was looking for a fugitive who may have come into this neighborhood. This put Appa flat-footed, since he assumed this man was out to get *him*. Appa told the agent to get lost, and he did, but now I was without protection. Appa and his men drove back over to my car. Appa got out and came up to my window. All these years later, I can still smell his breath, rank and sharp, like rotten eggs.

"There are some cops back there, but I don't think it's about us," he said.

"Why did you stop me from leaving?" I said. "I could've been caught with money in the car."

Before Appa could answer, another one of his men approached him. "I hear something in my ear," the man, who wore an earpiece of some kind, said to Appa. He looked at me. "I think he has a wire."

I knew, right then, that this guy had some sort of gadget that could detect remote transmitters or recording devices. My heart started to race. It was just me and a half-dozen drug lords with machine guns. I couldn't run. I couldn't break cover. I knew my surveillance was likely made, so I was operating blind and unprotected. *Stay in character,* I told myself. *You're still in control. You're still Manny.*

# THE WIRE

"Manny," he said, "I need you to get out of the car."

I did as I was told. Appa's men searched me. They rubbed down every square inch of my body, looking for a wire, a badge, any evidence that I was a cop. They found nothing. "Everything all right, Appa?" I said, trying to keep my composure, to not escalate the situation. His face fell. He knew he'd overstepped, nearly strip-searching a high-echelon money launderer like me.

"*Lo siento*, Manny," he said. "*Lo siento*."

"You better be sorry," I said, getting back into my car and slamming the door shut. "Toro is going to hear about this."

"He doesn't need to know about this," he said. "I can give you some money, for your troubles."

"I don't want your money," I said. I shifted into first gear and took off.

On my way out to this meeting, I couldn't shake the terrible feeling I had in my gut. There was something about this pickup that just didn't sit right with me: not meeting with Melenudo directly, being sent to a run-down part of the city, not knowing how my surveillance was able to protect me. Right before I turned into the neighborhood where Appa was waiting for me, I'd pulled over, ripped the wire off my chest, jerked the miniature recording device out of my pocket, and tossed the entire thing into the bushes. My car was still bugged, a tape deck and transmitter shoved under the dash, but I knew they'd never find that. But the wire, strapped to my chest? I couldn't take the risk. I knew in my heart that something was about to go terribly wrong. I was right. If I had kept the wire on me, I surely would have been executed. God was on my side that day.

After leaving Appa, I drove my car to the Toys "R" Us parking lot so I could hand the money over to Santo. Normally, we would meet at one of our undercover safe houses, but since it was such a small amount of money, we thought we'd save some time and do a quick handoff. Santo was hyperventilating again, that paper bag stuffed over his mouth. In and out. In and out. Trying to breathe his way around a panic attack. He rolled down his window and I handed him the money.

"Are you okay?" I asked.

He held up the paper bag and smirked, an admission that it was basically useless. "Mind over matter, I guess," he said.

"I made it work back there," I said. "We're good."

"We had a plane in the sky," he said, referencing surveillance aircraft that we sometimes used for more remote meetups. "You were entirely alone once they made our surveillance."

"And yet here I am, unscathed," I said.

"Let's just hope it stays that way," he said. "I'll get these checks going right now. You can pick them up later tonight." I bid Santo farewell and headed to my undercover apartment. It was time to finally meet Toro's courier: Julio Tamez.

\* \* \*

TORO SCHEDULED FOR ME to meet Julio Tamez the next day at Isla Verde, a downtrodden motel across the parkway from the high-end resorts that dotted San Juan Bay. Tony had already told the FBI the baseline contours of Toro's money-laundering scheme in Puerto Rico, but Tamez was the guy actually moving the drug money off the island. I was set to make multiple hand-offs to him over the proceeding months, and my plan was to act like we were old friends, quickly garner his trust, and gently push our conversations toward him revealing who else was involved—and how far up the food chain of the international banking sector this operation actually went. As things stood, we already had enough evidence for a handful of indictments. If he talked, we could have dozens more.

I stuffed my wire into my satchel, stacked the cashier's checks neatly in a second bag, and made my way to the meeting. I parked in the Isla Verde parking lot and quickly scoped out the location for any sketchy characters. It was clean. I went up to the room. I knocked and entered. Tamez rose from his chair and smiled. His clothes hung loose on his lanky frame, ringlet curls dangled atop his ears, and his skin held the hue of charcoal-stained wood, rich and black.

"Manny," he said, reaching out to shake my hand. "It's so good to meet you. Please, sit."

"It's good to meet you, too," I said, accepting his grip. "Toro says good things."

"And about you, as well," he said.

I raised my arms and gestured at the room. "Interesting choice of venue," I said, hoping to understand if this rinky-dink motel held any significance within his organization.

"Yeah, it's certainly not up to my standards, but Toro has instructed me to not draw any attention to myself," he said. "I hope you can understand."

"Of course," I said. "It's better to be safe than sorry, right?"

"Exactly," he said. "Do you have the checks?"

I placed the bag onto the table. "All there. One million, right?"

He smiled. "Exactly," he said, opening the bag and retrieving the checks. He stuffed them into his jacket pocket.

"So, where is Toro sending you with this batch?" I asked, making it seem as if Toro divulged more information to me about Tamez's routes than he actually did.

"Aruba," he said. "I'm bringing them directly to our bankers."

"Beautiful place," I said, teeing up another probe. "It must be nice to go there every few weeks."

"Well, I don't make deliveries only to Aruba," he said. "It could be Aruba, but it also could be Panama, Venezuela, Miami, or even directly to Colombia. It all depends on what Toro wants to do with the money. He offers different types of services and does a lot of favors for people."

*Interesting*, I thought to myself. *Bankers in Aruba, but contacts throughout North and South America.* "It must be tough to get the checks through Immigration and Customs," I said.

Tamez smiled, nearly laughing at the naivety of my statement. "Oh, that's not a problem," he said. "Toro has friends in many places. But just to be safe," he added, lifting up his pant leg and revealing a knee-high compression sock, "I put them in here. They don't come out until I walk into the bank. No one has a clue."

## CHAPTER 9

# DE NOCHE, TODOS LOS GATOS SON NEGROS

**THE FBI WANTED TO MAKE SURE MY HEAD WAS STRAIGHT.** Their chief concern was not whether I had gone crooked or become a double agent (although that was something for which all top brass had to be on the lookout; the money and power produced by the cartels was as intoxicating as a siren's song) but rather if, quite simply, the pressure was starting to get to me.

The FBI arranged psychological check-ins every few months. The initial sessions, when our money-laundering investigation first started, weren't difficult. I was much more excited to be burrowing deeper into a Colombian cartel than I was stressed about the demands of the task laid out before me. But, over time, as the operation became more complicated, my psychological state became more fragile. I didn't realize it at the time, but the threat of violence—and the number of years continuously working undercover—became a burden on my heart and mind. Despite this pressure, I never wanted to be pulled out, even for a few months. I was afraid that I would lose my edge if I became a traditional agent again; the only way to do my job well was to be Manny down to my bones. It's the ultimate contradiction of the covert technique: never again being an aboveground agent was the best thing for our case.

Moreover, it was not lost on me how important this case was to the FBI as a whole. Without me, we wouldn't understand how the cartel's financial stronghold over the international drug trade actually operated. Although every case for which I worked as a deep-undercover agent became one of my darlings, things for which I cared immensely, things through which I held a deep sense of pride and responsibility, the money laundering case was *mine*. I owned it. But the insanity of a case like this was that, nearly every day, I had $1 million in my car and didn't know if someone was about to knock on my window, raise a machine gun, and take my life. Being a money launderer exposed me to a more immediate form of danger than that of a smuggler; the closer I came to the money, the more risk I encountered. Maybe I should have been pulled out, given a breather. Maybe the FBI should've found another agent to embed with me, so I wasn't shouldering all the pressure alone—and maybe I shouldn't have put so much pressure on myself. But my ego wouldn't let a check-in get in the way of me seeing this investigation to its end. Plus, who would replace me now? I was in so deep that the cartels wouldn't work with anyone else. I couldn't bear to be pulled off the case, this thing that had become a crease in my heart.

To make matters worse, it wasn't Santo who would be checking in with me, but rather Special Agent in Charge (SAC) Dick Sanders, the big boss on the island. Although the

## DE NOCHE, TODOS LOS GATOS SON NEGROS

FBI sent me back to Quantico for formal psychological evaluations, it was Dick who checked in with me while I was in the thick of it; the FBI understood how important undercover agents were to the success of big cases like this, and it fell upon the SACs to meet with us and ensure that we were being placed neither in physical nor mental danger. I planned to tell Dick what he wanted to hear. I wanted him to know how thrilled I was to be doing this job, not to think that I couldn't handle it.

Jimmy, my administrative case agent and direct link to Dick, called me.

"Eleven p.m. Meet me behind the supermarket," he said, and hung up. I arrived as instructed and pulled my sports car up to his covert Toyota sedan.

"The old man wants to see you," he said.

"At the house, right?" I asked, referencing one of our safe houses in San Juan, where we held secret meetings and in which I would sometimes clean myself before going home to Maria and my boys.

Jimmy nodded. "Tomorrow, after dinner. He'll be waiting for you."

The following evening, with dusk firmly settled on the island, I crept down the block and toward the house. The home sat on a canal flanked by mangroves that stretched out to the bay, with one of our covert boats tethered to a pier off the backyard. I pulled into the garage and closed the door behind me. Jimmy's Toyota was already inside; he always shuttled Dick to these meetings, a security precaution since Dick was a public figure. His face was known to the cartels. We couldn't risk anyone seeing he was meeting with his prized undercover agent.

I walked into the kitchen to find Jimmy pouring three

glasses of whiskey. "He's in the dining room," he said. I turned the corner to find Dick sitting at the table.

"Hello, sir," I said. Dick was an old-school Hoover boy, and I always addressed him with the necessary formalities. But he and I shared a deeper bond. I had been in the academy with his son, and Dick kept an eye on my career as I rose through the ranks in Miami and made my way to San Juan. I extended my arm for a handshake, but he rose from his seat and gave me a hug.

"Take a seat," he said, releasing me from his grip. I pulled out a chair and sat down. Jimmy joined us and placed our whiskeys down on the table. We gently nursed our drinks. This was official business, not some cartel meeting. Plus, I was talking with the boss. I had to appear calm, professional, and not under some self-imposed order not to crack.

"How are you?" Dick asked.

"I'm fine," I said. "Things are going really well. I just met with Toro's courier, Julio Tamez. He seems ready to spill some details on the other big players involved in the scheme."

"That's great, Suarez. You've already ensnared so many major players. HQ is really excited. They are considering this a major case. In fact, this is now the number one case in the bureau, because of the cartel groups involved. We've never seen access like this before, and we have other intelligence from our contacts in Colombia showing that this money-laundering operation may reach up to the highest levels of the Colombian government."

"Are you sure?" I asked. I didn't doubt the intelligence—nothing truly surprised me anymore—but I was happily shocked that the group we had infiltrated may be the one to break open the entire Colombian narco-political establishment.

"We're confident, yes," Dick said. He took a sip of his whiskey. "We just need you to get it on the wire. That's how we prove this damn thing."

"I just need more time," I said. "The longer I spend with these people, the more they trust me."

"Time. That's what I wanted to talk to you about," Dick said. "How are you doing, really?"

Like in many other aspects of my life—how I communicated with my father, what I was able, or willing, to share with my wife about my job—there was always a code of silence when it came to speaking to my superiors about the stress of any undercover case. I knew in my heart that I could handle it, but I didn't want to risk overexplaining, overthinking, or over-contextualizing my experiences and my emotional perceptions of danger. The constant struggle of working undercover wasn't necessarily the prospect of actually being unmasked by criminals, but rather figuring out a way to manage the stress that came with trying to prevent that from happening, in that the stress of prevention almost outweighed the danger of the event I was trying to avert. Doing this type of work was balancing the duality of doing something no one else had ever done before—which gave me a pure, unadulterated thrill—with the fear of the repercussions if I slipped up. Not only could I personally be in danger, but the entire mission was on the line, too: something bigger than me but for which I was still, in some ways, responsible. So, with all that in mind, I just stared at Dick directly in the eyes and said, "I'm great."

"You certainly *look* great," he said. It was common knowledge I was burning the candle at both ends, and I probably did look exhausted, but he was commenting on my attire, which was completely different than when he saw me in the office: loafers without socks, blue jeans, and a silk shirt. I had also grown my hair into a pseudo-mullet, with thick curls that hung down the back of my neck. And, of course, my mustache, which danced atop my lip when I spoke. Dick may have been the big boss, but he wasn't averse to sarcasm, a willingness to bust my balls to make a point.

"Let me put it this way, Suarez: Do you see an ending to this case?" It was a trick question. He could see right through me—that adrenaline, and nothing else, was carrying me through this operation. What he really meant was: Who am I now? Manny, or Martin? And if the former, could I see myself becoming Martin again? With this question, he wasn't referring to my style of dress, or the lingo I used, but rather the emotional and psychological demands of assuming this character, the intangible effects of becoming someone else for years at a time.

"*De noche, todos los gatos son negros,*" I said. At night, all the cats are black. It was the most honest thing I had said to anyone in years. He sat with my words for what seemed like an eternity.

"Are you seeing Maria and the kids enough?" he asked.

"Yeah, I mean, when I can."

"You've been under a lot of pressure, Martin," he said, his tone softening. "A lot of close calls. I read the reports. Ella and Appa. Those really had me spooked."

"It was fine," I said, brushing it off. "They weren't a problem at all."

Dick turned to Jimmy, who was taking notes of our conversation. "Jimmy, let's make sure Martin gets his R&R. A trip to the States, a vacation for his family."

"You got it, boss," Jimmy said.

"I'll cover you with the brass in DC," Dick said to me. "They don't want you off this case, but you have a long career ahead of you. I need you alive if we are going to do this again down the road."

I kept my composure, but my heart had tied itself into a knot: A little time away with my wife and children was exactly what I needed right now. But I also didn't want to take a break when we were so close to nabbing the cartel's leaders.

"Where would you like to go?" Jimmy asked me.

"I don't know," I said. I thought of all the places we could visit, all the sites we could see, what would make me most happy and keep my family safe. I needed something secluded, peaceful, a sanctuary to take me away from this case, if even for a fleeting moment.

I rubbed my chin. "Maybe the Poconos?"

\* \* \*

AT ITS CORE, BEING an undercover agent is about double-crossing people. This nucleus of betrayal, so inherent to the covert technique, acts like a prism, and its refraction hits all aspects of an agent's life. Not only am I betraying the relationships I've built with drug lords and money launderers, but also that of my own family. Going undercover is a zero-sum game. Justice wins, but everybody else loses. And although I was relieved to be given time off to spend with my family, I knew that, even far away from the dirty streets of Puerto Rico, I wouldn't be able to turn off the switch of being Manny. He'd follow me, and stay in my heart, wherever I went.

Before I left for my much-needed vacation, I wanted to see my father. My house, like any house in Puerto Rico that withstood the annual hurricane season, required constant upkeep. And with me having been gone for the better part of a year, some repairs were necessary. Our drainage ditch had swelled with the seasonal rush of rainwater, and the roof above my patio leaked. I asked my father if we could spend a day together and do some domestic work. He didn't hesitate; anything to see his son.

He came over first thing in the morning, and we got to work. He brought his ladder, some roofing nails, gooey tar, and asphalt sheets. He manned the materials while I climbed onto the roof and fielded his directions. I was almost forty years old, and yet I was still in awe of his command and the knowledge he bestowed onto me. I had become an engineer for the Navy, a guy who made sure missiles launched properly, and here I was, listening to my dad tell me how to lay shingle. It reminded me of our time together when I was a boy, doing good in the community by helping out with home repairs for the needy. Now, the roles were reversed: I was doing the work and he was handing me materials. Back then, as we worked together, he shared words of wisdom on how to be a good man. Working undercover for the FBI had taught me similar lessons, but I knew, even in this private moment with my father, I couldn't share the specifics of the moral foundation that my job—a career that he wanted for me—had laid beneath my feet. Instead, I continued to crouch down on the roof and follow his instructions, one shingle at a time.

After patching the roof, we moved over to installing a drainage system. We made a trip to the hardware store and bought a few long PVC tubes, then came back to dig a deep trench that stretched from the side of my house all the way through the backyard. It was backbreaking work. As I shoveled scoop after scoop of rocky soil into a wheelbarrow, I thought back to pulling bales of cocaine out of the ocean. But here, I was making my father proud, not pleasing some drug lord. I was taking care of my family's home—which entailed more pressure than a covert smuggling mission.

By late afternoon, we had nearly finished. My father and I sat on the back patio together, both of us coated in sweat, and shared a couple of beers. I had put on some weight since becoming a money launderer (being fat was almost a projection of pride, knowing that manual labor wasn't required for getting rich). My lungs burned and my back ached. My mind whirled, knowing that my other life, as Manny, was still waiting for me outside the bubble of this normal afternoon. I was dead tired: mentally and physically exhausted. My father could tell.

"How's work?" he asked.

I looked up at him, trying my hardest to mask the pressure that the FBI had put on me—that I had put on myself. "Good," I said. "It's good."

He nodded. "Good," he said. "I'm glad." We sat there in silence for what seemed like a long while. I thumbed the label on my beer bottle and rubbed some dirt off my jeans. I took solace in this talisman, of a son's time with his father. I wondered if my own sons would be able to create similar memories with me. I wanted so badly to tell my father all the contours of this massive undercover money-laundering operation, to let him know that I had made it into the heart of a Colombian drug cartel, that I was doing my best to take down the bad guys, that I was doing all I could to make him proud. But I knew I couldn't. I knew it would put all that I had worked for in jeopardy, and possibly, endanger my father's life. I also knew that, if he didn't approve of how much danger I was in, my heart wouldn't let me continue working undercover. To be honest, since I became an FBI agent, there was never enough time for my father and me to be together in any concerted way. It was always a few stolen hours here, a few stolen hours there, the secrets I couldn't tell forming a space between us. Our bond was now defined by what wasn't said, versus what was. Silence—the failure of disclosure—had become the foundation of our relationship. It was a stalemate—that crude zero-sum game. So, we sat there and gently sipped our beers, waiting for the other person to change the subject.

"Maria says you're taking a vacation?" he asked.

"Yeah," I said. "We are going to the Pocono Mountains, in Pennsylvania, in two days."

"With the boys?"

I nodded.

"Good," he said. "You need some time with them." He leaned forward toward me. His body curled into the same posture when, almost thirty-five years earlier, he told me that, if I wanted it badly enough, I could be an FBI agent. I could see the scar that ran down his arm, which had always reminded me that he was a strong man. "Always remember, nothing is more important than family, Martin. Nothing."

\* \* \*

AS MY VACATION CREPT closer, my phone rang more and more. By mid-1993, the North Coast Cartel had, bolstered by their monopoly over the Caribbean smuggling routes, grown exponentially. The Snail's foresight in this regard paid him back in spades. At that time, a drug lord would pay roughly 50 percent of his load's worth in transportation fees if he sent it through Mexico. But for the Caribbean, the fees were only 20 percent. The Snail was a powerhouse now, and Toro's business grew along with it. Tony and I were doing multiple pickups a week, washing nearly $10 million per month, and Toro teased that our next contract would be for $300 million.

Their success, however, was a double-edged sword. On one hand, it gave our operation untold amounts of evidence linking the money-laundering ring to drug trafficking, but it also meant that Tony and I were working ourselves ragged. When I told Tony I had to go on leave for a week, he too admitted that he needed a break. We decided we would use our uptick in cash received as an excuse. Tony called Toro and explained that he had to send me to a remote area of the island to stash money, fibbing that we couldn't smurf it fast enough. Toro understood and told us we could take some time off to catch up. I went to Tony's house the day before I was scheduled to fly to Pennsylvania, to confirm that Toro was actually going to leave us alone while I was gone.

"Are you sure we're good to go?" I asked. "I don't want to have to rush back to San Juan because you're overselling this to me."

"Manny, *todo bien*," he said, spreading his arms wide, flashing that toothy smile. "You know I'm a good talker. I worked it out for us. Don't stress."

"Good," I said, standing up to leave. "I'll see you in a week. Santo will be keeping an eye on you while I'm gone. If you need anything, give him a call."

"Hey Manny," he said, walking me to the door, his voice softening. "You're coming back, right? This isn't a trick or anything."

"Of course I am," I said. "I'll be back in a week. I promise."

"I give you hundred percent, and you give me hundred percent," he said, referencing our first conversation together when I convinced him to flip.

## INSIDE THE CARTEL

"Exactly, Tony," I said. "From me, it's always hundred percent. Always."

* * *

MARIA AND I SAT our two sons down and told them we were going on a vacation to the Poconos. They didn't know the Poconos from Los Angeles. That esoteric region of the country was completely irrelevant to two young boys who only spent their toddler years in the United States. And yet they were thrilled.

"And *guess what*," Maria said, crouched down at eye level with them. "We're going to go to Hershey Park!"

"Hershey Park! Hershey Park!" my eldest son said. He started jumping up and down, shaking his fists in excitement. My youngest son followed his lead and started running around the house as fast as he could, scampering from room to room, yelling. He made the loop and came back to Maria.

"And guess what *else*," Maria said.

"What? What? What?" they responded in unison.

"We're going to go to Busch Gardens too, and go on *all* the rides!"

"Busch Gardens! Hershey Park! Busch Gardens! Hershey Park!" they yelped in excitement. I stood off to the side and smiled, basking in my children's joy. The boys ran off to their room and Maria looked up at me. She didn't thank me for making sure I could take this vacation, didn't stroke my ego when it came to my role as a father. Our family was bound together by duty and sacrifice, and no reassurance was needed for us to know that we were each doing everything we could—in our own way—to raise our sons with love and care. But her smile, curling from ear to ear, gave her away. I could tell she was truly happy. Finally, she said: "This trip is going to mean the world to them."

We rented a three-story log cabin on Big Bass Lake with a fireplace and a large backyard lined by blueberry bushes. Every morning, Maria and my two boys would pick fresh blueberries. We'd make pancakes, the fruit so fresh they oozed juice when we cooked them. The cabin boasted a half-dozen rooms with fancy beds, but we opted to build a roaring fire in the fireplace, curl up on couch cushions and under throw blankets, and let the snap and crackle of the flames lull us to sleep.

Good on our word, we took the boys to Hershey Park and Busch Gardens. We put no restrictions on the vacation and let them gorge themselves on all manner of chocolate and sweet treats being hawked at the amusement park. The rush of sugar and the adrenaline of the vacation carried them from ride to ride, game to game. Puerto Rico was fading away with every day passed at another tourist destination, every evening spent in front of the fireplace, every morning hunched over a stack of pancakes.

And yet my phone still haunted me, connected to my body and my mind. Tony called me every day. Although Toro largely left him alone, the traffickers with whom we had built relationships were contacting him directly, enticed by my background as a smuggler. They wanted to run loads with us, convinced that the methodologies I had previously employed were more seamless than the jerry-rigged systems on which they had come to rely. "He really wants to do the load! What should I tell him?" Tony said on one call. As part of his cooperation agreement, Tony was prohibited from acting autonomously.

## INSIDE THE CARTEL

We owned him, and he had to run everything by me. I stood out on the porch, phone plugged to my ear. I could see Maria eyeing me, her hopes dashed that I could leave work behind.

"Tell him we can do a thousand units, but it will take a while to arrange it," I said. "But I have to go now. Keep me posted." I hung up and went back into the house. The boys had completed their daily run through the blueberry bushes, and Maria was preparing the batter, the cabin's griddle heating up, smoke curling off its cast-iron plate.

I walked over to my wife, who was cracking an egg into the bowl. But before I could thank her for cooking, my phone rang again. I pulled it out of my pocket and looked at the number: a Washington, DC, area code. Why would someone from FBI headquarters be calling me while I'm on vacation? *This can't be good*, I thought to myself. I looked up at Maria. She nodded in resigned approval to take the call. I walked to the bedroom, closed the door behind me, and answered.

"Hello?"

"Agent Suarez?" the voice said. "It's Unit Chief Rob Green." Rob Green was a supervisor based at FBI headquarters on the drug and money-laundering desk. Because our case into the North Coast Cartel had grown so big and became a top priority for the FBI, more supervisors came out of the woodwork to join our team. Rob Green was a liaison between Washington, DC, and San Juan and, in my opinion, wanted to ride the coattails of our case, a typical careerist. He gave me grief every chance he could get, to make sure the case was making him look good. Frustratingly, Green found his way into my ear more and more often. But still: Why was he calling me now?

"What can I do for you, Rob?" I asked.

"How is everything going in San Juan?" he asked.

"It's going just fine," I said. "But I'm actually on vacation with my family right now in Pennsylvania."

"Vacation? Why?"

"I'm on R&R," I said.

"What? R&R? Why the hell aren't you in Puerto Rico? Suarez, shit is really heating up down there. We've already positively ID'd guys from ten different countries. You should be there, not on vacation."

"Well, we can do no wrong in the eyes of the Colombians right now. They trust us, and I used that as a wedge to get some time off. Now is the time to pace ourselves, too. We have already laundered over $25 million, with much more to come. I can't act too eager with them. It works best when I play hard to get."

"Suarez, we need you down there. When will you be back?"

"In about a week," I said.

"A week?!" he bellowed. "But you're the main guy down there! Tony is alone! The subjects are calling you! Does Dick know you're off the island?"

"He's the one who made me take the vacation."

"I want you to have some time with your family, but you need to get your ass back down to San Juan as soon as possible," he said. "You volunteered for this."

"I'll be back soon," I said, and hung up. I threw my phone down onto the bed and muttered *fuck* under my breath. This was the first time I had gotten angry with anyone at the FBI over a case. Normally, my bosses were cognizant of the stressors of working undercover, of the psychological resources it demanded. But as the money-laundering case grew and grew, and attracted attention from the highest levels of the FBI and the Department of Justice, I felt like the deskbound agents and supervisors didn't view me as a real person, but rather an asset to their own careers. I didn't like that at all. Nobility had brought me to this job, not ladder climbing, and I wanted that ethos to not only carry me through the case, but dictate the viewpoint of those who were looking out for me, too.

I walked back into the kitchen. A steaming pile of pancakes sat atop a plate, ready to be gobbled up.

"I'm sorry, sweetie," I said to Maria. "That was someone at HQ."

"What did he say?"

"He didn't know I was on vacation," I said. "He was pretty pissed off. He wants me back in San Juan as soon as we are done here."

"Wait a minute," she said. "They told you to take a vacation, but they aren't supporting you to actually take a break?"

"He's just one guy," I said. "Every team has that one difficult supervisor. It's just part of the job."

"I just wanted us to have some time away," she said, placing another flapjack onto the plate, "without any distractions."

"And we are," I said. "It was just one call, and I don't care what he thinks. I'm here with you and the boys, and that's all that's on my mind right now. This is the best week I've had in years."

She looked up at me. "You promise?"

"Yes," I said. "I promise." I grabbed a pancake off the stack and took a bite. "These are delicious, by the way," I said, reaching for a napkin.

Looking back, that week is one of my fondest memories, the stress from the case receding, if even for a fleeting moment, like the ocean tide.

## CHAPTER 10

# THE BLACK MARKET PESO EXCHANGE

**TONY TOLD ME THAT THE CARTEL NEEDED CASH IN MIAMI AS** soon as possible—and that Toro's Florida-based counterpart, a man named Daniel Mayer, would be receiving the money. I had just returned from my vacation in the Poconos. I fell back into being Manny with ease; I was eager to get back to work after having spent some much-needed quality time with my family. Dick Sanders even handled Rob Green's angry grumblings, which allowed me to finish out my trip with a quiet phone. And yet, as soon as Toro knew that I was ready to work again, the daily calls started. I was back in the thick of it. And now, Tony explained, I was to take the next step in our operation. Tony knew that if he was asked to meet someone with whom I hadn't yet interacted in person (and therefore got on the wire), he was to bend the conversation toward either me joining or, better yet, me going at it alone, so I could prove my worth to Toro and infiltrate even deeper.

"Let's send Manny," Tony said to Toro the day prior. "He

has spoken with Daniel on my phone already, and Daniel invited Manny to come." Toro agreed. I really had spoken with Daniel on the phone; that wasn't a lie. Now, he was going to meet me, the new expert launderer on the island, face-to-face.

Tony gave me the details. "You remember Daniel Mayer, yes? You'll be meeting with him. He needs $40,000," he said. "It should be pretty simple. You're just giving him the checks."

"Doesn't sound too difficult," I said. "What's the money for?"

"Toro was a little cagey about it," he said, "but it's for a drug load coming out of Colombia next week. They need the cash to buy some equipment for an airdrop operation. I guess something broke at the last minute, and they need some new parts or something. Call Toro and he'll confirm all the details."

"Perfect," I said, and hung up. I immediately called Toro.

"Tony says you need me to go to Miami with some money?" I asked.

"Yes, it's urgent," he said. "When is the soonest you can leave?"

"I have the money with me now," I said. "I could leave tonight."

"Tomorrow is fine," he said. "Call Daniel when you get there. But get ready: You're definitely going."

"You got it, *jefe*."

\* \* \*

THE FBI GAVE ME a very long leash for this operation, and I didn't need to obtain approval from the higher-ups to travel within the United States. I immediately called Jimmy and filled him in on Toro's directive. He made contact with my old colleagues at the Miami field office to let them know I was coming, and arranged for an agent in San Juan to assist me during travel and be the liaison with the FBI's team in Miami. I couldn't book the flight under my real name, in case the cartel obtained my boarding pass or the flight manifest, so the other agent took the money, my gun, and my wire and flew to Miami on an earlier flight. Once I landed, I drove to a Denny's. The agent was already waiting for me in a booth. We ordered pancakes, and he secretly slid my bag across the seat to me. I reassured him that this was an easy mission, that I was just dropping off money, and that there was no need to worry.

After finishing our breakfast, I made my way to the Fontainebleau on Collins Avenue, one of the most luxurious resorts in Miami Beach. I checked into my room, picked up the phone, and called Daniel Mayer.

"I've been waiting for you to call," he said. "You made it all right? No problems?"

"No problems at all," I said. "When do you want to meet?"

He gave an address and a room number for a nearby motel. "Come over whenever," he said. "I'll be here all night." I packed the money, made sure my wire was turned on, and headed to the meeting.

A Colombian national living in Miami, Daniel Mayer held deep, long-term relationships with Colombian drug cartels, and had been Toro's stateside partner for years. Daniel was also the careful sort. I knew that us meeting at a motel was a security precaution. There was no way, for our first meeting, that he would have me to his office, and certainly not his home. Although I had been working for him and Toro for over a year, he still needed to make sure I was clean. I showed up and cased the spot: I first drove around the perimeter of the hotel, following any roads that gave an entry or exit point, and then through every inch of the parking lot. I looked into all of the cars, searching for people who seemed suspicious. I never wanted to see someone at idle, watching and waiting. The coast was clear, so I made my way to his room.

The door was cracked, so I let myself in. It was a dumpy place. This guy was a multimillionaire, and yet we met in a grungy motel. I peered around: dirty carpet, scratchy sheets, yellowed wallpaper. The room was empty—this was a classic setup, something out of the Mafia playbook. I immediately turned on my heels, slammed the door shut, and locked it behind me. I tiptoed through the room, looking for my hidden attacker. My heart raced faster and faster. I peeked into the closet. Nothing. I turned the corner, looked into the bathroom, and saw two beady eyes peering out from behind the shower curtain.

"Daniel? What are you doing? Are you taking a shower?"

Daniel opened the curtain and stepped out. He was fully clothed, shoes and all.

"Is everything okay?" I asked.

"Oh, you know, just one of my things," he said. Daniel stood six foot two, square jawed and lithe, a soccer player through and through. His skin held a deep tan, his hair a thick wave. He had a thin nose and a long face, more Moroccan than South American. I could tell his roots likely came from the Middle Easterners who settled in northern Colombia over a century ago.

We sat down on the bed, the cheap springs creaking under our weight. I placed the money bag between us.

"What time did you get in?" Daniel asked.

He already knew the answer. He was trying to trip me up. I stuck to the truth. "Noon," I said.

"Which airline? Good flight?"

"American. And, yeah, it was fine."

"Beer?" he asked. Another test. Everyone knows smugglers drink Black Label whiskey.

"I'd prefer some whiskey," I said.

"Do you like Black Label?" he asked.

"My favorite." He poured two glasses.

"You should see the bottle I have at my house." He chuckled. "One day, I will have you over and show it to you."

"I'd love to see it."

"Are those the checks?" he asked, pointing to my second bag. I nodded. He picked it up, peered inside, gave a visual count, and seemed satisfied. He smiled, took a sip of his drink, and peered at me over the rim of his glass, trying to figure me out. He was shrewder than I had anticipated. I knew if I tried to excavate for details of what this money was for, or tried to talk about the laundering operation, he would clam up—and become highly suspicious of my motives. Moreover, he was technically my boss, and a subordinate spoke only when spoken to. But I knew that I had plenty of time to pry him open like a treasure chest. The crowbar of my patience was stronger than the locks of his reservation. I just needed to play the long game with him, to let him think that he was in control.

"Are we all good?" I asked.

"Yes, Manny," he said. "Big things." He tapped the bag full of checks. "We're doing big things."

"Do you need me to bring anything back to Tony?" I asked, at least hoping I could get more evidence of conspiracy during the meeting.

"No," he said, "but I am sure you will be back here soon. We will have some more whiskey together." He slipped off his shoes, removed the sole inserts, placed the checks inside, reapplied the inserts, and slipped his feet back in. He looked up at me. "You can never be too careful, Manny," he said. "You can never be too careful."

* * *

TONY PICKED ME UP at the airport when I flew back to San Juan. He recently ditched his old jalopy and purchased a brand-new GMC Yukon with the Eddie Bauer color package. "It's my country truck," he told me, with a shrug, when I got in. As we drove back to my undercover apartment, he explained that Daniel really liked me, and that Toro was thrilled that the meeting went well. No suspicions projected, no accusations lobbed: In their eyes, I was more than legit. I was reliable, followed through on my word, and didn't make any mistakes.

"Manny, you are *in* with these guys now," Tony said.

"You see?" I asked. "There's no way they think I'm a cop now."

By this point, I had laundered over $30 million for Toro and, by extension, the North Coast Cartel. We had more than enough evidence to show a clear link between the cash proceeds from drug sales and the initial laundering of those funds, but I was still working on getting Julio Tamez to open up about the other big players in the scheme, and how the cartel actually got their money back into Colombia. I wanted names of the bankers who sent the wire transfers, and the politicians who had been corrupted. I wanted big-ticket corporations that were involved. I needed it all. Luckily, upon returning from Miami, Toro delegated much of the coming cashier check drop-offs to me. It seemed that Julio Tamez, like Daniel, had taken a liking to me, too.

I had another $1 million in cashier checks stuffed into my

bag. I turned on my wire, hopped into my sports car, and made my way to Isla Verde, Tamez's favorite rendezvous spot. I didn't understand why he chose to meet at such a grimy motel until after meeting with Daniel in his own run-down room in Miami; it seemed to be a team-wide mandate. I had been so used to the world of smuggling—flashing cash and making a scene at the fanciest restaurants—that I quickly realized that money launderers were a different breed. It's a complicated business, one that requires a financier's knowledge of the banking system, a spy's handling of covert meetings, and a criminal's ruthless disregard for the law. Most of these dudes were highly educated. In fact, the Cali Cartel's money launderer, Franklin Jurado, studied economics at Harvard. They didn't need to flash their money. They just needed to not get arrested. And so, Isla Verde it was. Better safe than sorry.

Tamez poured a couple whiskeys when I arrived. I placed my bag onto the table between us, grabbed my drink, clinked his glass, and took a long, slow sip.

"Always on time, Manny," he said. "I appreciate that."

"We're running a business, right?" I replied.

"That we are," he said. "That we are." He grabbed my bag. "One million again?"

I nodded. "All there," I said, getting ready for my first probe. "I think all the company names on the checks are spelled correctly, so there won't be any issues getting them deposited into the right accounts."

He laughed. "Yes, there are so many companies. It's hard to keep track of them all."

"What do these companies do, exactly?" I nudged. "Why would Toro bring them into his operation? It's a lot of people to manage."

He laughed again. He seemed tickled to educate me, a

newbie who was still trying to figure this all out. "Manny, they aren't real companies," he said. "They're all fake."

*Interesting*, I thought to myself, frantically arranging the puzzle pieces in my head. *They have powerful bankers who oversee accounts for fake businesses, and they put drug money into those accounts. But how does that help them?* My mind whirled, trying to figure out how to keep the conversation going, but my face told a different story: I just stared at him, trying my best to look dumbfounded.

"Let me just put it this way, Manny," he said. "We *own* the bank."

Tamez explained that the companies to whom these checks were issued were merely shell corporations that were controlled by Toro and his offshore banking counterparts in Aruba. The small island nation, which sits a mere fifty miles off the northern coast of Colombia, was the perfect place to set up a cartel money-laundering operation (its name literally derives from *Oruba*, which means "well-situated island" in the language of the Caiquetío, its original inhabitants). A puddle jumper could take off from Maicao, where Toro was based, and land in Oranjestad, Aruba's capital, in under an hour. It certainly made sense that the majority of the bank accounts that Tamez mentioned during our first meeting were stationed there.

Twenty miles long and six miles wide, Aruba was first colonized by Spain in 1499, who enslaved the natives and forced them to mine gold in the present-day Dominican Republic. From there came a game of political hot potato: The Netherlands seized Aruba in 1636 during the Thirty Years' War but gave up control of the island to the British in 1806 during the Napoleonic Wars, only to regain control of it again in 1819. The island lay mostly dormant economically until the 1890s, when enterprising farmers discovered that aloe vera grew quite well atop its gently rolling hills. The soothing extract became Aruba's dominant export and largest contributor to its fledgling economy, which soon came to include oil refineries as a vertebra of its financial backbone. After Nazi occupation during the Second World War, Aruba was bundled with other Dutch islands to form the Netherland Antilles. This sister-island arrangement didn't last long. In 1986, Aruba broke off from its Caribbean counterparts and became a constituent country of the Kingdom of the Netherlands. As such, it continued to be governed by the Dutch, although their political system did establish some crucial autonomy—namely related to trade and banking, which, in the coming years, formed the crux of its money-laundering ties to Colombian drug cartels.

It was common knowledge that Aruban banks and businesses had ties to the narco-trade, and in 1989 a minister of Parliament even proclaimed publicly that his home country had become so infested with money launderers and drug traffickers that he vowed to fight "the washing machine." Despite his hard-line honesty, and claims of public corruption, nothing changed. The washing machine kept churning: Between 1992 and 1997, $1.4 billion flowed through Aruban banks, a massive sum for an island with a population of only 83,000 people. "Aruba has rented itself out to the bad guys," a US government official once told the *Wall Street Journal*.

Tamez also told me the names of the bankers with whom Toro allegedly collaborated: Alec sand Ethan Moore. They were cousins, and executives at SurBank, one of the largest financial institutions in Aruba. But these were not rogue employees who colluded with Colombian drug cartels on the down-low. Tamez wasn't being coy with his proclamation: their family *literally* owned the bank. In fact, the billionaire

Moore dynasty was known as the Rothschilds of Aruba, and their influence and fortune touched every aspect of the island's economy. Originally from Lebanon, the Moores were savvy businessmen who had built empires. The family patriarch, Jassy Moore, owned the island's largest newspaper and a seaside casino. But his greatest achievement was in trade. Jassy's family owned Moore Free Zone Trading Company NV, which dominated the country's imports and exports and operated under the free-trade zone, a special economic zone with a duty-free designation that allowed reexportation to third-party locations—including Colombia. Free-trade zone companies are exempt from local taxes and customs, allowing shipments originally bound for South America to make a pit stop on the island, avoid financial scrutiny and regulatory inspection, and then be rerouted, or reexported, to their final destination. The Moores also operated export businesses in Panamanian and Venezuelan free-trade zones, giving them unprecedented trade access with Colombia. This, combined with owning a bank that operated with very little regulatory oversight, allegedly allowed the Moore cousins to become, alongside Toro, the linchpin in the global narco-economy: the money launderers' money launderers.

I hadn't heard of the Moore family, but they had been on the US government's radar for some time. When drug traffickers were interviewed in the late 1980s during the fallout of the Iran-Contra Affair, one name kept popping up: the Moores of Aruba. "[They are] the big family in Aruba we used for laundering money and moving cocaine," one smuggler told an investigator for Senator John Kerry. It was later alleged, but not proven, that the Moores laundered money for a faction of the Sicilian Mafia that reportedly supplied 70 percent of the world's heroin. The Italian newspaper *Corriere della Sera* described Aruba as "the first state to be bought by the bosses Cosa Nostra," and a DEA agent once said, "[The Sicilian Mafia] phoned Moore's trading company and his place. They certainly talked to each other." (A descendant of the Moores was elected a senator of the Aruban Parliament in 2021; he has never been implicated in a crime.)

"Are you following me, Manny?" Tamez asked after explaining the seemingly incestuous relationship between the Moore cousins and organized crime.

"Yes, yes," I said, logging the words *SurBank* and *Alec and Ethan Moore* into my mind, hoping my wire also heard loud and clear. "Please, continue."

Tamez claimed that, after the North Coast Cartel's drug money was transferred into cashier's checks, he would fly to Aruba and deposit the money into various bank accounts at SurBank. "Toro and the Moore cousins use the money to purchase merchandise. It could be car tires, it could be washing machines, it could be cigarettes. They then ship that merchandise to their businesses that operate under the free-trade zones in Aruba, Panama, or Venezuela. The merchandise is repackaged and smuggled into Colombia, where it is sold to their contacts in respective markets for pesos. That money gets put into Colombian bank accounts, which Toro and the Moores also control, and then the cartels are given their money back. Toro and the Moores have their hand in every step of the process: smuggling routes from Colombia to the US, the banks where the money is deposited, the companies that purchase goods, the import businesses that move those products into Colombia, and the Colombian politicians that take bribes and turn a blind eye to their operation."

"It all seems very well thought out," I said, stunned at what I was hearing, hoping his claims about the Moores could later be proven in a court of law.

"It has to be, right? It's very tough to use American dollars in Colombia. And, I mean, how would you even get the money back from the United States, anyway? Put it on a plane? It's too risky and time-consuming. The cartels want to ship their merchandise out and, a few weeks later, see pesos in their bank accounts. Which is why they need Toro and the Moore cousins. They are the only people who can turn the cartel's cocaine, which is sold in the United States for American dollars, into pesos, which the cartels need back in Colombia to continue doing business. All the billions of dollars the cartels have made over the past decade? That's because of Toro and the Moore cousins."

"Wow," I said, making sure I heard him right: *billions*. Tamez claimed that these men didn't just launder money; they had seemingly created an entire shadow economy. "There must be a lot of risk for Toro involved."

"Yes," he said, "but also a lot of reward. Toro is actually taking responsibility for the Snail's cocaine shipments once they leave Colombia. He buys the account, basically a promise to pay the cartel back in pesos at some point in the near future, which is why he's controlling the delivery of the money from the smugglers, the picking up of the money by guys like you, and then routing the money back to Colombia himself. He makes a big cut at every step along the way. It's very lucrative for him. But you have to think of Toro more like a money broker rather than a drug trafficker. For example, a cartel will tell him that their load is worth $100 million. He'll take a flat-rate six percent fee off the top, and then he'll implement an exchange rate to transfer the remaining cash from dollars to

## THE BLACK MARKET PESO EXCHANGE

pesos. Through a normal, aboveground currency exchange—like if you're going to London for vacation and exchange your dollars for British pounds—you'd usually lose about five percent of your money's value through the transaction. His profit comes from the spread between those two prices, sort of like how traders and brokers do their jobs on Wall Street. He usually charges around eleven percent, about double what you'd pay if done legally. But since the cartels can't use traditional banks, they have no problem agreeing to Toro's terms. Hell, they would probably pay the same amount of money if they tried to fly their proceeds back to Colombia from the United States. This process, however, is much more reliable."

"So, it's basically a black market peso exchange," I said. "It's not like cartels can just go down to a big American bank in Miami with a truck full of money and exchange dollars for pesos and ship them home. This system is a way for the cartels to get money that they can actually use back in Colombia, to further their own goals and hold on to power."

He raised his glass and took down the rest of his whiskey. "Now you're catching on, Manny," he said. "Money is power."

# CHAPTER 11

# CARNAGE

**MY MEETING WITH JULIO TAMEZ PROVIDED THE FBI WITH** our most important breakthrough to date. As with all of my money pickups with Toro's drug smugglers, I memorialized my meetings with Tamez in written reports. They gave context to, and buttressed information gathered on, my wire recordings. But I couldn't just head back to my undercover apartment, pull out a pencil and a sheet of FBI letterhead, and write down what I had seen and heard. I never kept any FBI-related materials at my apartment in case the cartel hired a bagman or spy to break in and root through my belongings. At the start of the money-laundering operation, I secured a villa in Isla Verde, a high-end beachside community just east of San Juan. I dubbed it my "writing villa," which acted as my de facto FBI office. Part of a gated subdivision, it had a first-floor balcony that overlooked the ocean. It was surrounded by palm trees, thick vegetation, and a large privacy fence. I was safe from prying eyes. No one from the cartel knew that I had access to this property. Even Tony was in the dark. It was my tether to the outside world, a secure communication facility with my squad, and a place where I could basically keep a diary of what I had experienced day to day. For a life built upon secrecy, it was the only place where I was allowed to be open and honest about who I really was.

And yet, I couldn't just keep my reports in a desk drawer or strewn atop the dining room table. Santo, Jimmy, and I developed strict protocols for how my reports would be written, stored, and transferred back to the squad. The FBI gave me a bulky Dell laptop, its computing power on par with what you'd expect from a piece of technology from the early 1990s. It didn't even have an internal hard drive; we stored my reports on old-school floppy disks. I kept the laptop stashed in a hidden compartment within an armoire in one of the bedrooms. To retrieve it, I'd remove one of the shelves, unlatch the false back, and pull out the clunky machine. I'd insert a fresh floppy disk and begin typing. When I was done, I'd label and date the disk and place everything back into the secret compartment. The following day, Jimmy would pick it up, swap my floppy disk with a fresh one, and we'd start the process over again.

If the intelligence I gathered was groundbreaking, Jimmy and Santo would call a meeting with me to discuss the details more thoroughly. I had a feeling that they would want to meet after Julio Tamez revealed to me the explosive information about the Black Market Peso Exchange—and I was right. Jimmy instructed me to meet him at La Plazita, a weekly block party in San Juan. Thousands of people came every week. It was the perfect place to blend into a crowd for a quick meeting. "Santo is coming, too," Jimmy told me.

I made my way to the event at dusk, parked my undercover car on a side street, and looked for Jimmy as I wove through the crowd. He was the only FBI employee whom I could meet in public places; he had been a plainclothes agent, more or less a light undercover, since my smuggling days. Most cartel men assumed he was one of my associates, an ongoing legend that we continued to exploit throughout the money-laundering investigation. I spotted him leaning against a vendor's stand, sipping a beer, trying his best to blend into the crowd. We met eyes as I approached. He nodded.

"Drink?" he asked. "You look like you need one."

I laughed. He was always busting my balls. "Sure," I said, turning to the vendor.

"I'll have a vodka with grapefruit juice," I said, thinking it would be a nice departure from my steady stream of Black Label whiskey. I grabbed my drink and turned back to Jimmy.

"Where's Santo?" I asked.

"He's waiting for us in his car two blocks down," Jimmy said. "Let's go."

We walked through the packed crowd, dodging businessmen mingling with their mistresses, gaggles of teenagers enjoying a night on the town, and lovestruck couples falling in with the revelry. We turned down a side street. Santo's car sat in the shadow between two street poles, its taillights glowing bright red. We climbed in.

"You're partying without me, I see," Santo said, eyeing our drinks.

"You gotta go undercover," Jimmy said. "You're missing out."

Santo smiled and put the car in drive. "Let's go for a spin," he said, and hit the gas. "So, Martin," he said, "I read your report, but tell me again what Julio Tamez told you."

I explained what I knew so far: With the alleged help of the Moore cousins in Aruba, Toro had built a multibillion-dollar global money-laundering empire that disguised drug payments as legitimate import shipments. It was the first time in the history of the FBI that we had been volunteered this information directly from a criminal target. It was a groundbreaking piece of intelligence that changed the federal government's understanding of the narco-economy.

"You know," Santo said, after I finished reiterating what Julio Tamez told me, "we have over a dozen wiretaps running right now, and we've been hearing bits and pieces of this during conversations, but we really didn't know what it all meant."

"They are very cagey about it all," I said, "and everything is completely compartmentalized. I think Tamez and Daniel Mayer are the only people who know everything. But Tamez seems easier to crack."

"You need to keep working on him," Santo said. "Everything you're getting is supporting what our analysts are digging through, and what our surveillance is picking up on the wiretaps. We're proving the nexus between money and drugs—and more. This is going to be big, I know it. All of us just need to do our part."

I nodded. I knew exactly what he meant. Just because I was the lone deep-undercover agent on the team didn't mean that I was the only one establishing valuable evidence for our case. Each sector of our squad gathered their own puzzle pieces, but only when all of them were fitted together were we able to see the big picture of what the cartels were really pulling off. It was often the case, however, that the information I gathered from my conversations with smugglers or money couriers like Julio Tamez was the last piece of the puzzle that made everything come into focus. And yet I never forgot I was merely one piece in this massive jigsaw. We were all there, connected for a common goal: to take down one of Colombia's most powerful drug cartels.

"Tamez trusts me," I said. "Even Tony said that I am one of them now. It's just a matter of time before we get everything."

# INSIDE THE CARTEL

Santo pulled up to the curb on the edge of La Plazita, our little excursion complete. He put the car in park and looked back at me. "You are one of them now, Martin," he said, "but I still want you to be careful. You never know what could happen."

* * *

TORO HAD RECENTLY CONNECTED me with Jorge Sanchez, a drug smuggler who ran loads to the island from Colombia. I would pick up money from Jorge every few weeks, and we got to know each other. For our first meeting, he arrived in a suit with wide lapels and a starched collar that reached up to his earlobes. We met at El Padrinito, a fast-casual restaurant just outside of San Juan. He was clearly well-educated, and not someone I would expect to be a smuggler. As we got to know each other, he shared that he had previously been a captain in the United States Army.

"Can you believe that?" he said to me.

"You've obviously changed," I said.

"I developed a heart condition, and they kicked me out," he said. He hunched over the table, clearly wounded by the rejection. "All I wanted to be in life was an Army officer. My father, my grandfather: they were in the Army, too. But now that dream is dead, so I do this now."

It was strange to realize how easily one's life can transform—that, in an instant, a person can turn left instead of right, revealing just how slippery the moral slope can be. I saw so much of myself in Jorge; we both grew up in Puerto Rico and shared the idea that the military could offer us a path to success. And yet here I was, wearing a wire as an agent for the US government, trying to implicate him, a member of a drug cartel, in a crime. As I sat across from him, I wanted to turn back into Martin, grab his shoulders, remind him of his duty as a soldier, and shake some sense into him. But I stayed quiet, sipped my drink, and listened to his story. We finished our lunch. I took his money and brought it back to be smurfed, laundered, and routed back to Colombia, to the very men that paved Jorge's crooked path.

My second pickup with Jorge came a few weeks later. I was at Tony's house when my phone rang. It was Toro.

"Yes, *jefe*?" I said.

"You're meeting with Jorge again," Toro said. "You'll be getting $500,000."

"I'll be there," I said and hung up. I placed the phone down and met eyes with Tony. He knew what Toro had said without even hearing his voice.

"I can't come tonight," he said. "I have plans with my wife."

"I can do this one by myself," I said. "It's just Jorge again."

"Any progress with him?"

"I'm working on it. He mentioned drugs during our first meeting, so we have a wiretap on him now," I explained. "I'm going to try and see if I can get him to pitch me on doing a load together. He's a big player with the Colombians, so having him confirm again that the money he's giving us comes from drugs is going to make the case stronger."

"You're a whiz, Manny," he said. "I have full faith in you." It still felt strange to have Tony, a cartel money launderer, compliment me. And yet, I took it as proof of my approach to undercover work: getting criminals to like me, to work with me, was the only way I myself could succeed.

I left Tony and went back to my undercover apartment to prepare for the meeting. I packed my gun and my wire, and checked in with Santo, who confirmed that we would have surveillance on the meeting and that the wiretap on Jorge was up and running so we could cross-reference our in-person conversation with the phone calls he would make after the meeting. I then called Jorge to confirm the time and place.

I made my way to the restaurant and pulled into the parking lot. I saw his truck and parked next to it. He had a large cardboard box in the back, presumably filled with the $500,000 I was supposed to collect. It felt strange to see the money out in the open like that. In Puerto Rico, you never leave anything in the back of a truck; it would almost always get stolen. Its casual placement meant that he must have his own lookouts keeping eyes on our meeting—as did I. I hoped that his men wouldn't spot my own surveillance. I didn't want a repeat of the situation with Appa. I entered the restaurant and joined him at a table in the rear of the dining room. I shook his hand before taking a seat, the formalities of our previous meetings gone. We were just two buddies now, doing a business deal.

"Order a beer," he said, "and let's have something to eat. Today's special is fried chicken. We've got to try it." I followed his lead, ordered the chicken, and tipped back a beer to wash it down. I had mentioned in passing, during our first meeting, that I had access to nondescript boats outfitted with souped-up engines. I didn't elaborate, but I hoped it would plant a seed into his mind, a way to pry loose more information about his drug-running operation. Like I told Tony, I was waiting for him to pitch me on moving a load together.

"You still have those boats?" he asked, right on cue.

I nodded, taking another bite of my chicken. "We should go fishing sometime," I said.

"Or we could use them to do a load together."

I demurred. "Ah," I said, "I'm not *metiendo palos* anymore.

I get a good cut through Toro. I don't make nearly as much as I did smuggling, but at least I won't go to jail."

He laughed. "Come on, just one load together. You can make a little extra scrap. How did you move it before? Did you use containers?"

"I just picked it up at sea. Airdrops," I said. "I would usually pick up loads around Cuba and then bring them into Miami. Other times I would do pickups off the coast and bring them in through Maternillo," referring to a remote village within Fajardo on the eastern tip of Puerto Rico.

"Fajardo? Interesting," he said. "You know, I have a very large load coming in soon. I get skittish every time I get a big shipment. There's so much going on, so many things happening at once. I'm just trying to relax right now." He drank more and more, trying to calm his nerves and maybe suppress the excitement of the profit he'd make once the drugs landed. I tried to act uninterested. I couldn't understand why he was telling me this; smugglers are normally quite cagey about when their loads were being delivered. Maybe it was just a guy trying to shake his nerves. Or maybe it was Toro planting a false-flag operation, to see if I would betray him, to see if I was a snitch—in that, if his load were to be seized upon delivery, I would likely be the person responsible, because no one else had been told about the details. Or maybe he just trusted me now? I didn't want to get conned, so I listened, nodded my head, tried to gather more intelligence, and drank my beer.

"It's a pretty big load. Five hundred kilos," he said. "I wish it was more, though."

"All I ever dealt with was large loads," I said, trying not to be too specific, but also trying to keep him talking. My wire was listening. "It's not worth it to do anything under five hundred kilos."

## INSIDE THE CARTEL

"I totally agree, Manny," he said. "I get all of my shipments from El Caracol directly. He refuses to send anything under five hundred kilos."

"Smart guy," I said, trying to play it cool, but this piece of information was crucial. This was the second smuggler from whom I picked up money who confirmed that they received their drugs directly from the Snail, the top dog at the North Coast Cartel. It proved that these routes were controlled by North Coast, and that Toro was their money launderer.

"Very smart," he said. "He sends batches to Saint Nevis, and then they are broken down, repackaged, and shipped. He has a crew of Dominicans with speedboats that make the deliveries. But even five hundred kilos seems small to me now. That's why I'm hoping we could do some business together. Pull off something big."

"I've thought about getting back into bringing in *palos*, here and there," I said, "but I need reliable partners."

"After this is all said and done, we can do something together," he said, raising his beer. We clinked and finished off our respective bottles. The chicken was long gone. Jorge called over the waitress for the bill. I pulled out a wad of cash and threw it onto the table.

"All right," he said, "now let's go out to my truck and get the money."

\* \* \*

AS SOON AS I was on the road with Jorge's money in my trunk, I called Jimmy and told him to meet me behind the mall, at one of our covert rendezvous spots. He was already there, waiting for me, when I pulled into the parking lot. I crept up next to him and rolled down my window.

"What's going on?" he asked. I never called an emergency meeting unless it was important.

"Jorge is coming in with a big load soon," I said. "He might have just been boasting about it, but if it's for real, it's going to be big—at least five hundred kilos. And he said he's getting it directly from the Snail. It might be coming into Fajardo—he had this look on his face when I mentioned that area of the island, as if that was his entry point—but, regardless, I bet they are going to bring it to San Juan."

"Wow," Jimmy said. "That's great, Martin. We've had Jorge's phones tapped ever since your first meeting, and we were getting details of some type of shipment on the wire, too. But it's just been chatter. We couldn't make out any specifics. Let me talk with Santo and we'll let you know our plan. Hopefully we can track the load and find a way to seize it."

"I'll be at the apartment," I said. "Just call me."

"We will," he said. "Good job, Martin. This is big."

I sped out of the parking lot and made my way to my undercover apartment. I cracked open another beer and waited for Jimmy or Santo to call me with an update. It was now past 10:00 p.m. I paced around my living room, checking my watch, knowing that, if Jorge really was bringing in the drugs over the next couple of days, we didn't have much time to put a plan together. Finally, my phone rang. It was Santo.

"Tell me exactly what you said to Jimmy," Santo said. I reiterated all that I had learned from Jorge: five hundred kilos from the Snail, likely coming into Fajardo sometime soon and probably ending up in San Juan.

"I've known about it," he said. "We got it on the wire, but they never said when and where."

"Well, it's definitely on its way!" I said.

"Don't worry, Martin. We will have eyes all over the island.

We'll find them and figure out where they are taking it." I hoped we could make the seizure. And if we couldn't, I would at least be able to create a crucial nexus between the drugs that were coming in and the money Toro would direct me to pick up from Jorge a few days later.

\* \* \*

I WAS DEAD ASLEEP when my phone rang. I opened my eyes, and the clock came into focus: 5:09 a.m. I answered the call. It was Santo.

"Martin," he said. "Jorge lost his shipment. He got robbed. There was a shootout."

"What?!" I yelled. "Where?"

"Right after Loíza, by the mangroves."

"Goddamn it," I said. "Any idea who did it?"

"Not yet," he said. "We just heard about it. We haven't even gotten eyes on it yet. But I'm hearing that it was really bad."

"Let me see if I can get out there, see what happened, and gather some intelligence," I said.

"Be careful, Martin," Santo replied.

"I will."

I hung up the phone and threw on some dirty clothes that were strewn across my floor. I ran down to the parking garage and jumped into one of my backup covert vehicles. I left the city, careened through the forest, a skinny road flanked by palm trees and swamp, and then, at a break in the road, the bloody scene came into focus: more than half-a-dozen dead bodies strewn across the road, cars smashed into one another, the blue Ford Ranger that had been carrying the drugs flipped over in a ditch, the bales of cocaine spilling out of the bed. Most of the dead men had been covered in sheets by the local police, who were on scene, the fabric blossoming with their freshly spilled blood. One man hung out of the truck by his waist, his head blown apart, execution-style. I thought to myself: *Why hadn't the drugs been taken?* And that's when I realized, among the slew of dead bodies, the machine guns, the pools of blood: no one made it out of this shootout alive.

I went back to my undercover apartment and called Santo, to tell him what I had seen and try and parse out what was going to happen next.

"They're all dead," I said. "It's a bloodbath out there. And it doesn't look like any of the coke was taken."

"A couple of guys actually made it out alive," Santo said. "One of the ambushers was dropped off at the hospital. I'm trying to get a couple agents in there to interview him, but it doesn't look like he's going to make it."

"Good God," I said. "How did this happen?"

"We've had Jorge on the wire all night," he said. "I think he knew the robbers, as if he worked with them before but cut them out at some point. Whatever the connection, they knew Jorge's route from Fajardo to San Juan. It was an ambush. They were sitting ducks."

Revenge. Of course it wasn't random. This made perfect sense to me; there are no friends in the drug world, only opportunities. "What does Jorge have planned?" I asked.

"He's been on the phone constantly since it happened," Santo said. "He's calling every sicario he knows to find this gang and *kill every single one of those motherfuckers.* His words. We're trying to follow all of them. There's definitely going to be retaliation, and soon."

"This is the world we live in, Santo," I said.

"Tell me about it. Should you call him?"

"No," I said. "He was supposed to give me the money from this load next week. He'll call me. I'm sure of it."

"All right," Santo said. "I have some photographs of the victims with me. Meet me in a couple of hours so you can take a look. Maybe you can identify some of these guys." We set the meeting and I looked through the photographs: bullet-ridden bodies, pools of blood, faces destroyed past the point of recognition. A few of the victims had been shot in the eyes at point-blank range. It was carnage at its worst.

Seeing all that death and destruction made me shake with fear, knowing that one of those dead bodies could have easily been me. I knew that working with a cartel was a dangerous game, but I always made sure to maneuver in a way that avoided violence. That's always an agent's number one priority: get the goods without getting killed. I've seen death before, but this was surreal, realizing how vulnerable I actually was. If a gang of bandits could figure out when a load of cocaine was coming onto the island, they could also figure out that I was constantly carrying millions of dollars in my trunk. It wouldn't take much for me to end up like this, a dozen bullet holes in my chest, dead in a ditch. Tony had his own brush with fate a few weeks prior. He was set to pick up a small amount of money from a smuggler but got caught in traffic. He called his contact, who was waiting at a payphone, to relay that he was running late. Midway through the call, the guy was shot and killed. The traffic jam saved Tony's life.

\* \* \*

JORGE CALLED ME A week later, just as I had anticipated. I recorded the call. I needed a way to triangulate our conversation from dinner, Santo's wiretap, and his explanation to me about what happened.

"You already have the money?" I said upon picking up, making sure to cover my tracks with what I already knew about his delivery. "That was fast."

"I'm sorry, Manny, but I am going to have to postpone the money drop," he said. "I have a serious problem to handle."

"What happened?" I had to appear ignorant. Jorge had no idea that I knew about the shootout. Like with all of my conversations with drug smugglers and money launderers, I had to play dumb, to let them spill the details to me. "Anything to do with the load you told me about?"

"Yeah," he said. "I lost it."

"Damn," I said. "What are you going to do?"

"I still have to pay," he said. "Once I get a load, El Caracol expects his money, regardless of what happens. He doesn't care that I got robbed, and that it wasn't my fault."

"Do you have the money?" I asked, trying to appear sympathetic.

"No," he said. "I'm not in a good situation here, Manny. When you lose a big load, North Coast makes you work for them until you're fully repaid."

"So, you do one load for free and you're square," I said.

"No, Manny, you don't understand," he said, fear threaded into his voice. "I'll never get out from under this. I'll be their slave forever." I didn't know what else to say to him. The only thing running through my mind was picturing him as a soldier, his Army uniform perfectly ironed. How had he ended up here? That was the last time I ever spoke with Jorge. His fate was sealed.

\* \* \*

## INSIDE THE CARTEL

I NEEDED TO HEAR my sons' voices. I needed to feel safe, to remind myself why I was taking such a blatant risk with my life. I couldn't get out of my head how that could've been me on the side of the road, how at any moment Toro could turn on me, how any money pickup could instantly become an ambush. After speaking with Jorge, I drove down to my writing villa and walked into the bedroom. After making the recording of my son discussing the Batman play in the park, I had stored the cassette tape within the secret vault at the rear of the armoire. I pulled it out, put it into my tape deck, and pressed play, my anxiety fading with every excited lilt in his voice. I played it over and over again, reminding myself what really mattered here, who I had volunteered to do this for in the first place: my family.

# CHAPTER 12

# TWO WAGONS

*"¡PILAS Y MOSCA!"*

Toro's favorite directive: Get ready, be alert, and don't make any mistakes. I was driving around with Tony, having just dropped off $100,000 to be smurfed, when the call came in. "Prepare yourselves," Toro added, "because you're going to be picking up two melons."

"*Two* wagons?" I said through the speakerphone. A wagon, a melon: both meant a million bucks. But we had never before picked up two at once.

"*Sí*," he said. "You're going to see more wagons from now on."

Tony hung up the phone and looked at me. North Coast was making a run for it: larger shipments, more cash to wash. It was December 1993. Pablo Escobar, in a bloody shootout with Colombian special forces, had just been killed. It sent shock waves throughout Colombia. Although the Medellín Cartel was seen as a cutthroat competitor to other drug cartels, Escobar's presence created stability within the region. Now, with him dead, his faction was crumbling, and other cartels, like Cali and North Coast, were rising up in his wake. It also didn't help matters that a number of North Coast's core members, who worked under the Snail, had been murdered over the past two years—one of whom on orders from Escobar directly. Taking over Escobar's turf became a personal mission for the Snail. Moreover, the Cali Cartel was in active talks with the Colombian government to surrender their narco-empire in exchange for favorable judicial treatment. Everyone was on edge, unsure of what would happen next. Toro wanted control over as much of North Coast's drug proceeds as possible, perhaps to secure immense profit, but also to cement his power if Cali ended up disbanded.

Tony and I darted to my undercover apartment. I always drove my Nissan 300ZX on runs, which had a decent-sized trunk, but we would need a larger vehicle to carry this much cash. We hopped into my Mitsubishi Galant and made our way to the designated meeting place: Pizzeria del Diego, a downtrodden restaurant near the city center. Toro had referenced the man from whom we were picking up the money only by his code name: *Gutiérrez 14*. Tony and I had never met him, and had no idea which Caribbean cell of the North Coast Cartel he represented. After seeing the bloody shootout on the outskirts of Loíza, everything now felt like a setup to me. Maybe the turmoil in Colombia wasn't pushing Toro to launder more money, but rather to close shop and tie up loose ends—including us. Maybe rival drug lords were shifting their loyalties and wanted to send a message by murdering the launderers in San Juan. Or maybe I was just being paranoid, letting the stress of the situation get the best of me. Tony stared at me as I drove, clearly aware that I was on edge, playing out the worst-case scenarios in my head.

"Manny, I am thinking just like you," he said.

"What do you mean?" I said. "You're the one who is nervous."

"Yeah, just like you. But you're like a fly."

"A fly?"

"You can't catch a fly. When you're about to smack it, it darts away. That's the way I feel about you. You're never complacent, and you never fully trust a scenario. You are fully alert to the point of almost having a heart attack. Look at you. You're sweating."

I looked down at my shirt. It was soaked. "Well, it's hot as hell in here," I said, reaching to crank up the air-conditioning.

"After all of our pickups, we are always thinking we are going to get ripped off," he said. "We are relaxed, but we are always thinking of the bad things that could happen."

"It's all in the planning," I said. "We have the best support team, which is why we never get in trouble."

"Well, all these guys get fucking ripped off. They know they are safe, until they *don't* know they are safe. Every money robbery leaves no witnesses. Toro will never know how or why we got killed. These guys are not afraid of the FBI. They fear their own people—their partners, their enemies—more. If betrayal arrives, we will never see it coming."

"Are you saying you have a bad feeling about this pickup?"

"It's a lot of money," Tony said. "It doesn't feel normal."

"We'll be fine. We've done this a hundred times before. Just play it cool, and I'll handle it. But if I end up getting my ass kicked, and it's a matter of survival," I continued, pointing to the glove compartment, which held my secondary pistol, "don't hesitate to help me out."

"I know, Manny. I don't want to use the gun, but I will if I need to. It's just outside of our character. We aren't violent like them," he said. "But mentally, it's a different story. We change more with each pickup we do. We are becoming more and more like them, whether we know it or not." Tony was right: Every passing day that I continued to be Manny, the more my heart and mind molded to my alter ego's necessities. I never forgot my mission as an FBI agent, but the subconscious changing of the self was real, and I wondered if Manny would ever be able to truly leave my psyche.

We pulled into the restaurant's parking lot. It was empty. "He's not here yet," I said.

"Are we meeting him inside?" Tony asked. "Should we get a table?"

"Let's just wait here," I said.

Twenty minutes later, a Ford Bronco pulled up next to us. Gutiérrez 14, whoever he was, got out of the truck and came over to my window. I scanned his body, looking for a bulge under his shirt or within his pant leg. He didn't seem to be armed. In fact, he was smiling. I rolled down my window.

"I'm sorry I'm late," he said, with a degree of sincerity that took me off guard. This guy didn't know me or Tony; a sliver of reservation was usually in order, but he betrayed no nervousness. He must be a true professional, I thought.

"It's all right," I said. "We just got here ourselves."

"Good, I'm glad," he said. "It's nice to meet you guys. I usually meet with his other team on the island, the Argentinians and the Dominicans, but they were busy today." I looked over at Tony. Additional laundering cells on the island? Tony had mentioned early in his cooperation that this was a possibility. Toro severely compartmentalized his operation; no one who worked for him knew the true scale of his business. It was an insurance policy, a form of protection, that insulated him from risk. If one cell was compromised, his others could operate unscathed. This was a double-edged sword: not only could it expand our money-laundering investigation, but it proved that, in Toro's eyes, Tony and I were expendable.

## TWO WAGONS

"Good thing we had a few hours to kill, then," Tony said, flashing his pearly whites, trying to mirror the man's friendliness.

"You can put the money in the trunk," I said, "and we'll let Toro know that we met up."

"One more thing," he said. "I was only able to bring $1 million. The rest is still being counted." He had stuffed the cash inside three hulking duffel bags. They barely fit in my trunk. As he was about to leave, he added, "I'll let you know when the rest is ready."

We took the first million to the covert FBI warehouse to be counted and smurfed, and true to his word, I met up with Gutiérrez 14 again when he called a few hours later. He was prompt, every bill accounted for. We made the pickup and safely transported the money. We were alive.

"Manny," Tony said as we drove away, the money burning a hole in our trunk, "if I ever get out of this alive and free, I will never commit another crime as long as I live."

\* \* \*

IT WAS VERY DIFFICULT to give Maria advance notice if I was coming home. When I was an undercover smuggler, I had the benefit of a more formalized schedule. Although I met with drug lords regularly, the deliveries for which they hired me required a lot of lead time. I knew which weekends I had off as Manny and could pencil into my calendar a couple nights at home with my family. But money never slept—and now, under Toro's thumb, spontaneity controlled my life. The phone. It was always the phone. If Toro called, I had to answer. Even turning back into Martin was more precarious, more time-consuming, more stressful. Instead of just going to an underground parking garage and swapping cars, like I did when I was a smuggler, I now had to drive a second undercover car, one that no criminals knew I owned, to the parking garage. From there, I would switch to my initial Martin car, the windows tinted black. And then I would drive to a different location on the island and trade *that* car for my truly aboveground Martin vehicle: a simple Toyota minivan. The FBI knew that this operation was more dangerous than anything we had done previously. The precaution was mandatory. The whole process took hours.

One evening, after completing a $500,000 pickup with Tony, I sprawled out on the couch in my undercover apartment. I thought of my boys and how they must be, at that very moment, gathering seashells on the beach, or muscling through a homework assignment, or playing with our dog, Mushy (or "Doggy Mushy," as my youngest son called her). I missed them dearly. Over the past few months, ever since our vacation in the Poconos, I paid more attention to the surveillance put on me by the FBI. I realized that, if I sat in my undercover apartment for at least two hours after a pickup, it was highly unlikely that anyone, whether agents or sicarios or both, would still be following me. It became a game, the final score of which would allow me the freedom to turn back into Martin and go see my family.

I ate dinner and tried to watch TV, but I found myself pacing around my apartment for the next few hours. I lay back down and tried to go to sleep, but I couldn't stop thinking of my two boys, my wife, and how much I missed them. I lifted my head off of the couch and looked at the clock: 12:48 a.m. "Fuck it," I said to myself, and stood up. I drove my second undercover car to the parking garage. I switched cars and made my way across the island to where I stashed my minivan, switched vehicles again, and went home. By the time I pulled into the driveway, it was almost 3:00 a.m. The house

## TWO WAGONS

was dark, the lights turned off. I entered as quietly as I could, knowing that if I woke my boys, we'd be up all night. I walked into the kitchen and Mushy came scurrying over to me, her tail wagging, whimpering at the sight of her missing friend. I bent down and rubbed her head. I opened the refrigerator to make sure that my family had enough food to eat, that what I was doing provided for my family. It was stocked with groceries. A neat plate of leftovers, wrapped in tinfoil, sat on the middle shelf. Had this been prepared for me? Did Maria make me a plate every night, hoping I'd come home? And every morning that she woke up with me not here, did she have to throw it away? I peeked inside (chicken and rice) but placed the tinfoil back over the plate. I realized, at that moment, that I hadn't had dinner in our house, with my wife, in months.

I tiptoed down the hallway and peered into my sons' bedroom. Both of them had Batman posters on their sides of the room, purchased by Maria from the live-action play in the park. They were sound asleep, not even stirring at the presence of their father right behind them. I gently closed the door, careful not to wake them. I walked into my bedroom, took off my clothes, and crawled into bed. Maria stirred. "You're home," she said.

"Yes, sweetie," I replied. I leaned over and kissed her on the forehead. "I'm home."

"I'm so tired," she said. "It's been a long week."

"Just get some sleep," I said, caressing her head. She closed her eyes and drifted off. I lay on my back and stared at the ceiling for what seemed like hours. I couldn't shake off the stress. It coursed through me, vibrating in my chest. I replayed, over and over, all the close calls I had, all the quick-witted responses I shot back at the drug smugglers, all the maybes and what-ifs that had begun to control my psyche. I tossed and turned. I couldn't fall asleep. I got out of bed and walked into the living room. I turned on the TV, clicked over to the sports channel, and muted the volume. I sat in my leather recliner, propped up my feet, and thought again and again about details of the life that I had chosen to lead: the drugs, the guns, the money; Toro, the faceless specter that controlled me on the other end of the phone line. Finally, I drifted off.

I woke up to the sounds of my two sons yelling. "Dad is here! Dad is here!" they chanted. They ran over to me, and I gathered them up into my lap.

"Are you excited for school?" I asked.

"Yes!" my eldest said.

"Well, let's get you some breakfast first."

We rose out of the chair and walked into the kitchen. Maria was already putting hot oatmeal into bowls. We sat down and ate together, the first meal I had with my family, in my own house, in a very long time. After we ate, the boys gathered their backpacks and got ready to leave.

"You two be good at school," I said.

"Are you catching bad guys today?" my youngest asked. "Like Batman?"

I laughed. "Yes, just like Batman."

Maria smiled and ushered them out of the house. I watched as she walked them to the bus stop, which was outside of the entrance to our neighborhood. I couldn't take them myself, for fear of being seen. Although we lived in a safe area, the broader region was rife with cartel men and other criminals possibly on their payroll. In fact, one of the smugglers from whom I picked up money had a stash house just a mile from my home. He had installed a secret vault under the concrete of his carport. It could hold millions of dollars' worth of cocaine.

I went back into the living room and waited for Maria to return. She came back into the house, walked over to the sink, and began scrubbing dishes. I walked up behind her, wrapped my arms around her waist, and nuzzled my face into her neck.

"I wish you could've come to the wedding," she said. She was talking about an old Navy buddy who lived on the island and got married a few weeks prior. Like all personal events that were held in public, I couldn't attend. Maria's brother took my place, so she wouldn't have to go alone. "It was a really nice ceremony, and the weather was beautiful up in the mountains."

"I know, sweetie," I said. "I wish I could've come, too." Her tone wasn't resentful, and she didn't press further. She didn't become impatient. She didn't admonish me that my role as an undercover agent forced me to miss the personal moments that bound a family together. She didn't make me feel guilty at the choices that I had made. She just let me hold her as she scrubbed the dishes. I understood, in that moment, the strongest emotional thread that held our marriage together: Maria's restraint became a requirement of my job as an undercover agent. I always wondered how her silence stayed so steadfast for so many years, and then I realized what Maria had figured out for herself, without us ever needing to have a conversation about it: If she projected any undue stress onto me, I would carry it as a distraction back into the field. If she became resentful about what my career required of me, I could end up dead. I knew that my dream of becoming an FBI agent wasn't only about me. It controlled my family. Maria was the unsung hero of my undercover career. Her forced silence was the only way that I succeeded. The only way I stayed alive.

She turned to me, her hands covered in soap. "Are you safe, Martin? Tell me the truth."

I exhaled. "Yes," I said. "I promise."

She rested her weight onto my chest. "I hope so, Martin. I really hope so. Our boys need a father, and I need you."

I took her hands in mine and thought back to our wedding day in front of the judge. "We always said we would care for each other, right?" I asked. She nodded. "Well, I'm not going to stop now." We hugged, her soapy hands wrapped around my neck. "Christmas is in a couple weeks," I said. "I will be here. I promise. And everything will be just fine."

\* \* \*

I WANTED TO SEE my father. I assumed, if I could see him, I would feel less guilty about the position in which I put Maria—that searching for nobility through undercover work was a just cause. I left my house, drove across town, and pulled into my parents' driveway. I took a deep breath and walked through the front door. My mother stood in the kitchen, peeling fruit.

"Martin?" she called. "Martin, is that you?"

"Hi, Mom," I said. I walked over and kissed her on the forehead.

"What are you doing here?" she asked. "I figured you'd be working today."

"I took the day off," I said. "Where's Dad?"

She nodded toward the back patio. "He's outside."

I opened the door and stepped out. My father was hunched over, pruning a patch of flowers. He didn't look up as he spoke: "I didn't know FBI agents had sick days," he said.

"I just have a couple hours before I have to get back," I said. His sarcastic comment felt like a boxer's swinging hook. Maybe he knew something was wrong, that I wouldn't just show up like this without good reason. Anxiety rushed from my chest to my head. Was I doing the right thing? Would I die with regrets? I needed to calm down. I pulled a cigar out of my pocket and lit it. I took a deep pull and let the smoke pour from my mouth. I had smoked a few cigars in the Navy, but it never became a habit until I went undercover. Drug lords loved cigars. I had to play the part. My father craned his neck and glared at me.

"What are you doing?" he asked.

"What?" I said, a sheepish grin spreading across my face, like I was a child who had been caught doing something naughty.

"You're smoking now?" My father knew nothing about my work as an undercover agent. He had no idea who his son had become. Every time I saw him, I had changed a bit more. It was subtle to him, at first, but I knew that Manny had crept into the boy that he raised. He projected a look of concerned confusion, as if he didn't recognize the man standing before him.

"It's a long story, Dad," I said.

"Well, I hope you will be coming to your mother's event next weekend," he said. "Her artwork is being shown at the museum." My mother had started pursuing art after retiring from her job with a local heart surgeon. She joined boards and did nonprofit work for various organizations in the arts, and now she was being honored for all that she did for Puerto Rico.

"Dad, I can't show my face in public like that. If someone takes a picture and it shows up in the newspaper with my real name, it could be dangerous for all of us."

He didn't look at me, didn't say a word, just cast his eyes down at the ground. I took another drag on my cigar. I realized, then, that the one thing that bound me to everything that I held dear—my wife, my sons, my parents, my role in the FBI—was silence. I thought of my son, the recording I made of him gushing over Batman, and then I saw my father reach back into his flower patch, that scar that meant so much to me—that represented his entire being, his influence on me—running down his arm.

"Dad," I said, exhaling, "I'm just trying to catch the bad guys."

## CHAPTER 13

# VAMOS A MATARTE

**I MADE IT HOME FOR CHRISTMAS. I HAD PLANNED TO LEAVE** my undercover apartment after lunch on Christmas Eve, clean myself, and be home before dinner, but, like clockwork, Toro called Tony and me for a pickup. It was small compared to the wagons with which we were now handling—just over $150,000—but we drove to a grungy neighborhood in San Juan, had dinner with the smuggler, grabbed the cash, and dropped it off with the FBI to be processed. It was past midnight, and I was exhausted, but I wasn't going to break my promise. I wanted to be home when my children woke up on Christmas morning. Moreover, my car was stuffed to the brim with gifts for my boys.

I pulled into my driveway. The Christmas tree, covered in multicolored lights, beamed through the window. It was nearly two in the morning, the house still and quiet. I was exhausted, and didn't want to wake anyone up, so I left the presents—unwrapped—in the hatchback of my Nissan (a second one, much older than my undercover Nissan 300ZX, which along with my minivan I used as a personal vehicle). I snuck into the house, gently closed the door behind me, and walked into the living room. Maria had placed a few small gifts under the tree, but I was in charge of all the presents that Santa Claus was scheduled to deliver down the chimney. I lay down on the couch and quickly passed out, the tree's lights casting a red and yellow glow across my face.

I woke up to Maria talking with my youngest son. He knew that I was supposed to come home for Christmas, and when he awoke in his bedroom, he peeked out the window and saw all of the presents stacked in the rear of my car. His curiosity at the gifts' odd placement overrode his excitement at seeing his father, and he snuck out of the house to inspect the bounty. He was confused, devastated, and furious. He called for Maria in the kitchen. A heated discussion brewed.

"Does Santa Claus really exist?" he asked point-blank.

"Yes, he does!" Maria beamed, trying to cover up my mistake. "Go look under the tree to see what he brought you!"

"But there are gifts in Dad's car!"

"Oh, um, those gifts are for the poor kids in San Juan," she said.

"Oh, okay," he said, mulling over the facts at hand. "Wait a minute," he continued, his voice rising, "but those are the exact toys that we asked for! I see the football helmets sitting right there! Everything in Dad's car was on our list!"

I rose from the couch and rushed into the kitchen. I couldn't abandon Maria underneath the glare of his suspicion. "Those gifts are for you, but I had to help out Santa last night," I told him. "He was really busy."

"You mean to tell me that all these years have been nothing but lies!" he yelled.

My eldest son came scurrying over to his brother. "Who cares! We got presents! It's Christmas!"

## VAMOS A MATARTE

I went out to my car and brought in the boys' gifts: no wrapping paper, no surprises, just their father giving them exactly what they wanted for Christmas. They squealed at every present passed to them: GI Joes, Ninja Turtle figurines, and new football equipment. While they played with their toys, Maria and I made breakfast. In the afternoon, we made our way to my parents' house, my father beaming at being able to see his son on Christmas. True to his nature, he didn't say anything about how happy my boys were about the gifts I bought them. Instead, he watched them as they played, glanced at me, his eyes aglow, a smile spread across his face. I knew, then, that he approved of me as a father to my sons. As it did every time I got to see my family, the stress of being Manny faded away as the hours passed. I planned to stay at home, and be Martin, the whole week. I'd turn back into Manny after New Year's.

\* \* \*

THE HOLIDAY LANDED OVER the weekend, so the boys and Maria all went to school on Monday. They left the house shortly after 6:00 a.m. and I decided to take a long run through our neighborhood. I wanted to keep my mind settled, remind myself that I was safe here with my family, that I had the space and time to enjoy myself. I put on my shorts, laced up my sneakers, and grabbed my gun. It wasn't my formal service pistol, but rather a tiny, five-shot revolver that was issued to me when I went undercover. I secured the gun against my hip with a length of telephone wire run through the loops of my running shorts. It held five 38-caliber bullets.

I ran to the beach, down the waterline, across the boulder-laden jetty where the tropical forest began, and turned around.

## INSIDE THE CARTEL

I stopped at the center of the beach, did some jumping jacks, then muscled through some push-ups. Finished, I dusted the sand off my feet, put my shoes back on, and sprinted back toward my house. I looped around the edge of the golf course and through our neighborhood. As I came around the bend, I saw a red Honda Civic parked across the street from my house. Two men sat inside.

I immediately crossed the street, to have a better vantage point, and to put myself between them and my house. I didn't think they had seen me, but something in my gut told me that they were looking for me. My mind, however, had been playing tricks on me for years. As I told my boss, Dick Sanders: At night, all the cats are black. And I had been seeing red cars and black cats everywhere, thinking everything was a threat. My heart started racing. I put my hand on my pistol, felt the gentle curve of its trigger, the nub of its grip, the safety it provided me. I dropped my pace to a slow walk. The FBI trained me to never engage in a firefight without first taking cover. I stopped at my neighbor's baby blue Volvo sedan, crouched down, and peered at them above the trunk. I was close enough now that I could see their eyes. They were staring at my house. I stood up so they could see me.

"I live here," I shouted. "Can I help you?" They looked at me but didn't respond. "What are you doing here?" I said.

"None of your business," one of the men said. "We are waiting for somebody."

"Well, I live here," I said. "This is my house."

Both men got out of the car. The passenger stood by the Honda while the driver walked toward me. I looked at his belt and immediately recognized that it had some bulk to it. It could've easily been a weapon. I pulled my gun out of my waistband and held it down by my thigh so he could see that I was armed.

"What can I help you with?" I asked, again.

The driver, eyeing my pistol, stopped and turned around. He looked back over his shoulder at me and said, "We will see you later." They got back into the car, fired it up, and drove away. This could've been completely random, but I couldn't shake the feeling that my family was in danger. I didn't want to alarm Maria, so I didn't mention what had happened when she got home later that day. I just played my role as husband and father, trying to suppress my nervous energy.

* * *

TWO DAYS LATER, ON December 29, I came home very late after tying up a few loose ends with Tony. Since I was away, Maria and the boys had gone to her father's house in the mountains. As I parked in front of my house, an eerie feeling came over me. I knew something wasn't right. I grabbed my shotgun, stepped out of my car, and stood in the middle of the road. I peered into the night, my ears perked. I didn't see or hear anything amiss. I went into my house, watched a little television, and then climbed into bed. Not long after, a loud explosion, guttural and shrill, like a freshly detonated bomb, rocketed through the night. A massive white flash, followed by orange and red and blue flames, shot past my windows like a spotlight. The smell of gasoline and the sound of shattering glass filled the air. I jumped out of bed, grabbed my shotgun, and rushed outside to find my neighbor's baby blue Volvo on fire. The windows were blown out, the whole thing a raging ball of heat and smoke.

## INSIDE THE CARTEL

I ran over to the car, and my neighbor ran out to meet me. He called the police. As we watched it burn, he said, "I just put a new radio in. It must've been a short circuit or something." I didn't push back, but I knew this wasn't due to faulty wiring. The cops and fire department showed up a few minutes later. After putting the fire out, a few police officers inspected the wreckage. I approached one of the cops.

"This wasn't from a short circuit," the cop told me. "The windows were blown out." He started walking toward the car. I followed him. We peered into the back seat. "That could be some sort of accelerant," he said, pointing to a slick of liquid on the floor. "I think someone blew this car up on purpose." The cop relayed the same theory to my neighbor, but he refused to believe that someone had intentionally bombed his car. I didn't want to cause a scene, so I didn't tell them about the men in the red Honda I had confronted just two days prior. I needed to think.

Had I been made? Or was this just random violence? The funhouse mirrors of my life were warping again.

Maria and our sons came home the following morning to find the charred remains of the car still sitting on the street. The cops were gone by now. She spoke with our neighbor, who told her that it was just an accident, faulty wiring. It didn't take much to convince her. The only clue she had about what I was really doing came from when we ran into the cartel money launderer on the beach. It was a shocking pronouncement regarding what I had gotten myself into but, now, deep down, Maria didn't want to believe that members of a Colombian drug cartel could be hunting her husband—hunting *us*. She shared our neighbor's theory with me, but I didn't divulge my own suspicions. In some ways, I needed her to believe in her own reality—to believe a lie. I didn't want to make too much of it, either. If I formulated a firm theory as to who was behind the bombing, I could be pulled out, the case shut down—standard safety protocol when there's a credible threat on an undercover agent's life. I needed to keep my head straight, to not jump to conclusions.

I told Jimmy and Santo about the incident, just in case. They, too, brushed it off, chalking it up to a couple local hoodlums causing a ruckus or trying to intimidate my neighbor so they could rob his house. They had no evidence, from our wiretaps or other surveillance of the cartel's men on the island, that anyone knew who I was or that sicarios were after me. "You're fine, Martin," Santo told me. "Don't worry about it." I asked Tony about it, too. He seemed genuinely concerned, but offered a conclusion that honestly made a lot of sense: "We are so prosperous for Toro. At this point, if he thought the FBI was laundering for him, he would just keep it going because we are making so much money for him," he said. "These people, Manny, they are shameless." Tony had a point. Currently, there was no extradition treaty between Colombia and the United States. Moreover, if our cell of his money-laundering empire was compromised—by law enforcement, a rival faction, or otherwise—he had a dozen others operating in various countries that could easily take on more work. We weren't the engine or even the transmission of his machine, but merely a cog.

I tried to forget about the blown-up Volvo and enjoy the rest of the holiday week. But I was on edge, more vigilant than I had been in months. Every time my wife and children left the house, I peered out the window to make sure no one was following them. The next few days consumed me with a strange sense of floating: the desire to be Martin, the loving father and husband, coupled with the necessity of being Manny, the cartel money launderer always on the lookout, always peering over his shoulder. I was never ashamed of Manny, this alternative version of myself that I had created. I realized that my two sides had become the same; one had to be present for the other to exist. Martin and Manny had to live together simultaneously. Whenever I gazed through the looking glass of Martin, I saw Manny's reflection, and vice versa. I thought back to my neighbor's lack of concern, of Santo and Jimmy shrugging the explosion off, and forced myself to also dismiss the threats, to live in a perpetual state of denial. It was more comforting than the truth.

* * *

MY FAMILY WAS HOSTING a New Year's Eve party at my sister's house. It had been on the calendar for weeks, and Maria and the boys were excited to go. I was also looking forward to the gathering, seeing it as a symbol of normalcy to end a very abnormal year. Just before dinner, we loaded up the kids into our car and drove to my father's house for drinks and appetizers. It was a simple pre-party, from which we would carpool to my sister's place. My youngest son sprinted through the front door when we arrived, giddy to see his grandfather. I inherited my mother's body—broad, stocky—but my father's face. When my son saw his grandfather, he saw his father, too. My son also had our facial features, and when he was born, my father said, "This is a Suarez, no doubt."

My father, standing in the living room, scooped up my son into his arms.

"Did you get everything you wanted for Christmas?" he asked him.

"Yeah, I did!"

"Tell me the lemonade story again," my father said, putting him down onto the floor.

"This guy came and tried to take my money, and I told him to get lost!" my son exclaimed. My father roared with laughter, as if he was hearing the story for the first time. Earlier that year, my son had set up a lemonade stand in our neighborhood, charging a dollar per cup, and the gate security for our community approached and asked for a drink. My son handed him the beverage, and the guard gave him a ten-dollar bill. But my son, being so young, treated every bill as if it represented one dollar. When the guard asked for nine dollars back, my son thought the guy was trying to rip him off, and he told him to scram. The guard understood the situation, laughed it off, and let my son keep the change—a big tip for the little kid.

We hung around at my father's house, having snacks and cocktails while my kids played with him. Just after eight, we headed over to my sister's. Her street was closed off, as all the houses on the block were hosting their own parties. Everyone spilled out from their homes, onto their front lawns and into the street. Grills were aflame, the drinks ice cold. Fireworks were lit. Children were laughing into the night. It was the perfect evening, and my entire family was there, nearly two dozen people in all.

I sat in a lawn chair next to Maria and my boys, nursed a beer, and watched my brother set off fireworks. They shot into the sky and crackled into a flower of red and yellow, the sparks and flashes raining down above our heads. My sons loved it.

"Dad, let's do one together!" my eldest son said.

"All right," I said, standing up from my chair. "Go ask your uncle for one of his fireworks." He gleefully ran off, returning quickly with the tiny rocket. We bent down on the lawn and shoved its base into the dirt.

## INSIDE THE CARTEL

"For safety, once it starts burning, we have to step back," I told my son. He nodded in anticipation. I flicked a lighter and touched the flame to the fuse. It sparkled to life. I picked my son up and stepped back. The firework shot into the sky and dispersed with a loud, hollow pop. My son was thrilled.

And then, more pops in the distance: not fireworks, but gunshots.

After fifteen years in the military and law enforcement, I knew the sound as well as my wife's voice. I put my son down and immediately started casing the area. I hustled behind the house and circled around the line of cars on the street. I needed to make sure that a cartel gunman wasn't hiding, waiting for the perfect shot, my head at the center of his crosshairs. My focus was palpable, my training kicked in. I had to make sure we were all safe.

The area was clear. There was no threat. I walked back over to my seat, took a deep breath, and sat down.

But then: machine guns. At close range. I could tell by the sound they were AK-47s. I thought of the ambush on the side of the road and Appa's men holding their machine guns when they made my surveillance. Although many local bad guys had access to these guns, I could only think of the cartel.

I turned to Maria. She heard the gunshots, too. I didn't need to say a word. Our hearts and minds were connected in a way that only soulmates know—bound forever by our children. I knew our sons could be in danger, and she did too. As if by instinct, she calmly ushered our boys toward the house. I turned to my family, all two dozen of them, and started yelling: "Everyone in the house, right now! Come on, let's go!"

"What's going on, Martin?" my father asked me.

"I heard gunshots," I said. "We should be in the house, just in case. Stray bullets, you know." The front lawn stood vacant, quiet, the remnants of a family celebration strewn about the grass, abandoned. It was ten minutes before midnight. We turned on the TV and watched the countdown. I brought Maria close to me and forced a smile. Everything was fine. We were safe now. The boys sat on the carpet at our feet, and as the ball dropped and the clock struck midnight, I pulled Maria's face into mine and kissed her.

We left shortly thereafter. The boys fell asleep in the car on the way home. I pulled up in front of my house. Maria pulled our eldest son from the back seat, while I handled our youngest. As I cradled him in my arms, I heard a car creep up alongside me: the same red Honda Civic from a few days earlier. Inside was dark, I couldn't make out any faces, but today, thirty years later, I can still hear the guy's voice.

"*Vamos a matarte.*" We are going to fucking kill you.

My worlds were colliding. Did these men know that I was an FBI agent, or just as Manny, with more secrets than they could abide? Maria heard him too. She went into a trance, her face white as a ghost, frozen in place. "Maria," I said, "get inside the house. Now." She turned and ran and I followed her, both of us clutching our children. She sat down on the couch, my oldest son at her side as I placed my youngest son next to her. I ran to the closet, grabbed my shotgun, and made my way toward the front door.

"Martin!" Maria screamed. "Don't go out there!"

"I'll be right back." I wasn't scared. I was angry. I couldn't let these guys terrorize my family—to show up at our house on New Year's Eve. I had to show them that I was stronger than they were. I burst through the front door, shotgun raised up, ready to put my finger on the trigger. The men were gone, and I watched the blur of taillights down the street. I jumped into my car and chased after them, toward the ocean. The streetlights were sparser toward the coast, and all I could see within the glow of my headlights was an expanse of blackness that was the ocean. As I came around the bend, I saw two cars ahead of me at a stop sign. One turned left; the other turned right. I went right and followed the car I thought was the red Honda. But this area was even more remote. I was completely exposed, encased in nothing but my own anger and paranoia. I put my high beams on. I saw nothing. They were gone. I slowed to a stop.

I looked down at my shotgun. This wasn't how I had been trained by the FBI. This wasn't me. I put the car in drive, turned around, and went home.

# CHAPTER 14

# I AM NOT AFRAID OF DEATH

**I TOLD JIMMY ABOUT THE SECOND THREAT FROM THE MEN** in the red Honda Civic, but didn't emphasize the danger I felt. The blown-up Volvo, which I considered to be the most obvious evidence that someone was out to get me, couldn't be tied back to Toro or his men on the island. Why would this most recent threat be different? Violence had woven itself into the very fabric of Puerto Rico during the early 1990s. There were a thousand drug-related homicides in 1993—the same number as New York City. But whereas the Big Apple counted a population of 7.5 million, only 3.5 million people lived in Puerto Rico. Our drug-related per-capita homicide rate stood three times higher than that of America's largest city. What I had experienced, for many citizens living in San Juan, was commonplace. Moreover, I didn't want to set in motion a self-fulfilling prophecy by raising alarm bells with the bosses at the field office. If I convinced my superiors that there was a credible threat on my life related to our money laundering operation, I could be pulled out, the investigation closed down. This case was mine. I didn't want to let it go. I was too close to closing it.

And of course, being an FBI agent—especially one working undercover—came with risk. It was just part of the job, especially if you were working the streets. Even being out in public settings, especially in a place like Puerto Rico, raised an agent's susceptibility to violence. Gangs were everywhere on the island, and they attacked people indiscriminately. One of our agents got robbed while getting fitted for a new suit. It was completely random. Another agent was assaulted while making a call on a payphone. He fought off the assailants and they fled. In fact, avoiding violent situations became the exception, not the rule. Any agent—myself included—who had not yet been robbed, shot at, or threatened, found themselves engaging in a gambler's fallacy: we figured, just because we were on safety's winning streak, we would be shielded forever.

In one memorable story that got passed around my squad, a San Juan field office supervisor got robbed after buying milk at the supermarket. A few young gang members stole his unmarked FBI vehicle. We knew which gang the men represented, and the next day a few agents went to the crew's leader and told him to give back the car or they were in deep shit. That weekend, they found the agent's car in the airport parking lot. They also found the robber in a nearby neighborhood. He was wearing the agent's bulletproof vest, which had been in the trunk, with a single bullet hole in his head.

I didn't expect the two men in the Honda Civic to turn up dead, a cartel-imposed slap-on-the-wrist, but I did hope that they realized, seeing me armed and willing to fight, that I wasn't a sitting duck. Whether they knew I was an FBI agent or not, I wanted them to understand that threatening my family or me would have dire consequences. Of course, I didn't have much time to think about any of this because, after spending New Year's Day at home with my family, trying to forget what happened the night before, I turned back into Manny, reunited with Tony, and my phone started ringing again. Toro told us that we had a lot of work to do.

* * *

"YOU'RE SHORT." IT WAS February 1994, and I was on the phone with José Sarmiento, a big-time Dominican trafficker for North Coast whose money was managed by Toro. I had just received what was supposed to be $250,000 and had dropped it off with my case agents to be counted. They counted it once, twice, three times, and realized that he skimped roughly $40,000 off the amount Toro told me I was set to receive. Santo called me to give the update.

Honestly, I didn't care that much. I could just tell Toro and he would take care of José on his end of things, but I always gave the smugglers a chance to pay up before I called Colombia; you never knew what sort of mood Toro would be in. He could shrug it off, add the fee onto their next delivery, or he could take it as a personal affront and assume more drastic measures. Moreover, playing things like this out gave me more contact with the smugglers: more intelligence, more evidence, more opportunities to garner facetime with the drug lords outside of Toro's narrow directives. I called José.

"Meet me at Plaza de Americas," José said, referencing a shopping mall in San Juan. "We have to make this right before I report back to Toro."

"Sounds good," I answered. "I will be there."

I waited in the parking lot, and José drove up beside me. Strange, high-pitched Latin music blared from his speakers.

# INSIDE THE CARTEL

He turned off his car, rolled down his window, and called to me: "*¡Vamos!*"

"In your car?" I asked. I was spooked. Was this a setup? I hadn't dealt with José much before, and I couldn't find his angle. I had hoped that he would either have the money with him, or I could at least drive him to pick it up (my car was bugged, after all). But I had to act cool, play the part. As soon as I got into his car and we started driving, he blasted the music again.

"What is this?" I yelled. I really didn't like the tunes, but I had to fake some sort of enthusiasm to keep the mood positive.

"*¡Bachata!*" he said, turning up the dial even louder. "The best music in all of the Dominican Republic!" I groaned and kept quiet. Our conversation would have to wait until we got to where we were going.

We drove to the outskirts of San Juan: Puerto Nuevo, a typical working-class neighborhood. We pulled up to his stash house and entered. A parade of guards stood watch over the money and cocaine. They glared at me suspiciously. An AK-47 leaned gingerly against the wall, and each of the guards stored pistols in their waistbands. José walked over to a table, reached into a cardboard box, and handed me twenty small stacks of cash wrapped in rubber bands.

I thumbed through it. "This is only eight thousand," I told him. "You were short forty large."

"Okay," he said, "tell me when to stop." More stacks. More stacks. More stacks. When I placed the money into my bag and he flashed a guilty smile, it hit me: this guy couldn't count. And yet he was detail-oriented, a great leader to his men, and certainly trustworthy enough to be high up in the cartel. These contradictions bothered me at times. Most of these smugglers came from extreme poverty. They were men with nothing to lose by becoming a player in the international drug trade. If I didn't have the father that I did—a respectable man, dedicated to law and order—would I have turned out like them? I knew it was a conspiratorial thought. The odds that I would've turned out to be a cartel man were slim. But being around these men revealed to me cracks in society's fabric. It made me think that anyone, no matter their background or pedigree, could trip and fall in.

"The next delivery will come at the airport," José told me. "One of my men, Ceritt, will bring it to you."

"As long as the count is accurate, I'll go wherever you need me to go," I said.

"*Perfecto*, Manny," he said. "Now, let me bring you back to your car." We drove back to the shopping mall, that awful music blaring the entire way.

\* \* \*

EVERY COUPLE OF WEEKS, I would meet with Santo and Jimmy and discuss how much money we were washing per month. This type of operation—doing controlled money laundering for a Colombian drug cartel, where the money was actually fed back into the narco-economy—had never been done before, and the higher-ups in Washington, DC, didn't want to have to deal with the political fallout of having my team and me labeled undercover conspirators to the drug trade. Can you imagine the headlines? It'd be on the front page of the *New York Times*: FBI HELPS COLOMBIAN CARTEL LAUNDER MONEY. Congress would have a field day with us, every agent paraded down the gauntlet of the Capitol, C-SPAN cameras rolling, another Iran-Contra Affair playing out for the world to see. Yes, we wanted to break up the washing machine that stretched from Colombia to Miami to Aruba—which required actively participating in the narco-economy—but we also needed to protect our reputation. It didn't help that we were originally approved to only launder $5 million, just to see how the system functioned, and nab the immediate ring of people with whom Tony worked. By March 1994, the FBI had renewed our investigation five times, and I had helped launder over ten times that amount.

Our supervisors told us that we needed a seizure, at least for political theater. And they thought that our encounter with José's man Ceritt at the airport would be the perfect opportunity. I was against the decision. We were constantly identifying new cells that operated under Toro and doing a seizure could persuade him to adjust his methods, which would make our chase more complicated. I needed to penetrate deeper into the operation and expose the apparent connection with the Moore cousins in Aruba. I also knew Toro had government connections in Colombia. I wanted to find out what those were, as well. But our supervisors were steadfast in their conviction. We had laundered too much money without any seizures; we needed to slow down the amount we were funneling back into the cartel's economy. And taking down a cartel man was the only way to do so. I grumbled at the plan, but agreed. Anything to keep the operation going.

Santo and I went over the plan. "We will have a couple guys approach him and ask for his immigration papers," Santo said. "Once they get the money, you can beat feet out of there."

"All right. Sounds good," I said. "I'll keep an eye out for you at the airport."

*  *  *

## I AM NOT AFRAID OF DEATH

I RENTED A ROOM at the Sands Hotel for my pre-handoff meeting with Ceritt. We bugged the entire place and had robust surveillance not only around the perimeter of the hotel, but inside, as well. We wanted eyes and ears on the entire meeting, so we could prove that the money we were about to seize was, in fact, the proceeds from drug sales. I waited in my room until a knock came at my door.

I opened it up and shook Ceritt's hand. He was clean-shaven with short hair. He had a few inches on me, but stood thinner, ganglier. Most Dominican money launderers wore colorful, baggy dress shirts tucked only into the front of their jeans, the back flapping like a tail, with slip-on leather loafers and a gold Rolex watch. Ceritt fit the stereotype. "Drink?" I asked. He accepted. I poured two glasses of Black Label and motioned for him to help himself from a platter of chips and salsa that I had room service bring up earlier.

"So," I said. "José says we are meeting at the airport in a couple of days."

"Yes," he said. "A lot of people, a lot of commotion, so it should be safe for us. No one will notice what we are doing."

"Are you sure?" I asked. "I don't usually like the airport because there are a lot of cops around."

"Sure, but everyone has suitcases," he said. "We will blend in."

"If you say so," I said.

"Listen, Manny, I won't get ripped off," Ceritt said. "I am very careful, and I am not afraid of death. Someone will have to kill me to take this money away from me. I'll die before losing it. You have nothing to worry about."

If only Ceritt knew what was coming. I planned to use this conversation as a pretext for me to blame him after the FBI seized his cash and Toro started asking questions.

## INSIDE THE CARTEL

"Good," I said. "I trust you."

He smiled and lifted his jacket, revealing a pistol stuffed into his waistband. "Like I said, you have nothing to worry about." I glared at the gun. This plan may turn out to be more dangerous than I expected.

"So, what do you want to do, then?" I asked.

"It's going to be nice and clean," he said. "I will be wearing a nice suit. José will drop me off at the airport with my suitcase, which will be holding the money. I am going to go into the terminal like I am catching a flight. When you arrive, I will come back out like I've just arrived. It's better this way, because no one will think it's odd that I am giving you the suitcase. There are thousands of cars that pull up to that curb every day."

"So, I just park at the curb, pop the trunk, you put the suitcase in, and I'll take off? That sounds simple enough."

"Yes, Manny," he said. "Very simple indeed."

\* \* \*

I WAS SCHEDULED TO pick up the money at 2:00 p.m. As we discussed, Ceritt would be waiting for me inside the airport. José was also supposed to be there, watching from afar, in case anything went wrong. Santo was also stationed in the parking lot, monitoring the seizure. A team of FBI agents conducted surveillance, snapping pictures and taking video, while three plainclothes agents were designated to seize the money. I had given Santo a warning after my meeting with Ceritt. This guy is going to fight back. He's not afraid to die. He is armed and extremely dangerous. Santo assured me that the agents on the ground could handle it.

I pulled into the airport parking lot and crept up to the

curb. Ceritt saw my car and walked outside. He wheeled the suitcase behind him, which was filled to the brim with cash. I popped the trunk. Right on cue, the three plainclothes FBI agents approached him and asked for his immigration papers. They were supposed to spook him, let him run, and take the suitcase. But one of the agents inexplicably grabbed Ceritt by the arm, and Ceritt reared back and slugged the agent in the face. He split his forehead from nose to crown. The agent fell backward onto his ass. Then Ceritt ditched the suitcase and took off. The agents stumbled around, blood all over the ground and them. Eventually, they grabbed the suitcase, made their way out of the pickup area, got into their car, and left with the money.

I got the hell out of there, playacting as if I was as surprised as Ceritt by the confrontation. I had to act the part because José was watching from the parking lot. I nearly sideswiped a car as I careened toward the exit. José saw my car and flagged me down on foot. I stopped, and he approached my window. "Call your army!" he shouted. "Let's hit these guys before they get away!"

"I'm not in that business," I told him. "That's not what I do. I don't kill people. I am responsible for the money, that's it."

"We have to retaliate!"

"I'm fucking out of here. You're obviously hot. I can't be here." I zoomed out of the parking lot and went straight back to my undercover apartment. I didn't leave for over six hours, counting down the minutes for when I was supposed to debrief with Santo and Tony. I needed it to look like I was hiding out, in case the cartel was watching me.

\* \* \*

## INSIDE THE CARTEL

I WAS SUPPOSED TO meet Santo at Plaza de Americas, the shopping mall, just after dark. We had to take more precautions than previous meetings, considering that the cartel was surely suspicious that I had something to do with what they thought was a robbery. I pulled into the front parking lot, got out of my car, and entered the building. I walked through the mall, looped down this wing and that wing, and then exited through the rear entrance, into a different parking lot. I spotted Santo's covert car in the back, under a canopy of palm trees. I opened the door and fell into the passenger seat. He was heaving into his paper bag again.

"Everything all right?" I asked. "Does that even help?"

He pulled it away from his mouth. "It's the only thing keeping me from having a nervous breakdown," he said. He took a final deep breath and threw the bag in the back seat. "Let's go get Tony." We drove to another shopping mall on the far side of San Juan and found Tony waiting for us in the rear parking lot. We all drove to Tony's father's house, a secluded spot outside of the city, which had become another one of our covert meeting locations. We parked in the garage, closed the door, and made our way to the roof deck. Tony grabbed a couple of beers, and we gazed out at San Juan Bay, boats crawling along the shore like scurrying bugs, and went over what happened earlier at the airport. We couldn't help but laugh at the agent getting slugged in the face by Ceritt. Honestly, it was sort of funny and gave us some much-needed comic relief. In fact, over the years, that punch became a part of FBI lore. The agent still had a mark on his forehead decades later. He eventually became a high-ranking management figure in Washington, DC, the scar a testament to the risks he took to get there.

"What the fuck, you know?" Santo said. "Did he listen to instructions, to just let him run?"

"At least he earned the stitches!" Tony said, howling with laughter.

"Maybe it worked out for the best," I said. "Now, it's more believable that we weren't involved."

"Well, what is Toro's reaction going to be, being as we lost the money?" Tony asked. "This might make him suspicious of us, regardless if your agent got sucker punched."

"You have a valid point," I said, "but he's so happy with us. We've laundered so much for him. I bet he will get pissed off as a matter of principle, but this isn't a big loss for him. How much was in the suitcase? $150,000? He can easily absorb that loss."

"I agree," Santo said. "You guys should be fine."

"You might be right," Tony said, "but, again, it's a matter of principle, and a well-run organization doesn't even lose a pencil. I don't believe that he thinks we are cops, but maybe careless. We didn't have better control over the situation, to his eyes."

"Stop worrying," I said. "We will be fine. It technically wasn't even our fault. Plus, we are here to try and make a case, not make money for the cartel. If we have to seize some money, it is what it is. Because, in the end, when we arrest them, we are *really* going to rip them off."

* * *

DANIEL MAYER, TORO'S MIAMI-BASED counterpart, called me first thing the following morning. His tone was sympathetic, calm, like he cared about my well-being and, most importantly, didn't suspect that I was involved.

"So, what happened yesterday?" he asked.

"Only God knows what happened," I said. "If I can help it,

I don't want to pick up from them again. It's obvious that they have heat on them."

"Manny, it's your job to pick up the money."

"Well, I'm looking out for Toro and the organization," I said.

"What do you mean?"

"Can you imagine if José had killed those guys? Imagine he made me get involved? You think Toro would've liked that? Can you believe that guy? He ran in front of my car as I was trying to get out of there!" Daniel knew I was right. "Look, I need to make sure they didn't bring any of their heat onto me," I said. "I need to get a new car now."

"Do you have any idea who they were?" he asked.

"To me, they looked like street people," I said, planting some misinformation, "but I didn't stick around to find out. It could've been anyone."

Now that I knew that Daniel and Toro were investigating what happened, I booked it over to Tony's house. I had to make sure he wasn't going to say anything stupid if Toro called him. And I knew that Daniel was going to relay every word I said back to Toro, and Toro was going to call Tony to double-check my explanation. Tony and I had to keep our stories straight. I barged into Tony's house. He was sitting at his dining room table.

"Daniel just called me," I said. "Did Toro call you?"

He nodded. "What did he say?" I asked.

"He just asked what happened," Tony said. "I told him that it was just random, but that I wasn't there. He wanted to talk with you."

My pocket vibrated. My phone was ringing. It was Toro. I frantically plugged the phone into my recording device, made sure it was turned on, and answered the call.

"What the hell happened?" Toro asked, clearly frustrated.

"I popped open the trunk for him to put the suitcase in my car, but before he got to me, these guys approached him," I explained. "I could see in my rearview mirror that he was fighting with them. I don't know what they said to him, but he slugged one guy in the face and ran."

"What did they look like?"

"They looked like street guys. I think they might've been Dominican."

"What makes you think that?"

"I don't know," I said. "They looked Dominican."

"So, they weren't police? Did they look like detectives?"

"No," I said, further deflecting. "They were definitely not cops. I'm telling you the same thing that I told José. I couldn't help him. I am here to pick up money, not fight random people, which could compromise your operation. I am not responsible for money that I didn't receive."

"You're right," Toro said. "It's on them." I could hear him breathing on the other end of the line. And then he said, in a stern voice that haunted me from that moment on: "But if I ever find out you were behind this, you will be the one to answer for it."

\* \* \*

EVEN AFTER SPENDING SIX years working deep undercover, the man whose approval I sought the most, whose presence forced me to keep going with an operation that was getting more and more heated, continued to be my father. He stopped by my house at least once a week to see my boys, and my wife would take them to my parents' modest beach cottage on the weekends. My father walked them along the water's edge, scoured for seashells, and cooked fish over an open fire. He still had his plot of land up in the mountains, where he grew lemons, mangoes, grapefruit, and bananas. He'd carefully tended to it over the years and now, three decades later, the plot boasted nearly triple the amount of lemon trees from when I was a child. And, after hearing the funny story about how our neighborhood gate guard "ripped off" my youngest son, my father urged me to take him up to the grove so he could pick his own lemons for the lemonade stand.

I was able to take a few days off after the fallout from the airport seizure. I turned back into Martin and took my son to the lemon grove with my father. My son and I met him at his house and drove up into the mountains together. The plot was nestled in the central highlands, the island's most fertile region. As we made our way deeper into the tropical forest, my father once again brought up the lemonade stand story to my son.

"When you get back and set up your stand, you'll never let anyone steal from you, right?" he asked him. My father always talked to my son as if he were a little man, someone worthy of respect.

"Exactly!" my son squealed from the back seat.

When we arrived, I handed my son a small pail and sent him off to the trees. My father had recently built a brick firepit, and we filled it with wood. We lit a fire and grilled some hamburgers for lunch. This plot of land was a special place for my father and me. When I was a teenager, we would walk the land together and talk about building a house there: where it would sit, what the layout might be, how we would enjoy this little sanctuary. We built a shed on the land as a first project, which was meant to hold our tools and construction materials for the new house. We even built a scale model of the dream house on his sunporch. It was a two-story bungalow with big bay windows. We methodically carved each wall, roof pitch, and every nook and cranny out of cardboard, and assembled the structure piece by piece. We worked on the model continuously for over two years. When I returned to Puerto Rico after becoming an FBI agent, I went to my father's house and found the model on the sunporch. It was still there twenty years later, as clean and perfect as the day we'd finished, but he seemed to have lost sight of our dream to build the house when I left home. His interests had shifted to his beach house. But he still tended to the lemon grove, making sure the small token of what this land represented to us continued to thrive.

I hadn't told my father about the blown-up Volvo and the threats from the men in the red Honda or from Toro. I didn't want to worry him. He knew my line of work was dangerous, but he still believed that I was still working with the terrorism squad, investigating the Macheteros, an insurgent group on the island. I never explained that I had transferred to the drug squad and infiltrated a Colombian drug cartel. As we stood together under the shade of the lemon trees, a feeling of vulnerability came over me, and I desperately wanted to come clean about exactly what I was doing. I wanted to tell my father he was the reason why I took on the case. That I wanted to make him proud. But before my mouth got the best of me, my son came rushing over, holding a basket of fruit, and yelped, "Daddy, let's make lemonade!"

# CHAPTER 15

# SALUD

JUNE 15, 1994, WOULD GO DOWN IN HISTORY AS ONE OF THE most pivotal, and consequential, dates not only for the War on Drugs, but for the Colombian political establishment. Former senator Ernesto Samper, who was previously the Colombian ambassador to Spain, had just won the presidential election. It was a heated race against conservative candidate, and former mayor of Bogotá, Andrés Pastrana Arango. Samper eked out the win by only 2 percent.

Almost immediately after his defeat, Arango accused Samper of accepting drug money to finance his campaign. And he announced that he had tapes to prove it. They would come to be known as the "narco-cassettes," which featured a member of Samper's campaign speaking with a representative of the Cali Cartel. The scandal, dubbed "*Proceso* 8,000," snowballed over the proceeding months and revealed that Samper's campaign allegedly received $6 million from the Cali Cartel. At this time, the godfathers of Cali, who had come to control the majority of the country's drug trade after Pablo Escobar was killed seven months prior, were still trying to negotiate their surrender with the Colombian government. The alleged donation to Samper's campaign, which many credited as the deciding factor of his successful election, was presumably a quid pro quo to make sure that Cali's terms of surrender would be accepted. Both Samper and Cali denied impropriety, but the damage was done. To many, Samper's moral legitimacy was thrown into question.

* * *

I HAD LAUNDERED OVER $50 million for Toro and the North Coast Cartel at this point and delivered a mountain of cashier's checks to Toro's courier, Julio Tamez. We met more and more since the airport disaster, and although my assignment was to safely transfer the checks to him, my real mission was to push him to reveal more information about Toro's operational structure. I had already come to understand the Moore cousins' apparent involvement within the laundering operation over in Aruba, but there was definitely more intelligence to gather on how the Colombian political establishment was protecting them, and perhaps even which corporations were supplying their dirty merchandise. Julio Tamez was certainly a leaky faucet, but sometimes our conversations just didn't deliver. This put me in a tough spot. I didn't want to raise any red flags by coming across as pushy—someone mining for intelligence—but the threats against my family rattled me, and the Samper scandal created instability in Colombian politics and the narco-world. I knew we were standing on shaky ground. I needed Tamez to give me the information the FBI required so the Department of Justice and the US Attorney's Office could prepare their indictments.

Toro scheduled another meetup with Tamez, and I made

my way to our rendezvous point, that grimy motel near the ocean. I entered the room and handed over the checks.

"It never stops, the flow of money," he said.

"You're telling me. I'm the guy who has to pick the stuff up," I said. "So, what's being shipped to Colombia this time?"

"Cigarettes," he said. "You know, back in Colombia, Toro has a partner who they call 'the Marlboro Man,' right?"

I laughed. It was a funny nickname. "The Marlboro Man?"

"¡Sí! He's the king of cigarettes in Colombia," he said. Tamez was talking about Hector Lopez, who in 1986 was elected counselor for the city of Maicao, where Toro was based, and in 1988 was appointed deputy of La Guajira, the broader region that encompassed the seaside city. Lopez came from a family enmeshed in the shipping-and-receiving business, and he held a near-monopoly over imports and exports in the region. He became known as the Marlboro Man due to his prolific importation of cigarettes into Colombia. He also allegedly counted a key friend in Bogotá: Colombia's newly minted president, Ernesto Samper. Tamez explained that Lopez used his power and connections to act as the final chain in Toro's money-laundering operation. Lopez didn't only use his political contacts to protect the North Coast Cartel's turf; he actively participated in the narco-economy by importing the dirty merchandise and making sure it entered the Colombian supply chain. "And get this," Tamez continued, "Lopez is running for the Senate right now. With Samper in office as president, he's definitely going to win. We're about to have a lot of friends in high places, Manny."

I wanted to make sure I understood this correctly: The Snail, the leader of the North Coast Cartel, exports cocaine to the United States; his traffickers sell the load to kingpins in San Juan, Miami, and other US cities; the money is smurfed into cashier's checks and deposited into bank accounts allegedly controlled by Toro and the Moore cousins; and then they seemingly take the laundered money and, using shell corporations, buy cigarettes and other merchandise with it. Lastly, Lopez uses his political connections to import these goods into Colombia and sell them. And then Toro apparently uses the Moore cousins to route the clean pesos back to the cartel so they can keep producing cocaine and start the process over again?

"Exactly," Tamez said after my summation. "But that's not all. The Moores are direct clients of Philip Morris. They also know people at British American Tobacco and have been working with them for decades." (Neither company was charged with, nor convicted of, a crime.)

My heart nearly jumped into my throat. These were the two largest tobacco manufacturers in the entire world. "So, the Moores just call them and place an order?" I asked. "Don't they know that they are being paid with drug money?"

"It seems to me that they should. But it's not like a *cartel* is paying them," Tamez said. "It's one of the fake import businesses set up by the Moores, and the money is coming from SurBank, a very reputable institution. No one asks too many questions, and the deals go down."

"So, Toro and the Moores are insulated from all sides."

Tamez nodded. "Exactly. These aren't sketchy companies that he's buying products from. They are some of the largest corporations in the world—companies that have been around for over a century. And obviously they love the business Toro and the Moores bring to them. It's a well-oiled machine. The manufacturers are making millions of dollars per year in revenue because of Toro, the Moore cousins, and Lopez. You think they are going to turn down that business? Cigarettes are a massive commodity in Colombia and make up a sizable portion of its economy."

"It makes sense," I said, gearing up for the last piece of the puzzle. "And his contacts in Colombia must enjoy the business, as well."

"Well, Lopez has many people on the payroll, as you probably know," he said. "How else do you think he gets this stuff into Colombia and is able to make it look like legitimate sales? Where do you think all the money for Ernesto Samper's campaign came from? It wasn't just the Cali Cartel, I'll tell you that."

I couldn't believe what I was hearing. Tamez was claiming that major American corporations and the highest level of the Colombian government were allegedly on the take from Toro's money-laundering scheme. They were allegedly participants in, and instigators of, the Black Market Peso Exchange. "But why would the politicians want to be so involved with the cartels like this?" I asked. "They are just losing leverage, exposing themselves to cartel control."

"I mean, sure," Tamez said, "but you have to understand the bigger picture here. Yes, the politicians line their own pockets by being corrupt, but what do you think happens when all these useful products land on Colombian soil? Toro and the Moore cousins are buying them for a discount with the drug money because they are such good and consistent customers, and then they are selling the goods to businesses in Colombia more cheaply than local merchants can find elsewhere, and then that savings is passed along to the average consumer living in Medellín or Bogotá or Barranquilla."

"You mean that the drug trade actually helps people," I said, swallowing hard, resigning myself to the ironic truth of the narco-empires that controlled South America.

"In some ways, yes, when there's no violence involved, of course," he said. "You have to understand, the Colombian people are poor. If the Advil that their grandmother needs for her aging hip is half the price of what it normally would be, or the black market cigarettes are cheaper because they were smuggled in through the free-trade zone in Aruba without paying taxes, that savings can be diverted to put food on the table. At the end of the day, the average consumer doesn't care if these goods are the by-product of the cocaine trade, or if the money used to get them to Colombia is actually laundered drug money. Everyone is incentivized to keep this going, in one way or another."

"And if the music stops," I said, "everyone is screwed."

"Exactly," he said. "Without this underground system—or the Black Market Peso Exchange, as you call it—the Colombian economy could collapse."

* * *

TORO NEXT CALLED TONY and said that we needed to take cashier checks to Daniel Mayer in Miami. "He'll be coming to Colombia after you drop them off," he said. I told Tony that I would go alone. I needed more facetime with Daniel, to manipulate him both into admitting aspects of the scheme, and to confirm the bombshells that Julio Tamez had disclosed to me during our last meeting. I called Daniel the same day to arrange the details of my trip.

"Toro says I need to meet with you," I said.

"Yes, Manny," he said. "Come to Miami. It will be a good time."

"Sounds good," I said. "We'll get a few whiskeys under our belt."

## INSIDE THE CARTEL

"I'd like that very much," he said. "I want you to come to my office. It's in one of those high-rise buildings on Biscayne Boulevard. Can you handle that?"

I smiled to myself, eager to see what sort of evidence was stashed within the nerve center of their money-laundering ring. "Of course I can," I said. "I will see you soon."

Santo decided to travel with me. We put together the same clandestine arrangement as my last trip to Miami: I traveled under my covert identity, and Santo caught a separate flight and brought along my gun and the $1 million in checks that Toro directed me to give to Daniel. I landed at the airport, made my way off the plane, and stopped at a bar in the terminal, where I met with an agent from the Miami field office, who was also operating undercover. I grabbed a stool next to him at the bar and he slid me a key with a number stamped into its grip: 489. I took the key, finished my whiskey, and walked to a wall of lockers next to the baggage claim. After I made sure no one was watching me, I threaded the key into box number 489, opened it, and grabbed my gun and the cashier's checks. I took a cab to an Embassy Suites hotel, checked into my room, dropped off my bags, and made my way to Daniel's office on Biscayne Boulevard.

I took the elevator up to the floor. The doors opened to reveal an expansive office for a company called Carib-Foods. Their logo, curled letters and bright colors, anchored the foyer that led past a secretary's desk and into the cubicle-filled office floor. *This is strange*, I thought to myself. Daniel had never mentioned that he was an employee of an import-export produce company. Was it possible that Carib-Foods were also part of the money-laundering operation? The office, however, was empty; it was late in the afternoon and all of the employees had already gone home. I walked down the row of cubicles and saw Daniel standing in a glass-paneled executive suite overlooking the water. He waved me in.

He beamed a hearty smile, clearly happy to see me. He opened his arms for a hug, and I accepted. He clearly didn't find it necessary to hide in the shower anymore; we were friends now. His hands lingered on my back, running from both shoulder blades to the nook of my tailbone. He wouldn't find my wire, though; it was in my bag. "Take a seat," he said. "Whiskey?" I nodded.

It was a large office, with a wide wooden desk and hulking leather chairs. The furniture looked brand-new. The space was clean and organized, a businessman's domain. Two maps, their frames outlined in gold, hung on the wall: one of Panama, another of Colombia. I spotted a series of leather-bound books on the shelf that lined the wall behind his desk. They appeared to be trading ledgers labeled with their corresponding countries: Panama, Belize, Aruba, Colombia. I scanned for more evidence, but I wanted to play it cool. I couldn't seem too interested in what he had going on here.

"Macallan Eighteen?" he asked, standing next to his booze cart.

"I'll take some Black Label, actually," I said.

"I'm the same way," he said, reaching for the bottle. "I forgot you liked Black Label."

He poured two glasses and handed me one. I gave him the cashier's checks, wrapped in newsprint and secured with fiberglass tape. "One million," I said.

"Thanks," he said. "I appreciate you bringing them." He placed the bundle on his desk, not even bothering to make sure they were all there. This was a good sign. He fully trusted me now. We drank our whiskeys, and he started on a long monologue about all the women he was dating at the moment.

I nodded along, laughed at his jokes, and masked my alertness with relaxation. My goal, during any meeting within this investigation, was to establish a link between the money and the drugs, because that would give us the most leverage once my target was indicted. The possibility of decades behind bars—mandatory minimum sentences thanks to policies enacted under the War on Drugs—could force someone like Daniel to spill the beans on details of the money-laundering scheme that we weren't able to grab through my undercover operation. But I still had to play the long game with these guys. If I asked too many probing questions about Toro, the Moore cousins, Lopez, Samper, or other aspects of their apparent business model, Daniel would know something was up. I am merely a money soldier; why would I want to know these things? Still, I couldn't help myself to gently push his buttons.

"I can take this money to Toro directly, if you need me to," I said. "I understand this was a rush job. I could always go from Puerto Rico straight to Aruba or Colombia." It was a bluff. I would have to ask the FBI for clearance to leave the country, but I wanted to see what he would say, and for him to know that I knew about their contacts in Aruba.

"Oh," he said, taking a pause. "I needed this money here first." He didn't elaborate further, and I didn't push for more information. It didn't matter all that much. The men from whom I picked up this money, which the FBI turned into the cashier's checks that I'd just handed to Daniel, had already admitted to me, with my wire listening, that it was drug money. Ignorance didn't protect Daniel from the law. Moreover, we had his phone tapped. After I left, I knew he would make a call about my drop-off, which would be recorded. I didn't need to press him. We would catch him on the wiretap, anyway.

After we finished our drinks, I got up to leave. Daniel said it was nice to see me, and that he would have me do more drop-offs in Miami soon.

* * *

THE FOLLOWING WEEK, DANIEL called me and instructed me to bring more cashier's checks to Miami, but this time I was to have them made out to Carib-Foods. Bingo. I knew that the business was involved in some way, that Daniel wasn't merely a subletter. He instructed me to drop off the checks at their headquarters in Doral. He then invited me to come by his house when I was done and have another whiskey. Of course I obliged.

The Carib-Foods main office in Doral was as legitimate as their high-rise office on Biscayne Boulevard, only much larger. I arrived just after lunch on a weekday, and the space was bustling with dozens of employees. I met with the owner. He was a stocky Cuban American guy in his late fifties, dressed in a bespoke suit. His son, in his midthirties, accompanied him. It was a quick handoff, no pleasantries shared. The two men were curt but polite. Daniel had given me the boss's phone number, in case I needed it, and I handed the number off to Santo, for our records. Our surveillance revealed that Carib-Foods were certainly part of the Black Market Peso Exchange. They apparently shipped produce to the Moores' company in the Aruba free-trade zone, which was then sent to Colombia and sold to regional distributors, with the proceeds deposited into the cartel's bank accounts.

I left the office and drove to Daniel's house, a luxurious mansion near North Miami Beach. It was a lovely part of the city, quiet and pristine. Mangroves surrounded his home, which sat on the edge of the intercoastal waterway with direct access to the estuary from the backyard. You could get on his boat from the rear dock and be in the open ocean within a few minutes. I walked up to the front door and knocked. Daniel's wife, a flashy American woman with bleached blond hair and long legs, opened the door. She looked like a model. She greeted me cordially, but I could tell she was guarded. It was clear that she knew how her husband made his money and had a clue as to my part. (She was never charged with a crime.) Daniel scurried to the door and ushered me in. The interior of the home was more gorgeous than the exterior, with a massive kitchen outfitted with brand-new stainless-steel appliances.

We walked into the den, which faced the backyard and his private waterfront dock. "Black Label?" Daniel said, smirking, remembering my drink of choice.

"Sure," I said.

"You have to see this," he said. Against the far wall sat a massive bottle of whiskey, over four feet tall, holding thousands of dollars' worth of liquor. A gyroscope centered the stand that cradled it. With a gentle tip of the neck, the bottle tilted forward, and the liquid rushed into my crystal tumbler. I didn't see the massive bottle as a kitschy item to show off. To me, it symbolized just how far removed from street dealing these money launderers lived.

"*Salud*," Daniel said, raising his glass.

"*Salud*," I repeated, taking a long, slow slip.

"How did it go with Carib-Foods?" he asked.

"I met the old man and his son," I said. "No issues there."

"Good," he said. "How are things going in San Juan?"

"Just fine," I said. "Tony said you lived there for a period of time, too?"

He nodded. "I set up the entire operation there for Toro," he said.

## SALUD

"Did you have the same problems with the guys talking about drugs when you picked up the money?" I asked. My first nudge. "They always mention how the money comes from drugs."

"Yes, they always did that," he said, "but don't mention it to Toro, and obviously don't talk to anyone else about it."

"Why don't you instruct these guys not to bring it up to us? It just muddies the waters. They even ask for my help with smuggling. I always deflect, but these guys just keep complaining to me about their issues getting the drugs onto the island."

"Don't engage with them," he said. "We are not in that business. Manny, I really don't know where this money comes from, and I don't want to know. We can talk about money all you want, but let's not discuss dope."

"Listen," I said, eager to keep pushing him, "I deal with these guys on the street. They bring guns to every meeting. I need to be able to tell them that I at least passed along the word to you and Toro that they are having delivery problems, so they'll get off my back."

"Refer them back to the people who delivered the load to them," he said. "It's not our problem. We are not responsible for the merchandise. Our only problem is getting the money back to Colombia."

I needed to keep him talking. "Are we getting more wagons?" I asked, speaking in code, referencing the million-dollar deliveries.

"Yes," he said. "Our other men aren't as professional as you and Tony. The guys in Haiti, Dominican Republic, Saint Martin, Saint Nevins: they can be unreliable. We want to shift more money to you."

"At least you have Julio Tamez," I said, pushing further. "I like his style. He's very cautious, dresses like a businessman when he travels, stashes the checks very well on his body. He moves through security like nothing."

"Yeah, he's a good guy," Daniel said. "He's related to Toro, did you know that? Tamez is married to Toro's niece."

I had more than enough evidence on my wire for one meeting, but I needed to push just a little more. I wanted to know it all. "He really likes Aruba," I said.

"Yeah, it's a gorgeous place," he said. "You should come sometime soon. We can meet Toro there and introduce you to all of our partners. We'll have a good time."

"The Moore cousins?" I asked. I needed him to confirm it on the wire.

"Yes," he said. "We can go to their casinos. It will be great. They will take care of us. And while you're at it, you can bring some money for Ethan and Alec. They'd really appreciate it."

\* \* \*

AFTER I LEFT DANIEL'S house, I immediately called Santo and told him that I had been invited to Aruba to meet with Toro and the Moore cousins. "We're going to get access to the big guys," I told him. "We'll talk more when I'm back in San Juan." I then called Tony, who said he had already spoken with Daniel, who told him that we met at his house. Tony was thrilled. The climax of his cooperation was on the horizon.

I made my way back to Puerto Rico and called a meeting with Santo and the other case agents at one of our safe houses in San Juan. I explained that everyone would be in Aruba: Daniel, Toro, Julio Tamez, and members of the Moore family. I also told them that Daniel asked me to bring money to give to the Moores directly. Here was the missing link of our entire

# SALUD

investigation. We were thrilled, everyone convinced that this was the right move to make. Our request quickly made it up the chain to Washington, DC, who gave their blessing. I was going to Aruba.

As I prepared for my trip, SAC Dick Sanders requested my presence. It was the same setup as last time: Jimmy drove him to the safe house, parked in the garage, and I met them there. We sat down at the same dining room table. Jimmy took notes.

"How are you doing? How are things with the family?" he asked.

I kept hidden the full truth about the threats I had received. I didn't want to be denied the opportunity to go to Aruba because of a misplaced hunch. "We're great," I said. "Everything is going really well."

"Martin, you've gathered more evidence than we could've ever dreamed of when we first started this case," he said. "Are you sure you want to go to Aruba?"

Dick had a point. We had traced every phone number, every check, every shipment to Colombia. In many respects, I didn't need to go to Aruba. We had more than enough probable cause to draw up an indictment and get convictions at trial. Plus, the fallout from Ernesto Samper's presidential campaign was piling up. Even more narco-cassettes had been released, one of which included an alleged conversation between Elizabeth Montoya, the wife of a Cali Cartel deputy, and members of Samper's campaign, where a $500,000 donation was allegedly arranged on behalf of Senator Hector Lopez and the Moore family. Julio Tamez was telling the truth. After Samper took office a few months later, the Moore family was allegedly awarded a monopoly over the Colombian gambling market.

"Yes, of course," I said. It was unthinkable that I would give up the opportunity to get the entire group on my wire. "This case is my baby. I should go."

"Everyone will be there?"

I nodded. "Toro, the Moores, Julio Tamez, Daniel Mayer—everyone. And Daniel told me that Tony and I were going to be given a lot more money from now on. I think Toro and the Moores will want to discuss that with me while I'm in Aruba."

"You have my full support, Martin," he said. "Whatever you need. Once you're back from Aruba, we can close the case. We'll have more than enough to indict. You'll be done, and you can go back to your family." To satisfy Dick, a role model for all FBI agents, made the stress of the case worthwhile, especially with the finish line in sight. In many ways, Dick assumed the role of a father figure for me. I was close with his son, so there was a transferable respect, and an element of protection, extended to me. He was a tough boss, to be sure, but he treated me tenderly, like he really cared. Moreover, he was a proxy into the transparency that I wished I could have with my own father. When he and I discussed the details of the case, and of how much I was doing to further it, I pictured myself sharing the same details with my dad. I hoped, one day, I would have that opportunity.

I looked at Dick straight in the eyes and said, "Thank you, boss."

* * *

WITH MY TRIP TO Aruba confirmed, I took the following weekend off and went home to see my family. My boys and I went out to my father's private beach house. It wasn't in a public area, so I could be out in the open and feel safe. Maria and

## SALUD

my father joined, and we even brought our dog, Mushy. She sprinted up and down the waterline, and my sons played fetch with her. We fired up the grill. I felt calmer and more confident than I had in months. The money-laundering investigation was reaching its climax, and my efforts had exceeded the FBI's wildest expectations. My father noticed this change in my demeanor. Although no words were exchanged, I knew he could tell I was happy.

We drove back to our house just after sunset on Sunday. Maria put the boys to bed, and we retreated to our bedroom. I crawled in next to Maria, the sheets clean and cool, my heart full. The next chapter of our life within reach. Although I couldn't share any details with Maria, she, like my father, sensed a shift within me. I wasn't putting on a front. I wasn't pretending. Martin seemed to be winning the tug-of-war. I held Maria close and the sound of the ocean lulled me into a deep sleep.

A few hours later, I awoke to the sound of my pager beeping. *Who's calling me in the middle of the night?* I grabbed it from my nightstand and looked at the number. The area code and first three digits were from the FBI's San Juan field office. *Maybe it's Santo*, I thought to myself. *Maybe he's in trouble and needs my help.* I lifted myself out of bed, walked into the kitchen, and grabbed the phone off its receiver. I dialed the number that showed up on my pager. After a couple rings, someone answered.

"Hello?" I said. "Hello?" But whoever had paged me didn't respond. All I heard was slow and methodical breathing. I quickly hung up and stared down at my pager again. Yes, the area code and first three digits were the same as the field office, but the last four numbers didn't match any line from the FBI that I remembered. I instantly panicked.

Was this a setup? Was my family in danger? My adrenaline spiked and I quickly switched into agent mode. I closed all the blinds in the house, locked all the doors, checked to make sure my children were safe in their beds, and let our dog, Mushy, out into the backyard to keep watch. She was a barker and would alert me if anyone was coming. I grabbed my pistol from the closet and placed it on my nightstand.

Maria stirred when I got back into bed. "Who was that?" she asked.

"No one," I replied. "Santo paged me by mistake. Everything is fine." She rolled over and fell back asleep, but I lay awake until dawn. I couldn't shake the feeling that the cartel was onto me, that the page wasn't an accident, but an omen.

\* \* \*

I CALLED JIMMY EARLY the next morning. "I got a strange page last night," I told him. "I called the number, but no one answered." I relayed the number that paged me.

"I'll take it to the office and run it through the system," Jimmy said. "Santo and I will let you know what comes back."

Santo called me that afternoon and told me to go to our covert meeting place behind the shopping mall. I raced down to meet him. He explained that the team had traced the number back to the local jail, which sat just down the street from the field office. That's why the numbers were so similar.

"How the hell does someone at the jail have my pager number?" I asked.

"I don't know," he said. "We had two local marshals from the task force go down to the jail and talk to the supervisor. He denied knowing anything, but explained that, in the past, inmates have bribed the guards to use the phone."

## SALUD

"Fuck," I said. "I called back from my house, not my undercover phone."

"Don't worry about it, Martin," Santo said. "We have no reason to believe that this was any type of threat. Like with the Volvo, we haven't heard anything on the wiretaps that would confirm the page as a credible threat. We'll take some precautions, just in case, but they could've just dialed the wrong number, and by chance it was yours."

"Yeah," I said, looking at him. "You're probably right." But inside I knew the truth: Toro was connected to that page somehow. Outwardly, I agreed with Santo. But in my head, I wondered: *Did I just get made?*

## CHAPTER 16

# SICARIO

**MARIA AND OUR BOYS COULD BE IN DANGER. I HAD TO GET** them somewhere safe. After I left Santo in the parking lot, I drove around for a few hours, making sure I didn't have a tail. I couldn't risk being followed back to my house. I swept the entire neighborhood before entering my home. I drove around and made sure no one—especially the two men in the red Honda Civic—were lying in wait. My block was clean. By the time I was done, Maria and the boys were home from school. With our sons playing in the living room, I pulled Maria aside.

"I have to get you up to your father's house in the mountains," I told her. It was a place that no one knew existed, a hideaway where they would be safe. "You need to pack a few bags for you and the boys."

"What's going on, Martin?" she asked, dismayed, a blanket of fear falling over her face.

"It's nothing, sweetie," I told her. I wasn't technically lying, but rather hiding my suspicions. "I just have to clear something up, and I don't want you and the boys in the way while

I do it." She didn't say a word—just hustled into the bedroom, packed a bag, and started loading up the car.

As Maria packed up and my two sons continued to play with their toys, FBI SWAT team member Ron Montblanc showed up at my house. Ron was a burly dude: squat, broad, and laced with muscle. He walked through the door and handed me an AR-15 machine gun, a fully automatic weapon with a scope that could spray nearly a thousand rounds per minute. "The squad is still looking into it," he told me. "They don't want to make a big deal out of it, but I'll hold down the fort until you get back from dropping off Maria and the kids."

My two sons came wandering into the kitchen to find their father holding a fully automatic rifle. Thankfully, they knew Ron. He was a local football coach, and he gave them on-the-field tips. They waved to him, innocently.

"Are you guys excited for football season to start?" Ron asked them.

"Yeah!" my youngest son squealed.

"Remember what I taught you," Ron said. "Make sure to use your legs and lead with your shoulder."

"All right boys," I told them. "Let's get in the car. You're going to go visit *abuelo*."

"Cool!" my eldest son shouted.

"In the mountains, or at the beach?" my youngest asked.

"In the mountains," I told him. "It's going to be fun! Now, help your mother bring your bags into the car, okay?"

They scurried off to find Maria. She came out of the bedroom, and I helped her load their luggage into the car. Ron followed us out. "I'll be here when you get back," he said. I nodded, got into the driver's seat, and sped off. I careened through the dark mountain roads, my two sons asleep in the back seat. Out of nowhere, a car came speeding up behind us, headlights blazing. I held steady, but every turn I took, the car followed. My training kicked in: Don't panic, just observe and internalize the facts at hand.

"Oh my God," Maria said, her voice cracking. "I think he's following us! Don't let him get too close, Martin." I pulled over. I wanted to see what the driver would do. He came closer, closer, closer—and then sped past us. I kept driving but held a safe distance behind the vehicle. And then the car stopped. I kept driving, ready for a gang of gun-wielding cartel hitmen to jump out and start shooting. As I drove past, however, all I saw was a drunkard hunched over the steering wheel. He was just taking a breather, trying to get home safe. Relief washed over me. We continued through the woods, getting closer to safety. At least, I hoped.

I looked over to Maria. "I feel like something is about to happen," I said. "I hope God gives me the strength and the wisdom to deal with it."

Maria reached over and grabbed my hand. "You do have the strength, Martin," she told me. I wanted to believe her.

We arrived at the secret mountain house. We each pulled a sleeping child from the back seat and took them inside. I kissed my two boys on the forehead and gave Maria a hug. I told her there was nothing to be afraid of, and that she should be able to come home soon. Then, I got into my car and drove back to my house. Over the next four days, Rob and I guarded the place, but no one came. No more beeps on my pager from the prison, no men creeping around my house, no threats and no violence. Nothing. Finally, my case agents decided that the coast was clear, and Maria and our boys came back home. The call was chalked up to coincidence. Nonetheless, I needed to be sure it was still safe for me to go to Aruba. I didn't want to be walking into a trap.

## SICARIO

* * *

SANTO AND JIMMY CALLED a meeting with office management. We laid out all of the evidence regarding the threats against me and cross-referenced it with the intelligence we gathered on our wiretaps. We tried our best to play devil's advocate, but it was hard to find a link. Maybe we were all operating under an illusion of safety, excited at what we hoped to achieve, trying to convince ourselves that this trip to Aruba would bring down the whole machine. There were two sides to the argument—nothing had happened yet, so nothing was going to happen. Or, we were being naive.

And still, Toro stayed in touch. I did a few more money pickups for him over the next week. Everything seemed clear. We decided to tell SAC Dick Sanders that I was going to Aruba.

Although Dick initially supported my trip to Aruba, he changed his mind after the prison page. Whether or not the threats were real, sending an agent to Aruba was still a very big risk. The FBI didn't hold a lot of sway on the island. If I was walking into a trap, I could be kidnapped, taken back to Colombia, tortured, and killed. We were in the same situation as when I had been called to Colombia and Diego went in my place. I wanted so badly to meet Toro face-to-face and get the shadowy, billionaire bankers on my wire—but Dick told me that it was just too dangerous. He explained to me that the entire premise of our case was to aim high. At the start, we were merely smurfing money with Tony at the street level, and now I was firmly tied in with Daniel and Toro and had implicated not only dozens of drug lords and traffickers tied to the North Coast Cartel, but members of a billionaire banking dynasty that controlled Aruba. He assured me that, even without my trip to Aruba, we had enough to start making arrests. "We got there,

## INSIDE THE CARTEL

Martin," he told me. "We aimed high, and we achieved our goal. We've done what no other team of agents has done before. Money laundering is complicated. But you made the case, whether you go to Aruba or not."

I basked in the glow of my boss's compliment. But I couldn't shake the itch to finish what I had started, by my own definition. "I understand why I can't go," I told Dick, "but maybe we can work something else out? Maybe we can meet them in Miami or Panama, a place where we have more control."

"I don't even think we need to do that," Dick said. "I talked to the US attorney, and he said we have enough to indict them all. There's no need to put you in harm's way. I'll line up a meeting between you two. He'll want to talk to you about the evidence."

Dick made good on his word. The following week, I met with US Attorney Guillermo Gil at the El San Juan Hotel. Gil was no stranger to investigating Colombian drug cartels. A staunch crusader against the narco-trade, his truck had once been blown up by local drug lords. Despite the danger Gil faced every day, he was undeterred. My case was set to be his crown jewel, a chance to dismantle the North Coast Cartel and the Black Market Peso Exchange in one shot.

"You've done an outstanding job, Agent Suarez," Gil told me. "We have firsthand intelligence. We have thousands of hours of tapes and hundreds of photos and documents. This case is already a slam dunk."

"Thank you, Mr. Gil," I said. "I really appreciate that."

"No, thank you," he said. "Don't worry, Martin. I'm not going to let you down. These guys are going to get what's coming to them."

I let Gil's words settle onto me, a blanket of relief. The

case, in many ways, was in his hands now. I had done what I set out to do.

* * *

IN AUGUST 1994, SHORTLY after my meeting with US Attorney Gil, the FBI called the investigation complete. I could finally become Martin Suarez again. We were done. I never went back to my undercover apartment. I threw away all my doper gear and money-laundering garb. I crushed my undercover phones and turned my wire over to Santo. I would never again need to visit the restaurants, bars, and shady neighborhoods where I picked up money. I did my last switch into Martin, and this two-year saga was over. For all intents and purposes, Manny had disappeared. I erased him. He was a ghost.

Honestly, I felt a little sad to leave Manny behind, that persona, that portion of myself, who I'd become over time. And yet there was still a piece of him that lived in my heart. Emotionally, he was still there, tugging at how I viewed the world around me. I still looked over my shoulder in public places, still maintained best practices, still became suspicious whenever someone held my eye for too long. The shotgun stayed in my car, the pistol on my hip, the hypervigilance wrapped around my mind like a helmet. I tried my best to suppress Manny, to make him vanish, to fully become Martin again. I told myself that, because of him, I had fulfilled my dream, and that it was time to let him go. I felt proud at having brought him into the world, as if he were my third son, and even more proud that we had made it out of this mission alive. And yet I knew that his shadow would forever be cast over my life.

I still had to deal with Tony. As part of his cooperation

## INSIDE THE CARTEL

agreement, the FBI had secured a spot for him in the Federal Witness Protection Program (WITSEC). He, too, would become a ghost: a new identity, a new job, a new life. A few days before he was scheduled to be relocated, I went to his house. We sat on the patio and shared one last drink together. We talked about everything we had accomplished, our unlikely alliance that was on the verge of dismantling a Colombian drug cartel. We laughed about his jalopy, shook our heads at our close calls, and excitedly anticipated the indictments that would be unsealed in a couple of weeks. But a sour taste of resignation settled in our mouths. We had both sacrificed so much to get to this point, and in some ways, we relied on each other throughout the operation. None of this would have been possible without Tony and me. We were the stars of this investigation, and now it was over. In a couple of days, he would be gone. I wouldn't even be told where he'd end up.

"WITSEC is not an easy life," I told him, trying to be honest. "But it beats going to federal prison for twenty-five years, and it's certainly better than being killed by the cartel."

Tony nodded solemnly. "My wife doesn't want to go," he said. "I told her that she can't tell anyone, that we just have to disappear. She was crying. She doesn't want to leave her mother behind."

"It was a decision you made," I told him. "And, honestly, it was the right decision—the noble decision."

Tony looked at me and nodded. "I gave you a hundred percent and you gave me a hundred percent," he said, smiling, remembering our first conversation in the FBI parking lot.

I smiled back. "Did you expect anything less from me?" We clinked glasses and drank. Two days later, Jimmy and I took Tony to a safe house in Houston and handed him over to a team of US marshals.

## SICARIO

\* \* \*

IT FELT GOOD TO be done, to wake up every morning next to my wife, to have breakfast with my children, to be there for them every afternoon when they came home from school. We found the routine we had wanted for so long. It was the prize I had been working for. One morning, I slept in a little later than I usually do, my body still adjusting to a normal nighttime schedule. I walked into the kitchen to find Maria making pancakes for the boys, as she had done back in the Poconos.

"We want syrup!" my youngest son yelped.

"You can have syrup," I said, sitting down next to him, "but you have to drink your milk, too. Football practice starts next week. We need you to be big and strong." After Maria and the boys left for school, I decided to go on my usual morning run through the neighborhood. I had been letting our dog, Mushy, run with me, but today I kept her inside the house. I also left my small, five-shooter pistol at home. I had gotten tired of the crude strip of telephone wire that I used to hold the gun to my hip. I just wanted to relax and run.

I put on my shorts and laced up my sneakers. I ran alongside the golf course, under palm trees and through the hot tropical sun, toward the beach. Halfway there, however, a sinking feeling formed in my gut. I glanced into the golf course's fairways, peered over ridges into its bunkers, and scanned the greens. My heart beat faster than my running pace. A few cars passed by me, and I craned my neck to get a good look at the drivers. The sound of my own feet against the pavement tricked me; I kept thinking their echo was someone coming up behind me. I couldn't understand why, but I felt danger chasing me.

I made it to the beach. I continued my normal routine: I ran down to the jetty, did jumping jacks, muscled through a series of push-ups, and dunked myself in the ocean. I headed back to my house, running in intervals: sprint, jog, sprint, jog, sprint, jog, sprint. I saw my home from around the bend and I pushed my legs: faster, faster, faster. I sprinted to the head-high concrete retaining wall that stretched left from the front of my home and toward my neighbor's house; it separated the street from my outdoor patio. I opened its wooden gate and walked in. I bent over, my hands on my knees, and panted. I had pushed my body. A good run well done. I took deep breaths, in and out, and tried to quiet my heartbeat. Sweat coated my brow and dripped into my eyes. I forgot how good it felt to be in shape. I forgot how good it felt to be Martin. I grabbed a chair, took a seat, and kept breathing.

But then I heard it: *"Tsst! Tsst! Tsst!"*

The voice came from behind me, the venom on his tongue unmistakable. When I turned around, I knew he was a *sicario*, a hitman sent to kill me. He wore black gloves and a gray mask, two black-marble eyes staring back at me. He raised his arm and pointed his pistol, a Smith & Wesson revolver, at my chest. I could see the bullets in the chamber. He had been waiting for me, obscured within a low-hanging row of cat palms.

I raised my hands above my head, the universal signal that I was submissive to him. And yet the rest of my body betrayed what I really wanted to do: run.

"Don't run, motherfucker," he said. "You know what's going to happen to you if you do. You aren't going to outrun these bullets." I stared at him directly in the eyes. "Don't fucking look at me," he said. I dropped my sightline to the ground. "Sit down," he said, pointing to one of my patio chairs.

"What do you want?" I asked.

"Are you the owner of the house?"

I paused. At that moment, I knew this wasn't a robbery. This specific question, irrelevant to a thief, confirmed this man was sent here to kill me. I wanted to figure out a way to either run or fight him, but I was trapped. The sicario was too close for me to run, and too far away for me to overpower him. His operational tactics spoke volumes: he had done this before, and he was a professional. "I'm not the homeowner," I said.

"Let's wait for him inside the house," he said.

"I don't have a key to get in," I said. "He'll be back soon. He went out to buy bread and coffee for breakfast. He said he would be gone only for a few minutes."

"What are you doing here?"

"I'm visiting from Miami," I said. "I was just on a run, and I'm waiting for my friend to get back."

I wanted to keep him talking, to hide who I really was. It was clear why he hadn't just shot me in the back of the head when I came in from my run and sat down in my patio chair: he needed to confirm that it was really me.

"Sit the fuck down," he said. I turned around and raised my arms higher, signaling I wasn't about to put up a fight. I glanced at my sliding-glass door, our reflections beaming back at us. I glared at his face, searching for any hint of recognition. Who was this guy? Had I seen him somewhere before? He caught me looking at him. *CRACK!* He pistol-whipped me in the back of the head.

"Motherfucker, I told you not to look at me!" he said. "Keep your fucking head down!"

I stared down at the ground. I glimpsed his legs behind mine. He wore shorts; tattoos of naked women crawled down his calves and into his boots. They were poor-quality prison tattoos, muddy and splotched. I tried to burn their images into my brain, so I could figure out who this guy was. But, in the end, it didn't matter. I knew who sent him. The only thing running through my head as I waited for death was Toro's words: *At any time, I can reach across the world and tap you on the shoulder.* The sliver of time between disappearing from the criminal underworld and the FBI making their arrests was always the most dangerous part of working undercover. You had no idea what the criminals would do. Toro was still out there, the full power of the cartel behind him, wondering why one of his best money launderers had vanished—and wasn't listed on the indictment, which had surely leaked to him by now.

"Listen, I know the guy who owns the house, but I am not close with him," I said. "I met him in Miami, and he invited me here to stay with him, but I don't know him that well. I'm not going to get shot for someone I barely know. I'll give you whatever you want."

"He's coming back soon?" he asked.

"Yes," I said. "He just went to the bakery."

"When you hear his car pull up, wave him back here."

"Why don't you just let me go?" I asked. "I won't tell anyone that you are here. You can just stay here and deal with him."

"No," he said. "We will wait."

"Come on, man. Just let me go. This doesn't have anything to do with me!"

"Shut the fuck up!" he said. "Get down on your fucking knees." I dropped to one knee, and then the other. I knelt there in silence, his pistol inches away from my head, for what seemed like hours. The sweat that covered my skin from my run had gone cold, my flesh covered in goose bumps, my adrenaline morphing into resignation. I thought to myself: *This might be the day that I die.*

Eventually, he spoke again. "Get up," he ordered. I complied. "Walk." He led me around the house, and he checked all the doors. They were locked. "Do you have a key?" he asked. "I want to wait inside the house for the owner."

"I don't have a key," I said.

"If I find out you are lying to me," he said, "I am going to fucking kill you."

I had a shotgun in my backyard shed, and two guns in the house. One was in my bedroom on the top shelf of my closet. The other gun was in my satchel, which I always stashed in the mudroom closet, right inside the front door. I kept thinking about how I could get one of my guns and turn the tables on this situation. We walked over to the shed. If he opened it, I might be able to push him inside the shed, slam the door, and run. Or dash in front of him, grab my shotgun, and blow a hole through his chest. But he was too smart for that. "Step the fuck back," he said, keeping me five feet away from him. He tried to open the shed, but it was locked. The assassin then walked me back over to the patio and told me to sit down in the chair. He never lowered his gun, never gave me a chance to make a move. The pistol was always pointed straight at my head.

My neighbor, a woman whose property abutted ours along the backyard, came out onto her patio. She was talking on her phone, an early cordless model with a pullout antenna. I could see the shiny strip of metal over the top of our communal fence. She and I had a rapport, mainly because she was so nosy. Anytime she heard Maria or me on our patio or in the backyard, she would poke her head above the fence and chitchat. The sicario tapped my head with the barrel of his gun. "Sit down and don't say a fucking word," he said. "You know what will happen if you do." I prayed that the woman would peek into my yard. *Come on! Look! Look! You look over my fence every day! Please, look!* But she just kept chatting on the phone. Still, her voice was soothing, someone without a care in the world, a phone call to pass a slow morning. Within her voice, I found confidence that I would make it out of this situation alive. I knew that even if I was shot, she'd hear the commotion and call an ambulance, and I'd survive.

It was clear by now that the "owner" of the house was not going to show up, and the hitman knew it. He muttered to himself, running through the facts at hand, trying to convince himself I was the man he had come for. "He has the same eyes," he whispered. "He has the same eyes." At that point, I knew that he knew I was the owner of the house—that I was the man he had been hired to kill.

"Get up," he said. I stood and he began to pat me down. He pushed on the tops of my sneakers, ruffled my socks, and ran his hands along the band of my running shorts. And that's where he found it: my house key. I had lied to him. The key was for the gate that separated the patio from the front door. "You piece-of-shit liar," he said. "Get in the fucking house!"

I knew what he wanted to do: he wanted to take me into the house so his gunshot would be muffled, so my neighbor wouldn't hear, so my family would come home and find my body lying in a pool of blood. I slowly walked toward the gate. I knew that this would be the only chance I had at putting some distance between us, so I could run into the house, grab one of my guns, and defend myself.

A small, three-step staircase separated the landing between the patio floor and the gate. I took each step slowly, the sicario close behind me, his gun shoved into the small of my back. I threaded the key into the lock. I felt his body against mine. I could smell his breath. The gate swung out, toward us, and as I slowly opened it, my body leaned back to give the gate room. I was pressed against him now, and then I went for it: I let go of the gate and tried to grab his gun. He moved his hand, I missed his weapon, and then I shoved him. He lost his balance and stumbled backward down the steps. I immediately flung open the gate, ran to my front door, threw it open, and dove onto the floor. And then his gun went off. My back seized up and I felt blood on my face. I thought I was shot, but when I ran my hands over my face and skull, all I felt was the cool slick of blood from when we scuffled and he busted my nose. He missed. I wasn't dead yet.

"This motherfucker," I said under my breath. "I got this guy now."

I kicked the door closed behind me, stood up, and started running toward my bedroom. It was then that I saw his shadow through the glass doors that led from the living room and onto the patio; like any good hunter, he was trying to ambush me from a different direction. I knew that if I ran down the hallway, I would be fully exposed, and he would have a clear shot at me. Instead, I crouched down against the doorjamb. His shadow faded, and I knew he had gone around the back of the house. I ran into my bedroom, where I kept a pistol in my closet. I blindly grabbed a clip from the shelf—not realizing that it held a measly three rounds—and slapped it into the gun. I took a deep breath and tried to still my racing heart. I was ready to defend myself, my family, my home. I crept back down the hallway toward the kitchen and again perched myself against the doorjamb, which gave me valuable cover, and waited for the firefight to begin. I glanced over my shoulder into the living room and saw the toys, my sons' Christmas gifts from last year: the GI Joes, the football gear, the little tokens that bind a father and his children together. If for no one else, I needed to survive for them. I told myself that this sicario wouldn't steal their father, that when my boys came home from school, I would still be here, ready to take them for a walk on the beach. Martin would live.

"I am coming to get you, motherfucker!" I yelled.

And then I heard my neighbor, the woman who was on the phone, screaming for her husband. "There's a shooting at Martin's house!" she hollered. "Call the police! He's in trouble!"

I stood there for what seemed like an eternity. No shots were fired. We were at a stalemate. I peeked through the doorway, but didn't see the assassin on the patio. I started clearing the house, checking every room to make sure he didn't sneak in and try to ambush me from behind. The rooms were empty. I ran out the front door. Just as I jumped down the steps, he appeared in my path. I charged into him at full speed, our bodies crashing into one another. He stumbled, but I fell backward onto my back, pinning my hand—which still held my gun—under my ass.

The hitman regained his balance and stood up. His body hovered over mine. He raised his gun, the barrel pointing directly at my face, the hammer cocked, his finger on the trigger. In a flash, I lifted my hip, freed my arm, and started shooting. I didn't take aim. I just squeezed the trigger, trying to get this man away from me. He ran into the street. I stood up and chased after him. He sprinted as fast as he could onto the golf course. I raised my pistol, put my sights onto his back, and pulled the trigger.

*Click.*

I was out of bullets.

## CHAPTER 17

# INDICTMENTS

**I RAN TO THE SHED AND GRABBED MY SHOTGUN. I PLANNED** to get in my car and hunt this monster down, but the local cops showed up before I could. Within an hour, twenty FBI agents descended on my house, led by Ron, our SWAT team member, and Jimmy, my administrative case agent. Jimmy ran up to me. He was crestfallen, concerned, hoping I wasn't hurt. He kept asking me what happened, over and over—it was his only defense mechanism. Facts, not emotions, were our guiding light. He wanted to know every single detail. But I needed to calm down first. My hands shook and my vision was blurry. I was a sack of flesh coursing with adrenaline, my soul floating ten feet above my body. Another team of agents scoured the area for the sicario. They wanted to catch him even more than I did. This wasn't typical police work; this was personal.

I didn't call Maria. I didn't want her to rush home sick with worry. I also didn't want my boys to experience the trauma of being yanked out of school midway through the day with no explanation. When she did come home that afternoon, my two sons in the back seat, I saw the three of them enter the house—the three people for whom I had fought, the three people who meant more to me than any undercover operation. Maria came up to me. The fear was still radiating from me.

"Are you okay, Martin?" she asked. I didn't answer, my eyes cast off into the distance, still dismayed by what had happened that morning. And then I looked back at my wife and told her I was fine.

"What happened?" she asked.

"A guy showed up here with a gun, but I was able to fight him off," I told her, deliberately vague. "Jimmy said that they just found him. He's under arrest." My two sons broke away from us and started wandering around. They thought it was cool, seeing all the agents at our house. They didn't know how much peril their father had just been in. Ron knelt down and kept them occupied while I followed Maria into the bedroom. I sat down next to her on the bed.

"Should I leave?" she asked.

"We'll find a place for you and the boys to go for a couple nights," I said.

"What will we tell them, Martin?"

"Let's treat it as a miniature vacation," I said. "Just a little getaway."

\* \* \*

I SPENT THE NEXT few hours in conversation with Jimmy. He wanted to debrief me as quickly as possible, to cement all the details of the attempted assassination. Over two dozen agents stayed at the house and documented the crime scene. They scoured for boot prints and dug for bullet slugs. Around 6:00 p.m., the phone rang. Maria answered it.

"Hi, this is Louis Freeh. Can I speak with Martin, please?"

## INDICTMENTS

He declined to explain that he was *that* Louis Freeh, director of the FBI. In fact, Freeh and my boss, SAC Dick Sanders, were old friends; Freeh had pulled Dick out of retirement to run the San Juan field office when our money-laundering operation began. To Freeh, my case was the most important on the FBI's docket. He had been keeping close tabs on it.

"Well, he's busy right now," Maria told him, having no clue who he was. "He's talking to his colleagues about something important."

"No problem," Freeh said. "I will call back in thirty minutes."

Exactly thirty minutes later, Freeh called back. Maria came over to me and Jimmy, her hand covering the phone's mouthpiece. "Some guy named Freeh is on the phone," she said. "He's already called once."

Jimmy looked at me, and then at Maria. "Who?"

"Louis Freeh?" Maria said. "Do you guys know him?"

Jimmy cracked a smile. "Martin, you might want to take that."

I rose from my seat and grabbed the phone. "Hello, Mr. Freeh, this is Martin speaking."

"Martin, I heard what happened," he said. "Are you okay?"

"Yes, sir."

"Are Maria and the kids okay?"

"Yes, they are fine."

"You did well, Martin," Freeh said. "You are doing some truly heroic things down there. When you're done, I want you to come see me at Quantico. We can go for a run together in the morning. I want you to relax and be among your peers." I thought, perhaps, that Freeh was just paying me lip service, trying to smooth things over after I was almost murdered by a cartel sicario. But the next day, Jimmy called me and told me that my trip to Quantico was booked.

### INSIDE THE CARTEL

* * *

THE SHOOTING MADE THE newspapers. My brother was the first to see the article. It recounted the entire event—and included my real name. The cat was already out of the bag from me being in the press, so I guess the San Juan field office corroborated the story. The FBI, however, was careful not to reveal to the reporter the true nature of my work in Puerto Rico. My attempted assassination was chalked up to a home invasion gone wrong, another example of violence on the island. The article, however, did paint a flattering portrait of me, writing that "shrewd, fast-acting FBI Special Agent Martin Suarez thwarted the assailant." My brother shared the clip with my father, who called me and asked that I come see him. He wanted to make sure his son was safe.

After I walked through his front door, I followed my father out onto the patio. A cool breeze rustled the trees, and a scrum of birds chirped from their highest branches. The model of the house we had planned to build still sat on the table, as pristine as ever. My father pursed his lips, furrowed his brow, and stared down at the ground. I could tell he wanted me to tell him everything, all the darkest secrets and traumas that I still carried with me from my time as Manny. But all he said was, "I saw your name in the newspaper today."

"I was hoping it would stay quiet," I said. "Having my name in the paper could interfere with my work."

He rubbed his chin. "What happened, really?" he asked.

"Oh, it was just random violence," I said. I couldn't tell him that a Colombian cartel had tried to hunt me down. For a life lived within the valley of deception, I couldn't tell my father this one truth. To me, in that moment, I was protecting him. And yet, now, all these years later, I wonder if I had truly opened

## INDICTMENTS

up to my father, he would've been able to reciprocate. I wonder if the sharing of our truths would have allowed our bond to grow. But I couldn't do it. Maybe I was ashamed that I had let my guard down, that I let the cartel enter my home, that I had come so close to losing everything I loved the most. Or maybe I was still under the illusion that silence and obfuscation was the only way to sustain a relationship with my father, that the way he raised me to communicate was the healthiest way to show that you love someone—more telepathic than auditory, more heart than mouth.

"Well," he said, "any help you need, I am here to support you. I can watch over the kids."

"Don't worry, Dad," I said. "I'm not in any danger."

He looked up at me. "I hope not," he said. "I don't know what I would do without you."

* * *

MY TRIP TO QUANTICO wasn't to shoot the breeze with FBI Director Louis Freeh and to be patted on the back for a job well done. I had been exposed to a traumatic event and, as such, the FBI had mandatory protocols, including a psychological evaluation with the behavioral science unit and a post critical incident seminar with other agents who had been through similar ordeals. I was also told that Maria had to come with me. Maria's father took the boys, and we boarded our flight to Virginia. After so many years working undercover, I was excited to go back to where it all began. Quantico was a comforting place to me; I was born there, in a way.

Two FBI agents were waiting for us when we got off the plane. Fall had begun to descend on the region, and the agents brought us windbreakers, knowing we'd be dressed in the warm-weather gear of Puerto Rico. A few other agents and their spouses were also at the airport, and we all took a bus to Quantico together. There are few opportunities for a spouse to enter the FBI's nerve center, and Maria was excited to see my career up close. She had been to Quantico before, when I graduated from new agents class, but I gave her the grand tour of the vast complex anyway: the law library, the outdoor track, the swimming pools, the gyms, the classrooms, all the locations where I had trained to become an agent. It was a proud moment for me, the air electrified, the camaraderie of a shared purpose buzzing all around us, something I left behind when I decided to work undercover. Although she had already seen everything that I pointed out, it still felt like she was experiencing it for the first time.

After giving Maria a tour, we were shuttled into an auditorium with the other agents and their spouses who had recently experienced violence. Twelve agents in total joined, including two from the Washington, DC, bureau. They had recently been subjected to an ambush. The gunman, Bennie Lee Lawson, who was a suspect in a triple homicide, barged into the Washington, DC, police headquarters wielding a semiautomatic pistol. He entered the cold case squad room, to which the FBI agents were assigned, and opened fire. Special Agents Martha Dixon Martinez and Michael John Miller were killed. Their families came to the seminar, alongside the two agents who had been shot but survived. They were in wheelchairs and were later given the Medal of Valor. I felt ashamed. *These men are much worse off than me*, I thought to myself. *I wasn't even injured, at least physically.*

I leaned over to Maria and whispered in her ear, "I don't deserve to be here among these heroes."

## INDICTMENTS

"Nonsense," she said. "You should be here. People who are wiser than us invited you to come."

I was so consumed by the scene that I didn't see Louis Freeh walk up the aisle and stand before me. "Martin," he said. I looked up at him and immediately rose out of my seat.

"Director Freeh," I said. "It's nice to see you."

He smiled. "And you as well." We shook hands. "I just want you to know how impactful this case has been. The intelligence you gathered, the number of indictments we were able to secure, the amount of assets seized—great work."

"Thank you, sir," I said.

"It was pretty heroic what you did out there."

"Thank you," I said. "That means a lot."

"You should run with me in the mornings while you are here," he said.

"I'd be my pleasure," I said.

"Good," he said. "I'll see you out there bright and early." With that, he walked away. I turned to Maria, who sat quietly and listened to the exchange. She was in awe. She smiled at me and placed her hand in mine. She now knew every contour of the case I had been working on, of the secrets I had been keeping, and how far up the chain my efforts had been noticed. But, like always, no words were shared as we watched Freeh walk away, just the warmth of her hand in mine, her eyes gazing at me.

And then the seminar began. Everyone took turns at the podium. They introduced themselves and told their stories about the violence they had endured, why they were here, what sort of case they were working on and how it all went so wrong. A team from the behavioral science unit observed our presentations and took notes. When it was my turn, I walked up to the podium. Maria stood next to me.

"Hello, everyone," I said. "My name is Martin Suarez. I am from the San Juan division, and this is my wife, Maria. Thank you for having us." I paused, took a breath, and looked around the room. I was overcome with emotion, being forced to finally say out loud what sort of life I had been living all these years. I glanced at Maria, her chin held high, proud at the man her husband had become. She nodded, projecting confidence, and it all came spilling out: "I don't think I deserve to be here," I began. "There are some people here that have done some very heroic things, and my incident doesn't compare to that. Nonetheless, I will tell you what happened." My throat clotted up, my hands shook, and my voice wavered. "I was an undercover agent in a long-term money-laundering and narcotics operation that targeted a Colombian drug cartel. I spent two years infiltrating that world. It was a very successful case, but after it was closed down, a perp showed up at my home and held me at gunpoint for hours. That animal infringed on our peace, coming to where my wife and kids lived. Honestly, it felt like our family had been violated. Our house will never be the same. I used to rest in the hammock in my backyard and take a nap, but after the incident, there's no way I can do that again. I can still hear the *tsst, tsst, tsst* from him as he emerged from the bushes and ambushed me. I hear it everywhere I go. That house will never be a home again, even though my wife and my children love that house. I fought the guy off, but he was able to hit me a few times. In the struggle, I was able to obtain a firearm and chase him away. It's too bad that I ran out of ammunition. I wish I would've killed him."

I stepped from the podium; it was Maria's turn to speak. "Hello, everyone," she said. "Thank you for having me here today. I am very lucky to have not been at the house that day, because if I was there, our children would've been there, too. I left early to take the kids to school, where I am also a teacher. I'll be honest. I haven't felt safe since it happened, either. But I've always had complete trust in Martin's ability and his judgment. I've felt this way since the day Martin joined the Navy in 1978, almost twenty years ago. I will always be proud of everything he does as a representative of the FBI. I will always support him in whatever he wants to do."

Listening to Maria speak, my face twisted as I held back tears. I turned away so the crowd wouldn't see my face, but I felt prouder to hear aloud my wife's support of me, and her admiration of what I had done, than any other time throughout the investigation. Many wives would never have supported their agent husbands to the extent that she did for me.

We both were sent for one-on-one psychological evaluations with counselors from the behavioral science unit. They wanted to make sure that I wasn't permanently scarred from my experience. They also hoped to learn how this type of work affected my wife. After an oral examination, I was given a long written test, and my results were the same as when I first joined the FBI: honest but shrewd, perfect for working undercover. The psychologists asked me about my feelings, how I perceived the case and how it affected me. I was honest. I explained that I had been experiencing hypervigilance for years, especially with anything—a car, a person—approaching me from behind. But I told them that I was slowly beginning to feel better, and that I was ready to start working again. The shrinks informed me that I was surprisingly well-adjusted considering the amount of stress I had experienced. I was cleared to go back into the field—including working undercover, if I chose to do so.

Maria and I had a day to ourselves toward the end of our trip. We walked the grounds and talked about our respective interviews. She told the counselors that, although she sometimes felt unsafe, her confidence in me outweighed the threat of violence that my job entailed. In a way, coming to Quantico made her calmer. Perhaps it was seeing the apparatus that supported me firsthand. Perhaps it was hearing me speak about my work so candidly. Perhaps it was Louis Freeh saying that I did heroic work. Whatever it was, everything we had been through over the past few years had come full circle. Maria saw that my role as an undercover agent was not only recognized but commended by the highest levels of the FBI. She had confirmation that my case had serious implications not only for federal law enforcement, but for the cartels whom I had infiltrated. She knew that all we had experienced had been worthwhile.

* * *

**WE WENT BACK TO** San Juan. While I was gone, SAC Dick Sanders and my case agents tried to elicit a confession from the sicario. They wanted proof that Toro was behind the order. But the hitman wouldn't budge, codified in silence, his allegiance to the cartel unbreakable. Despite our lack of hard evidence, a piece of my heart told me that Toro sent this man to kill me, that he made good on his threat that he could reach his arm across the world at any time and touch my shoulder. I knew, and Dick agreed, it was too dangerous to have me stay in Puerto Rico. The FBI wanted to initiate a safety transfer for me and my family. I was going back to Miami.

While my transfer was being processed, the FBI sent me back to Quantico to teach at the FBI National Academy, a symposium on cutting-edge investigative techniques for high-ranking national and international law enforcement figures. My role would be that of a guidance counselor. I was to make sure they were absorbing all the tactics we employed at the FBI. In fact, I was sent to educate the Colombian general prosecutor who helped investigate—and eventually kill—Pablo Escobar. It didn't feel like a demotion; I felt privileged to be a guiding force for these men.

We sold our house in Puerto Rico before I reported for duty at Quantico, and Maria and the boys moved into a protected condo just outside of San Juan while we waited to relocate to Miami. It was a nice place. They had a pool, my boys made friends, and Maria taught at the elementary school at the nearby Army base. After the shooting at our house, Maria knew our days in Puerto Rico were numbered. The mandatory move was bittersweet for her. She loved the island and the proximity to our family it afforded us, but she knew that leaving was for our own good. When I told her my transfer was official, she said the same thing she told our son when we first moved to San Juan: "Wherever we are, we will be home."

"I know," I said. "We'll make a home, no matter the location."

"We've done what we came here to do," she said. "It's time to go."

Those years in Puerto Rico, despite the stress of working undercover, were some of the best times of my life. I watched my sons grow up. I formed lifelong bonds with my coworkers. And I spent invaluable time with my father. My two sons remembered living in Florida, however, and were excited to move back. They were both in middle school now, and we knew they'd get a better education on the mainland. They weren't little boys anymore. They were emerging as young men. Maria and I quickly found a one-story tropical ranch–style house in Fort Lauderdale, in which we still live to this day.

*   *   *

IN AUGUST 1994, ONE month after the operation ended and shortly after the sicario came for my head, the US Attorney for the District of Puerto Rico Guillermo Gil officially stamped the indictment and filed it into federal court. It made a bigger splash than a bale of cocaine falling from a plane and into the ocean. The document included a who's who of the North Coast Cartel's inner workings: all the traffickers from whom I picked up money, Daniel Mayer, Toro, Julio Tamez, and the Moore cousins. In total, fifty-two members of the cartel and their associates were charged with crimes, ranging from money laundering to drug trafficking. Gil had always been an ally to my undercover operation, a cheerleader who told the FBI that he would absolutely bring charges if we gathered enough evidence to support them. But even my jaw dropped at just how detailed his indictment was—and how it was a direct reflection of all the work my team and I had put in to truly understand how cartels moved their drug money between the US and Colombia. It would take many more years for law enforcement, policymakers, and academics to truly understand the scope of the Black Market Peso Exchange. It came to be known, however, that, throughout the 1980s and 1990s, this shadow money market became the backbone of the transcontinental drug trade and processed over $5 billion in illicit proceeds each year for Colombian cartels. I opened the door for those revelations.

"It was part of the conspiracy," Gil wrote, "that Toro and Mayer, and others, represented various Colombian-based

## INDICTMENTS

owners of United States currency collected from the sale of controlled substances in the United States." In layperson speak: Toro, Mayer and others ran the cartels' money machine. Gil went on, giving a nod to me: "They would deliver to Tony and an undercover FBI agent large amounts of United States currency, which constituted proceeds from the sale of narcotics, so they could transmit, transport, and/or transfer it to the Colombian owners of such proceeds." And Gil nailed Julio Tamez and the Moores down, too: "It was further part of the conspiracy that Ethan Moore and Alec Moore would receive in Aruba cash, money orders, and manager's checks from Julio Tamez and others so they could deposit them in bank accounts and/or transfer them to the Colombian owners of the proceeds."

Nearly all of the defendants were arrested and pleaded guilty, including Daniel Mayer and Julio Tamez, both of whom corroborated, and expanded on, all the intelligence I had gathered while working undercover. Daniel, having read the indictment and seeing that Tony had been working with an undercover FBI agent, put two and two together and realized I was a cop. The first time I sat down with him after his arrest, I asked him, "Did you know that I was an agent?"

"No," he said. "If I knew that, I would have flown back to Colombia and never showed my face again."

"Why do you think you overlooked the obvious?" I asked. "I could never have been absolutely perfect."

"There were no signs."

"Well, perhaps it's because you only saw the money and not the reality of the situation," I said. "Money can blind people. When you see money, you see nothing else."

He nodded, accepted defeat, and told us all that he knew. Julio Tamez was also helpful. But he told us, over and over, to focus on Colombian Senator Hector Lopez. "He's important in all of this," he told me. "He's my real boss."

Alec and Ethan Moore were notified that they had been indicted in US federal court, but the FBI was unable to arrest them because Aruba doesn't have an extradition treaty with the United States. The revelations from our investigation, however, became politically toxic, and their reputations suffered greatly. In 1996, President Bill Clinton took a jab at them publicly, writing in a letter to congressional leaders that Aruba was "a major drug-transit country," adding that "a substantial portion of the free zone's businesses in Aruba are owned and operated by members of the Moore family, who have been indicted in the United States on charges of conspiracy to launder trafficking proceeds." Jonathan Winer, deputy assistant secretary of state for law enforcement and crime during that time, would tell the *Washington Post*, "Moore family members have been involved in money laundering over an extended period of time throughout North and South America."

It took nearly four years of legal wrangling, but the Moore cousins were finally extradited to Puerto Rico in March 1998. They posted $1 million bail and were kept under house arrest in Miami for three years, but were allowed to go back to Aruba in 2001. They never spent a night in a jail cell, and the court records related to their arrangement with the government are still sealed, nearly twenty-five years later. After I'm done with an investigation, I'm on a need-to-know basis regarding the details of a deal between the government and a defendant, but it wouldn't surprise me if the Moore cousins, seemingly the nexus of this money-laundering system, agreed to be government informants for the rest of their lives.

After the indictment was made public, El Toro Negro disappeared. We never found him. He slipped into the darkness of Colombia's criminal underworld and never touched American soil. We were never even able to figure out his real name. The fallout from *Proceso* 8,000—the release of narco-tapes that implicated the highest reaches of Colombia's political establishment—however, was swift: President Ernesto Samper turned his back on many of the cartel godfathers who allegedly helped him get into office in the first place. Starting in 1995, a slew of the country's most formidable cartel leaders were arrested and extradited to the United States. This included Alberto Orlandez-Gamboa—El Caracol, the leader of the North Coast Cartel. The Snail was arrested in June 1998 by the Colombian National Police and extradited to the United States in 2000. It was the first extradition by the Colombian government in more than a decade. Once he was gone, North Coast fractured, dismantled by the FBI and one lone deep-undercover agent posing as a money launderer in Puerto Rico: me.

A few of the defendants in the case, however, pled not guilty and decided to try their luck in front of a jury. The cases moved slowly. In the meantime, I reunited with Ricky at the Miami field office and we worked on a few cases together, including an investigation of Los Pepes, the paramilitary group founded by the Cali Cartel that helped bring down Pablo Escobar. By 1995, Los Pepes themselves became formidable drug traffickers, and we had developed sources deep within the organization. We tracked shipments, set up wiretaps, and conducted seizures. I was only a case agent, however. I didn't go undercover for this operation. In many respects, I couldn't afford to: US Attorney Guillermo Gil had me on call to come to San Juan when needed, as we prepared for the trials related to the money-laundering investigation. The case was so sprawling and complicated that the Department of Justice even sent a team of prosecutors from Washington, DC, to the island to help out. We'd sit in Gil's office for hours and go over the most minute details of the case. We listened to tapes, went over my reports, and made sure there were no outstanding issues about anything I experienced. Gil also secretly flew Tony back to San Juan from his covert WITSEC outpost to corroborate my evidence and, if needed, prepare to take the witness stand. Being with Tony on the other side of the operation was a strangely festive experience. We reminisced about pickups and close calls, about how he had eventually decided to wear the white hat. Gil was impressed with our friendship, the collaboration between an agent and a source, something rare within the world of federal law enforcement that had proven to be so vital.

In late 1996 and early 1997, I made my way back to San Juan to take the witness stand. When the defendants saw me enter the courtroom in my G-man garb—slick suit, trimmed hair, clean-shaven—they knew they were in deep shit. *Manny, a federal agent? It couldn't be!* They knew, seeing me walk into court, that the evidence against them was substantial. After all, they had confided in me. In their minds, I had been running the operation in San Juan for Toro. But in reality, I was a federal agent.

Many of my peers watched in court as I testified and we presented the evidence I gathered. It was a proud moment for me, my final duty in a yearslong operation. And to be honest, it was an experience I thoroughly enjoyed. It felt good to raise my right hand and swear to tell the truth. When you have the facts on your side, you know you're going to win. But I never sneered at these men in court, never showed them contempt.

## INDICTMENTS

We had been bonded through their crimes. I knew their stories, all the good and the bad of their lives. I simply sat there and stoically answered every question asked of me.

The evidence I gathered, the nucleus of which were the tapes I recorded on my wire, spoke for itself. It was the nail in so many coffins. The smugglers sat there, listened to their own voices, and deflated. They knew they were going to jail. I had put my life on the line to catch these men, and the jury understood why. I followed the facts, told the jury my story, and came across as open and honest and calm. I was never frustrated or defensive with defense attorneys who pushed back against my undercover methods. I took my time. I'd pause for nearly twenty seconds before giving an answer, letting a pregnant pause fill the courtroom, ratcheting up the drama. The jury hung on my every word.

During one lunch break, US Attorney Gil approached my squad and told them, "You want to see how you're supposed to testify in a big trial like this? You watch Martin—and you take notes." All of the defendants who went to trial were found guilty and sentenced to decades in prison.

* * *

I TOOK MARIA AND our boys to Puerto Rico when I had to testify. It was a good excuse for a trip, to see our parents, to enjoy some time at the beach cottage and in the mountains. My youngest son, now a preteen remembering the joy of making homemade lemonade, wanted to go up to my father's grove, pick some citrus, and create a pop-up stand down the street from my parents' house so he could hawk the sugary drink for old times' sake. I drove him up into the mountains, and my father met us there. My son ran off into the scrum of trees, basket in hand, and began picking, searching for the ripest and juiciest lemons. My father and I hung back and watched him. It was a Saturday, and I had been in court every day that week—reliving my time as Manny, trying to do right by my father, to be Batman for my sons, to finally put the bad guys away.

"How did it go this week?" my father asked me.

"It's been tough, Dad," I said, a deep desire for honesty coming over me. I thought back to years prior when we had been standing in this same exact spot, and how I wanted, then, to tell him everything. I remembered how it felt to slowly morph into a character who wasn't me, someone my father and I didn't recognize. "The defense attorney is a real jerk."

"But you know the truth, right?" he said. My father was more correct than he ever knew.

"You know, Dad," I said. "I worked undercover with some really bad people. The shootout at my house? That was because of me working undercover. These people, they tried to have me murdered. I was nearly killed more than once for this case. It's personal for me."

"Martin, based on what you've told me, I don't know a single person who has had more of an impact on liberating the earth of this kind of scum."

"A lot of people do this type of work with me. It's a team effort."

"Well, son, I am very proud of you." I didn't respond, just stared off into the distance and let the weight of his words settle on me. "You've become the man I wish I had been."

## CHAPTER 18

# NEVER ENOUGH TIME

**THE INDICTMENTS, THE DOZENS OF GUILTY PLEAS, AND THE** handful of trials didn't spell the end of the government's probe into the Black Market Peso Exchange. My infiltration of the North Coast Cartel and Toro's money-laundering empire revealed the intricacies of how Colombian drug lords routed their money back to South America—the money brokers, the smurfs, the shell companies, the bankers—but one piece of the puzzle still remained hidden to domestic and international law enforcement: the blue-chip corporations who allegedly supplied the goods enlisted to mask the flow of drug money as legitimate business imports. In the eyes of the government, these companies surely knew from where the money that paid for these massive orders came. They vowed to get to the heart of that question, and install safeguards that prevented cartels from participating in the aboveground economy with dirty money.

## INSIDE THE CARTEL

Investigators at the European Union and the Colombian government zeroed-in on Philip Morris and British American Tobacco, which, based on the evidence I'd unearthed, were allegedly the largest clients of Toro and the Moore cousins' apparent money-laundering shell game. Their alleged relationship was, in fact, even cozier than I realized. The Moore family had allegedly been clients of Philip Morris since at least 1966 and acted as their exclusive distributors of cigarettes into South America, whose sales in the 1990s reached into the billions. Colombian authorities would later claim that roughly 90 percent of all cigarettes imported into Colombia came from Philip Morris and British American Tobacco—and were purchased with, or at least compromised by, drug money. (Philip Morris and British American Tobacco were never criminally charged with wrongdoing, and neither corporation admitted guilt in any civil proceeding.)

Authorities even accused Philip Morris, after discovering that their business partners were a cutout for the cartels, of creating even more circuitous means under which they could do business, with the explicit goal of evading law enforcement detection. In some cases, Philip Morris would allegedly make a single transaction of cigarettes, and then, for future orders, simply update the old purchasing agreement to not raise suspicion. That way, auditors would not find it strange that the same company, which really wasn't a company at all, was ordering a massive amount of product bound for Colombia over and over. In other cases, Philip Morris would allegedly ship cigarettes from their plant in Virginia to Europe, where the order changed hands to a middle-man company, and from there the cigarettes were sent to Aruba, where the Moore cousins, using their Colombian connections, would apparently import the contraband into Maicao—where Toro and now-senator Hector Lopez, the Marlboro Man, were based. It was revealed that Philip Morris employees allegedly paid bribes to Colombian officials so they could covertly enter the country and make sure that the orders were fulfilled successfully, and British American Tobacco employees were accused of driving from Colombia to Venezuela to swap cash for cashier's checks, which were then deposited into bank accounts in Miami and eventually routed to British American Tobacco's official business accounts. This certainly sounds insidious and overtly criminal, but the most shocking part of the Black Market Peso Exchange is that many other big-name corporations unwittingly participated in helping cartels launder their money. The *New York Times* reported that General Electric, Microsoft, Apple, and General Motors had sold goods to import companies that were, in fact, cutouts for the Cali Cartel. (These companies were never charged with wrongdoing, and it was never proven that they were aware that their products had entered the black market supply chain.)

But one name, possibly the most crucial aside from Toro and the Moores, came to the fore as investigators continued their work: Senator Hector Lopez, the Marlboro Man. He was the same person whose name Julio Tamez spilled to me during one of our meetings, and someone whom we highlighted for further investigation after my probe concluded. We didn't have enough evidence to indict him directly, but Santo made sure to publicly expose the senator's role in court papers, even if he couldn't be charged yet. "Lopez told Tamez that he was involved in the pool system of drug trafficking, whereby he would combine his load of drugs with those of other drug dealers into a single large shipment destined for the United States or Puerto Rico," Santo wrote in a 1997 affidavit meant to extradite the Moore cousins out of Aruba and to Puerto Rico so they could be brought to justice. "Individual traffickers in the United States received the drugs and sold them for US currency. The traffickers would then deliver the cash to couriers approved by the drug lords who would convert the cash into cashier's checks made payable to specific businesses owned by Lopez and the Moores." Lopez was also allegedly listed in internal Philip Morris documents as being a customer of the corporation. What's more: a tape-recorded conversation caught a friend of Colombian President Ernesto Samper allegedly pressuring him to meet with "the presidents of SurBank" in Aruba—the Moore cousins. And the $500,000 that the Moores allegedly gave to Samper's campaign? In all likelihood, this money came from a pickup that I conducted in Puerto Rico, and possibly could've been handed over during the trip to Aruba to which I was invited but wasn't able to attend. Can you imagine? I could've witnessed the president of Colombia accepting drug money from billionaire international money launderers.

And yet, even without my presence at this meeting, I was able to not only severely cripple the world's most insidious money-laundering apparatus but also expose it to the entire world. Philip Morris and British American Tobacco vowed to stop drug money from entering their supply chain, but the Colombian government and the European Union remained skeptical. The EU later sued Philip Morris and, in their lawsuit, wrote: "Throughout the 1990s and continuing into the year 2000, the Philip Morris Defendants continued to knowingly sell cigarettes to smugglers, or distributors who sell to smugglers, and have gone to great lengths to conceal this fact from the various law enforcement agencies and customs agencies around the world charged with the monitoring of cigarette sales. For example, throughout 1999 and into the year 2000, the Philip Morris Defendants on numerous occasions notified prosecutors and customs officials within the government of Panama that there is currently no authorized dealer in the Colon Free Trade Zone in Panama for the tobacco products of the Philip Morris Defendants. However, the Philip Morris Defendants continue to sell their products to persons in the Colon Free Trade Zone and conceal these." Their claim was clear: the money was just too good for those involved to stop working with the cartels. (Philip Morris denied the claims and never admitted any wrongdoing.)

* * *

THE TRIALS IN PUERTO Rico concluded in the summer of 1997. The case was officially behind me. But I didn't have time to mourn, or celebrate, or process the five-year ordeal that had consumed my life. I had more police work to do. I was still working on the Los Pepes investigation, but the gravity of going undercover again began to pull me into its orbit. Our source for that investigation, a high-level deputy in the Los Pepes, continued to feed us promising intelligence, and I began traveling with him to Costa Rica and Panama to coordinate shipments of cocaine into the United States. I became "Diego." It was a different name, but the same mindset. I was Manny once again. I dipped in and out, made cameos when necessary, and helped the case move forward. The contours of this case, however, allowed me to spend more time with my family—to fully assume the role of husband and father.

Maria got a job as a teacher at a local school in Fort Lauderdale, and I began coaching my sons' roller hockey teams. They had learned to skate when we lived in San Juan, but the roller hockey craze had recently swept across the United States, and they wanted to play competitively. Soon they were playing in tournaments. Every weekend, we traveled to games all over Florida. My eldest son was a reckless skater, but a prolific points-scorer; my youngest son was a graceful skater, someone with great style on the court (he also scored his fair share of goals). My eldest son's team even made it to the state championship in Tampa. When the last few seconds ticked down off the clock, and his team won a spot at the national championships in Chicago, I ran out onto the rink, picked him up, and held him in my arms. It was a moment of triumph and I was there.

* * *

AS TIME WENT ON, however, my parents got older, and their health became precarious. By 1997, my mother entered a decline. Her doctors put her on dialysis, which eventually gave her an infection that swiftly poisoned her body. When she became too sick to eat or drink water, my siblings took her to the hospital. I flew to San Juan to be with her. Coincidentally, my father was scheduled to receive open-heart surgery that same week. They were in different hospitals, across the city from each other. It pained my father to leave his sick wife to receive treatment that could prolong his life. While my father was in the middle of his surgery, my mother died. He wasn't present to see her into the afterlife.

I sidled up to his bed and waited for the anesthesia to wear off. His eyelids gently opened. Sun poured from the window, covering his face. He looked so old and fragile in that hospital bed, so different from the stern former soldier from my youth. He placed his hand on top of mine and said, "Martin. You're here."

"I'm here, Dad," I said.

"How is your mother?" he asked me.

I couldn't tell him. I ignored his question. "I want you to come live with me in Miami," I said. "We can be together. I'll take care of you."

He stared beyond me, through the window, to the palm trees that swayed in the distance. This was his home, and yet he knew his days were numbered. "I'll go," he said. "I'll go with you, Martin."

"Good, Dad," I said. "Good."

He looked me in the eyes again. "But you didn't answer my question," he said. "Your mother. Tell me."

It was as if he already knew. "Dad," I said. "Dad, she died. Mom is dead."

His eyes became glassy and wet. His lip quivered. "Son," he said. "Will you get me a cup of coffee?" I knew he wasn't supposed to have any caffeine, but I went down to the cafeteria, filled a cup to the brim, and snuck it back into his room. I handed it to him, and he took a sip.

"I wasn't there to see her," he said, handing me the cup. I placed it on his bedside table. "Life is so strange."

"I know, Dad. I know." My eyes brimmed.

He put his hand on top of mine again. "Can you do one thing for me, son?" he asked. "Take care of your sister." It was a request embedded in tradition, and a moral lesson that he tried to teach me all his life: Look after your family. They always need to come first.

My siblings and I took my father back home, where he was supposed to make a full recovery. For the first few weeks, he showed promise. He dutifully wore the compression socks that were supposed to prevent any arterial blockages. He took his medicine and drank plenty of water. He slept and ate well.

He could walk, but slowly. He couldn't stand up safely in the shower, however, and needed help bathing. I would sit him down in the tub and scoop water over his back, the soapsuds washing down the drain. He detested it: the scar on his chest and the fact that his son had to wash him. He felt weak, that he had lost control of his life. And yet I dutifully cared for him, as he had done for me when I was a small child. Now, the roles were reversed.

Our entire family came to see him, and my dad spent his days surrounded by his children and grandchildren, siblings and friends. Maria and my kids flew down to visit; she propped him up in a chair on the patio and gave him a haircut. She always called him "my handsome father-in-law." While I was working undercover, Maria and my father formed an unbreakable bond, a connection steeped in making sure my sons were getting the life they deserved. They had worried about me as a unit: a father for his son, a wife for her husband.

A few weeks later, I went back to Miami and started my latest undercover operation. I was driving down the highway in my doper car, jewelry flashing in the tropical sunlight, when my phone rang. It was my sister. I figured she was calling with an update about my father, as she was his primary caregiver. I picked up the phone and put it to my ear.

"Dad had a stroke," she said. "It's bad, Martin. The doctors don't think he's going to make it." I screeched to a halt, highway traffic rushing past me, and burst into a wail. I was crying for the man that made me the person I had become. This wasn't typical sadness or grief, but a physical pain. A death cry. I knew that I would never have a true moment with my father again.

He lived bedbound and helpless until he passed away a few weeks later. I couldn't bear to see him like that, a vegetable, and I knew he wouldn't want that either, so I never visited my father at the end. I wanted to remember him as the man he was, guiding me through life: the nights together watching Hollywood FBI agents in our living room; the weekends helping the needy in San Juan; the smile on his face when I became an officer in the Navy; his hand on my shoulder, grip firm, when I became an FBI agent; and the words that came out of his mouth, dripping with fatherly approval, as if all of his struggles in life had been worth it: "Martin, I want you to know that I am proud of you." I can still hear his voice, all these years later.

We buried him at the National Military Cemetery in Puerto Rico, the island's equivalent of Arlington. The entire FBI field office on the island arrived in a procession of blacked-out SUVs. Every agent who had supported me in Puerto Rico lined up at his grave: Santo, Jimmy, and Dick Sanders, the men that helped make my father proud of me. I knew, in that moment, that my peers saw who my father was, and what he meant to me.

My father had six siblings, and each brought their families to the funeral from all across the country. Over a hundred people gathered in total. The formal procession of patriotism and service began with soldiers raising their rifles and firing three shots into the air. My father had chosen me to receive the American flag that is given to a veteran's children. The soldiers, swords in hand, knelt in front of me and raised the neatly folded flag. Tears streamed down my face. I reached out, grabbed the cloth, and brought it to my chest. Then, I walked over to my father's grave and put my hand on his casket. When I couldn't hold it in anymore, I broke down. After my father was lowered into the ground, Maria held me for a long time.

## INSIDE THE CARTEL

* * *

MARIA AND I STAYED in Fort Lauderdale. For the next ten years, I worked hundreds of undercover cases, many of which were being conducted simultaneously. At one point, I was working undercover on ten cases at the same time. I traveled all over the world as one of the FBI's top covert agents: Spain, Holland, Germany, the United Kingdom, Thailand, Philippines, Japan, Poland, and more. I was highly selective of the cases on which I worked, and only dedicated myself to those that I believed would produce the most impact. But the investigations ran the gamut of the criminal underworld: art theft, kidnapping, homicide, counterintelligence, human trafficking, weapons smuggling, and white-collar crime. But I always returned to drug trafficking. I was older now and could pass for a narco-boss. I went undercover for hundreds of cases, made thousands of guest appearances in other agents' cases, and helped bring charges against many more criminals. In the end, I worked undercover for twenty-three years straight. But the length of time spent undercover is nothing compared to the depth of penetration. I was a top-notch drug smuggler, arms dealer, and money launderer—often all at once. I was known all over the world as one of the most prolific criminal masterminds of all time. In fact, my legend was so convincing that the DEA and CIA investigated one of my alter egos and confiscated $400,000 from one of my undercover bank accounts, never realizing I was an FBI agent. I called a meeting with the DEA. The agents told me that they were on the verge of arresting my alter ego, not realizing that we were the same person. The FBI let them know that the account was an asset in their covert operations division, and they gave us the money back.

## NEVER ENOUGH TIME

I eventually graduated into a more important role: teaching other promising recruits how to infiltrate criminal organizations, as I had done with the Colombian drug cartels. I was promoted to lead the FBI's covert operations for the southeastern United States, and eventually became the de facto national coordinator. I had five agents working under me, with five additional support employees, and organized any operation that had a covert element. I taught dozens of agents the tricks of the trade and built up a vast network of assets to ensure their undercover identities stayed intact. Moreover, these assets required me to stay undercover in order to maintain them: international bank accounts, yachts, planes, houses, fleets of cars. The assets I offered to other agents were only as reliable as the amount of time that I spent caring for them. I built the house; they were just living in it. My dedication to working undercover laid the foundation for hundreds of fellow agents. For my performance, I received special achievement awards. Some agents go through their entire career without ever receiving one. I was given six.

\* \* \*

I EVEN MADE MY way back to Puerto Rico. It was 2007, and I was tasked with giving new agents at the San Juan field office the lay of the land on undercover work. They hosted me in a hotel conference room, and I began my presentation by focusing on legal guidelines. "A case lives or dies by the rules," I told them, adding that nothing can be done while working undercover without written authorization by both the Department of Justice and the US attorney's office. "All of this work doesn't mean anything if we can't prosecute." I then explained all the assets I could employ to help them deepen their cover. "But the most important part of going undercover is the *story*," I said. "Any agent can jump in and become a character, but it's the legend surrounding them that tricks the targets into believing that an agent is really a criminal. That's how you truly infiltrate."

I also shared lessons I had learned. First and foremost: don't be a cheapskate. "Only cops check the bill. What millionaire drug lord checks the bill?" I also made sure, every time I gave a presentation, to relay Diego's directive from all those years ago, when I first became a drug smuggler: never wear resoled shoes while meeting with a kingpin. "Don't act like somebody you're not," I went on. "Stay close to your true self. And don't volunteer information if you don't know what you're talking about. Above all," I told them, "never break cover."

The next morning, I got dressed in my hotel room, grabbed my briefcase, and headed out for a meeting. When I entered the hotel elevator, a familiar face stared back at me: Tony, my cooperating witness from the money-laundering investigation. He wore a name tag on his suit lapel and stood next to two of his coworkers. They were running security for the hotel. We met eyes. I flashed him a smile.

"Good morning," I offered. He just nodded in return.

Later that day, back in my room, I heard a knock on my door.

"Security!" a voice shouted. I opened the door. It was Tony. I reached out for a hug and invited him in.

"So, you're Martin today, huh?" he said. "No more Manny."

"You're right, Tony," I responded, a tenderness coming over me. "No more Manny."

# EPILOGUE

**I RETIRED FROM THE FBI IN 2011. IN THE MONTHS LEADING** up to my official departure, I was given a lifetime achievement award by the Federal Law Enforcement Officers Association and, for the fourth time, the Department of Justice's outstanding law enforcement officer of the year award. Once I officially hung up my hat, the Miami field office threw a huge party at the Hard Rock Hotel and Casino in Fort Lauderdale. Ricky was there, along with two hundred other agents, half of whom had worked undercover and learned much of what they knew about the role from me.

The banquet team erected a makeshift stage and, after mingling in the crowd and enjoying a few drinks, I was ushered up to give a speech. I adjusted the microphone and took a piece of paper out of my pocket. Maria stood at the foot of the stage and gazed at me, pride emanating from her face like sunlight. I began to speak.

"A couple of months ago, as it dawned on me that I was about to retire, I started to reflect on my twenty-three-year-long career. Some people would argue that your career is not your life. I beg to differ. When you've lived the career that I've had, it becomes a part of who you are. Believe me, extensive undercover work changes you and, to some fools like me with a passion for the covert technique, it becomes, perhaps, too big a part of your life. And as I thought of my twenty-three years in the bureau, most of it spent in the undercover arena, I started to think of all the accomplishments, all the setbacks, and especially all of the significant cases. I realized I have no regrets. Hell, we did things that people write books about. How can I have regrets about that? How could I have any regrets when I've been so blessed to have met and worked with all of you? Now that I'm retired, I'm taking these special bonds with me. When I look around and I see a room full of my colleagues, I realize that you have become like family to me. I think I've worked undercover in some capacity with every one of you. Some of you have been my undercover girlfriends, undercover wives, undercover brothers, undercover colleagues. And we always looked out for each other—and in some cases depended on each other for our very lives. We looked out for each other in far-off places, away from what we know, in other countries with no protection but each other, cocaine bales thrown from planes and flying over our heads, smuggling loads in stormy seas two thousand miles away from home. Sometimes, we thought we wouldn't make it back. When personal integrity, safety, and lives are at stake, you depend on each other and special bonds are forged. How can I have regrets about that? It was a privilege and an honor for me to have served our country with you. I want to take this opportunity to thank all the wives and husbands who have let their spouses take time away from home and endured hardships in assisting our operations. I want to thank my wife, Maria, and my children for unselfishly accepting my career, and loving who I am and what I did, and enduring my absences while I indulged in my passions and lived this fascinating life and career. Thank you."

A chorus of applause filled the room, and I was overcome

# EPILOGUE

with sadness—at all I left behind, at having to finally let Manny go, at understanding that a fulfilled dream meant that, one day, it must come to an end. I stepped off the stage and fell into Maria's arms. I had made a difference in the world, just as I had hoped.

\* \* \*

**MY TWO SONS FOLLOWED** in my footsteps and became military men after the September 11, 2001, terrorist attacks. My eldest son, who got married directly after college, joined the Army and eventually became a captain, and my youngest enlisted in the Marines. They both fought in Iraq—my youngest in the battles for Fallujah and Ramadi—and MSNBC, the Associated Press, and CNN even broadcast a photograph of my eldest son steeped in battle in Sader City, Iraq. Afterward, my eldest son worked for the State Department in Afghanistan, focused on negotiations with the Taliban, while my youngest son landed a position with the Department of the Navy, tasked with classified operations. But they wouldn't stop there. Both of them would eventually become federal agents, just like their father, which is why I haven't used their names in this book.

In 2015, they both applied to be lawmen: my eldest son with the FBI, and my youngest with the DEA. In 2016 they were both accepted and were slated to officially join their respective agencies one month apart. To say that I was happy with their decision would be an understatement. I no longer had to worry about them being killed in the Middle East, and they both would be stationed in the United States. My youngest son was the first to receive his credentials. Maria and I flew to Virginia for the ceremony. Coincidentally, the DEA and the FBI both still used the same auditorium from when I'd become an agent. Normally, the director of the DEA hands each new agent their credentials but I was allowed to give my son his badge. After I gave it to him, he embraced me in front of the crowd and whispered in my ear, "Thanks, Dad." Maria and I stayed with him at the reception afterward, but he kept stealing time with a girl he'd met while enrolled in the academy. They later got married.

A few weeks later, my eldest son graduated from the FBI academy, and it was his turn to officially become an agent. (His wife also joined the FBI, as an analyst, shortly thereafter.) The FBI also let me bestow my son his credentials. But it wasn't just any old badge: it was my badge from when I was an agent. I stood on the stage, watched him walk over to me, and gave him a piece of myself that I'd carried in my heart for decades. But it was no longer mine. The tales of being an agent, of working undercover, of bringing down the bad guys, of being Batman for my sons, had now become memories. This token of all that I had sacrificed and accomplished belonged to him now.

*  *  *

AFTER RETIRING FROM THE FBI, I thought about my money-laundering investigation often. It always felt that there was one loose end that needed to be tied up: El Toro Negro. I never knew what had happened to him. To my knowledge, he was never arrested nor brought to justice, the voice on the other end of my phone never fully identified. The Department of Justice thought they found his real name, and I would Google it every few years. Nothing ever came up. Toro became a ghost, never to be found.

# EPILOGUE

The US government did, eventually, arrest Hector Lopez, the Colombian senator and importer who allegedly colluded with Toro and the Moore cousins. He was captured in 2002, charged with drug trafficking and money laundering, and extradited to the United States the following year. When he was handcuffed and paraded in front of the press, he wore a matching Marlboro hat and windbreaker, red with white stripes, living his role as the Marlboro Man until his last day out in the free world. In 2006, he was found guilty of the charges against him and, the following year, was sentenced to twenty-five years in prison.

\* \* \*

**AS MY RETIREMENT STRETCHED** on, I began to experience issues with my health. Starting in 2017, my speech became slurred, my muscles lost mass, and I moved much more slowly than even a few years before. I began seeing a series of neurologists, both through Veterans Affairs and the University of Miami. At first, they couldn't provide a shared diagnosis. The majority of the doctors, however, believed that I had amyotrophic lateral sclerosis (ALS), also known as Lou Gehrig's disease. Due to my time in the Navy, however, a couple physicians suspected that I may have been exposed to toxic chemicals, such as the flame-retardant foam that we used on ships in the 1970s, which could also explain my symptoms. As time went on, however, the diagnosis of ALS became a certainty. I quickly was made aware of my own mortality—and the value of my life story. Many undercover agents, the vast majority of whom I trained, had already written their own memoirs, and for years they pushed me to do the same. With my future uncertain, I felt it was time to share some of my own experiences within the FBI, especially my early days, where I infiltrated the cartels.

In 2022, I began collaborating on this book with my coauthor, Ian Frisch. One of our first orders of business was to look into Toro again. Ian and I wanted to see if I could bring some closure to the end of my story. I found a recently published article in a Colombian newspaper that made a shocking claim: El Toro Negro and Hector Lopez were the same person. I was dumbfounded. During my time undercover in Puerto Rico, I hadn't merely been working for some shadowy money broker at the heart of the Black Market Peso Exchange; I was likely dealing with one of the most powerful men in the Colombian government. But there was another shocking fact: Lopez was released from prison in August 2021 and sent back to Colombia. He quickly wove himself back into the Colombian political establishment and ran (unsuccessfully) for local office. In 2023, the *City Paper Bogotá* wrote that Lopez "remains a dangerous warlord."

Lopez, the Marlboro Man, Toro—whatever you want to call him, he's still out there. I suspect that he never forgot about me, the lone undercover FBI agent who crumbled the ground beneath his feet. I sometimes wonder if he continues to plot revenge, his long arm still laced with muscle, ready to tap me on the shoulder once more.

## ACKNOWLEDGMENTS

**THERE ARE MANY PEOPLE WHO HAVE MADE A LASTING IMPACT ON MY LIFE** and work, but none compare to my wife. Maria, as I reflect on our incredible journey over the past forty-eight years, my heart is filled with love and appreciation for you. Although I have had my shortcomings, your boundless patience and unconditional love have illuminated my path, especially during my long absences with the Navy and the FBI. Your unwavering support in high-pressure situations has been nothing short of remarkable. You have kept our family united with grace. Your devotion to our love and family has truly enriched our lives and demonstrated what commitment means. Thank you for being my soulmate, my rock, and my greatest love. Here's to many more years filled with cherished memories and a love that continues to grow stronger.

To my father, Angel, and my mother, Ariadina. To my siblings, Janet and Angel. To my brother Gilbert, who, in his way, always has my back. To my brothers-in-law, Nelson and Julio.

I am incredibly proud of my sons, Martin and Gio. Martin was an Army Ranger, and Gio was a Marine. Both men displayed true patriotism on the battlefield, and have since become federal agents, just like their father. Your strength and resilience inspire me. Your commitment to service encourages everyone to embrace their challenges. You continually remind me of the courage it takes to serve. I love you both more than you'll ever know.

To Nicole and Brittney "Little Hercules," my daughters-in-law. Brittney encouraged me to tell my story, but both of you consistently offer kindness, happiness, and support—both to me and my grandchildren. We are lucky to have you in our family.

I want to extend my heartfelt thanks to my partner, Henry Mercadal (Ricky). I am grateful that you chose me to be the

## ACKNOWLEDGMENTS

godfather of your first child, Nina. Your unwavering support and camaraderie have not only made my journey manageable but also truly rewarding. Thank you for being such an incredible partner in our mission.

To former Marine Captain and Special Agent in Charge Kenneth McCabe, code-named "El Cojo." You recognized that undercover work is among the most reliable investigative techniques, even knowing it could jeopardize your career. I appreciate your commitment to our safety as we traversed the world doing what we did.

To Anibal Gonzalez, also known as Gonzo (Antonio Ross), my undercover brother. You have been a fearless companion, and your courage and dedication have had a profound impact on me. Your commitment to our mission has been truly inspiring. To Vincent, Carlos, and Todd. We accomplished remarkable and innovative things together; together, we brought our dream to life. To Nicole Cruz, operational psychologist and behavioral scientist, thank you for believing in us and offering your unconditional support.

To former undercover colleagues: Daisy Güell-Hester, Lisa Wall, Lisa Beard, Lynnette Karnes, Omayra Soto, Colleen Cunningham, Jackie Suarez, Candace Calderon, Henry Mercadal, Gonzo, Vincent Pankoke, Jack Garcia, Scott Payne, Bob Wittman, Bob Bettis, Bo Loggins, Steve Salmieri, Joe Pistone (Donnie Brasco), John Legatto, Joe Phan, Joe Yazstremski, Jerry Bermudez, Jose Olivier, and Michael Hunt. My mentors: Wayne Jackson, Pete St. Pierre, and Timothy McNally. Exceptional role-players: Ronnie Bobbitt, Barb Smith, Liz Aviles, Yvonne Alduende, Carla Sena, Alexandra Montilla, and Frances Bourgeois.

Special thanks to Maria Alonso, our engineer; Carlos Gamez; and Captain Ivan Montilla.

Special thanks to my agent, Larry Weissman, and editor at Dey Street Books, Carrie Thornton. And to my talented coauthor, Ian Frisch, who taught me to be vulnerable and helped bring this memoir to life.

Thanks to my retirement domino partners, former Special Agents Carlos Monero, Eric Rivera, Carlos Cintron, and Gil Vasquez.